G000139423

Helena Pastor is a Dutch-Australian writer who is passionate about the social justice possibilities of her work. Through memoir and fiction, she hopes to influence the way people think and feel about topics including troubled youth, pregnancy and birth choices, growing up in an immigrant family, and recovering a lost Jewish identity. Her writing has attracted two Australian Society of Authors' Mentorships, along with a number of residencies at Varuna Writers' House and Bundanon. She has extensive experience as an educator, and has worked with groups ranging from Bosnian refugees to university-level creative writing students. Helena is also a songwriter and performer. She lives in Armidale and has four sons and a grandson.

STIRLING
LIBRARIES

- - JUN 2015

HELENA PASTOR

Wild Boys

UQP

First published in 2015 by University of Queensland Press
PO Box 6042, St Lucia, Queensland 4067 Australia

www.uqp.com.au
uqp@uqp.uq.edu.au
helenapastor.com

© 2015 Helena Pastor

This book is copyright. Except for private study, research, criticism or reviews, as
permitted under the Copyright Act, no part of this book may be reproduced, stored in
a retrieval system, or transmitted in any form or by any means without prior written
permission. Enquiries should be made to the publisher.

Author photograph by Simon Scott Photo
Photograph on page 299 by Brendan Read Photography
Cover design by Christabella Designs
Cover photographs: people by Ivan Montero Martinez / Shutterstock; corrugated wall by
Somchai Rakin / Shutterstock
Typeset in 11/16.5 pt Janson Text by Post Pre-press Group, Brisbane
Printed in Australia by McPherson's Printing Group, Melbourne

asa
Australian Society of **Authors**

COPYRIGHTAGENCY
CULTURAL
FUND

This publication has been supported by the Copyright Agency through the Australian
Society of Authors Emerging Writers' and Illustrators' Mentorship Program.

Cataloguing-in-Publication Data
National Library of Australia
Pastor, Helena, author.
   Wild boys: a parent's story of tough love / Helena Pastor.
   ISBN 978 0 7022 5365 2 (pbk)
   ISBN 978 0 7022 5539 7 (epdf)
   ISBN 978 0 7022 5540 3 (epub)
   ISBN 978 0 7022 5541 0 (kindle)
   Pastor, Helena.
   Mothers and sons – Australia.
   Motherhood – Australia.
   Youth – Services for – Australia.
   Youth workers – Australia.
   Youth – Australia – Life skills guides.
306.8743

University of Queensland Press uses papers that are natural, renewable and recyclable
products made from wood grown in sustainable forests. The logging and manufacturing
processes conform to the environmental regulations of the country of origin.

The author has changed the names of some characters in this memoir.
This has been done to protect their privacy.

For Pup and Joey with love,
for my boys at home and elsewhere,
and for Bernie and all the boys at the shed.

CONTENTS

CONTENTS

PROLOGUE

In the bathroom of the bakery house, the bare-chested boxer fronts up to the mirror. He adjusts his stance, raises his fists and tucks his chin. His face takes on a faraway look, like he's back in the ring perhaps, in another time and place. His hands flash through the air, accompanied by short tight breaths. *Phh phh phh* goes the right fist, *phh phh* goes the left. Right – *phh*. Left – *phh phh*. The punches and breaths have a rhythm, a timbre, like music. His children wander in and use the hand basin, where they brush their teeth and prepare for bed with the familiar sound of *phh phh* coming from the other side of the bathroom. They know not to interrupt their father while he boxes with his other self.

*

I take out a photo of Joey and his opa at the beach, and put it on the wall above my computer. They've just made an extravaganza of a sandcastle and are sitting back on the sand, looking pleased with themselves. When I was a child, my father built me similar sandcastles – huge mounds covered in turrets and decorated with shells – that stood grandly on the shore. He was always good like that with Joey, too, even though Joey didn't make it easy for him. When Joey was a baby, he often struggled and screamed at sleep-time, but my father would sit in the room with him and play classical guitar until Joey fell asleep. The crying never seemed to bother him. As a toddler, Joey liked to run away from his opa when they were at the beach or the park – and my father, who had bad knees, couldn't chase after him. He'd be calling for him to come back, petrified that Joey would fall from the rocks into the sea, or run across the road into traffic. One time, when Joey was eight, he and my father were playing cards, and when Joey didn't win, he kicked his opa in the leg. My father didn't get angry. He just said in his thick Dutch accent: 'That was not a very nice thing to do, Joey. You can't always win in life.'

My father wasn't always so calm and measured. He was once a boxer, and a baker, and the master of any fight with words. After a long day in the bakery, he would hang over his plate at the end of the dinner table and bait and criticise my three siblings, who were already teenagers by the time I was five. My father's recurring themes centred on how ungrateful his children were, how they didn't help enough around the house or try hard enough at school, and how their friends were the wrong sort of people. 'Is this what we came to Australia for?' he would ask. I lived through years of yelling and arguments over dinner, watching as my siblings tried to oppose my father, while my mother sat by and said little. Every time, my brothers or my sister – big, strong teenagers – crumpled before him, often running from the table in tears.

As a child, I cried to our corgi. I curled up with him in his kennel as the fights raged inside the house. By the time I was a teenager, I knew not to fight.

I

Autumn–Winter 2007

Joining the pack

The Iron Man Welders meet on Sundays in an old council depot on the edge of Armidale, a university town in northern New South Wales. I recently volunteered to help out with this program for troubled teenage boys, an initiative led by a maverick youth worker called Bernie Shakeshaft. Not that I'm a welder or a youth worker – I'm a trained English language teacher. But I only work part-time these days because I'm also a part-time PhD student, a wife, and a mother of four boys who range in age from two to sixteen. I was just looking for some answers.

About a year ago, Bernie had a vision of a welding project that would build on the strengths of a group of young men who had dropped out of high school but weren't ready for work. He asked the Armidale community to help out. The local council offered him the depot, which had once been a welding workshop and was lying empty, as if waiting for Bernie and the boys to come along and claim it.

There was nothing in the huge shed, not even a power lead. The boys turned up each weekend and worked hard to clean and create their own workplace. They borrowed nearly everything, from brooms to welding equipment, and started collecting recycled steel for the first batch of products they planned to make and then sell at the monthly markets. Local welding businesses gave scrap metal; people lent grinders, extension cords and old work boots.

Then the money started coming in. A local builder forked out the first five hundred dollars. The bowling club gave a thousand and a steel-manufacturing business donated a MIG welder. The credit union offered to draw up a business and marketing plan, organised insurance, and contributed a thousand dollars for equipment. A nearby mine donated another thousand and raised the possibility of apprenticeships for the boys, and the New South Wales Premier's Department handed over a grant worth five thousand dollars. It seemed like every week Bernie and the boys were in the local paper, celebrating some new success.

I saw a photo of Bernie in the paper, surrounded by a group of boys, their faces beaming with happiness and pride. At the time, I was having a lot of trouble with my sixteen-year-old son, Joey, who had left home but boarded in a house nearby. I was worried about him and didn't like the way he was drifting through life – no job, no direction, living off Centrelink payments, sleeping in till midday. As I looked at the happy faces in the photo, something stirred inside me. I wanted to be part of it: the Iron Man Welders.

The next day I heard Bernie on the radio, seeking community support for the project. 'We'll take any positive contribution,' he said. His words sounded clipped and tight, like he wasn't one for mucking around. 'Whether you've got a pile of old steel or timber in your backyard, or if you've got an idea, or if you like working with young people and you're prepared to come down to the shed and work one-on-one with some of these kids ...'

On impulse I rang. I was interested in learning more about boys and alternative forms of education – for both personal and academic reasons – but I'd never used power tools, let alone done any welding. I liked bushwalking and baking cakes. I enjoyed order, cleanliness, silence. What was I thinking?

Right from the start, though, the boys were gracious in accepting a 41-year-old woman into their grimy world. With my short brown hair, and in my King Gees and work boots, I don't stick out too much. The boys find easy jobs for me to do – like filing washers for candleholders or scrubbing rust off horseshoes. I sweep the floor, watch what's going on, listen to what they want to tell me. The fellas who come along are the sort of misfits you see wandering the streets of any country town, with nothing to do, nowhere to go. Once, I might have crossed the street to avoid them.

Most of the Iron Man Welders didn't 'engage positively' with the education system. Not one finished Year 12 and some barely made it through Year 10. One was expelled in Year 11 for 'kissing his missus in the schoolyard', another told a teacher to 'fuck off' on a ski trip because the teacher wouldn't stop hassling him, and another finished Year 10 at TAFE because he was about to be kicked out of school and reckoned the teachers didn't like him anyway. The welding shed is a different story. They love it. Bernie gives them the chance to take responsibility for their lives, to engage on their own terms with the community.

The first Sunday I joined them, it was the middle of autumn. I walked in carrying a tray of freshly baked brownies. Self-conscious in my new dark-blue work clothes, I huddled from the cold in the open-sided tin shed. Music blared from an old radio, and thumping and grinding noises came from the machines. Sparks flashed; everyone dragged on rollies, littering every sentence with 'shit' and 'fuck'. Taking a deep breath, I forced myself not to panic.

Thommo, a stocky bloke in his late teens, took me on a tour. His voice rumbled softly, and I could barely hear what he was saying as he showed me the kitchen area, the main workspace, and a forge he'd built in a dark side room that brought to mind a scene from the Middle Ages: flickering fire, hammers and anvil, dirt floor, open drain, a rusty tap jutting out from the wall.

He led me towards a shelf at one end of the shed to show me a range of candleholders, nutcrackers, penholders and coat hooks made from horseshoes. I noticed a smartly presented copy of the Iron Man Welders' business plan, and several glass-framed photos: Thommo bent over the anvil, hammering a piece of glowing-red metal; Bernie and about eight boys slouched in front of his yellow ute; and a young bloke with curly hair using a grinder, a halo of sparks around his head.

Bernie doesn't actually seem to know much about welding. Every so often I hear him say, 'No point asking me questions about welding shit' – but that might be his way of throwing the decision-making back onto the boys. He knows the basics, like what processes are involved in different jobs, but most of the fellas have the edge on him. Some are doing TAFE certificates in engineering courses, following on from their school studies.

Along with learning to understand the welding and power tools, I'm also keen to learn more about boys. You'd think I'd know enough with four of my own, but I've probably made every mistake there is, especially with Joey.

Joey moved out of home when he was fifteen, just over twelve months ago. Years of anger and rage, windows getting smashed and police knocking on the door had forced the decision. Thinking back, it was just crazy adolescent behaviour. I probably had similar scenes with my parents in my teenage years, but I didn't break things and I wasn't as loud or angry. My husband,

Rob – Joey's step-father – and I could have handled the conflict better, but we didn't know how back then. We didn't understand Joey and he didn't understand us. Our home life was an ongoing battle of wills, with escalating scenes of conflict occurring on a daily basis.

Joey used to play thumping loud rap music in his bedroom. Although he never played it at full volume, it was always too loud for me, and if Rob or I asked Joey to turn it down because the baby was sleeping, he'd rant about how 'unjust' we were. Whenever we attempted to impose some sort of control over his behaviour, Joey would go wild. I've never been good at confrontation, and I found it impossible to reason with him. He'd stand over me, his face close to mine, and yell so loudly I'd just give up and walk away, anxious to keep the peace. One day he shouted so much that a neighbour called the police. When I saw the police at the door, I waved them inside – 'Please explain to my son that it's not appropriate to yell so loud the whole street hears.'

Something had to change. Neither Rob nor I were good at handling stress; we were like two nuclear reactors heading for a major meltdown at any moment. The tension in the house was tangible. I didn't want my younger boys growing up in an environment where people were always fighting and angry, and I didn't want my relationship with Joey to be based around anger. I wanted to see him do well in life – he had a lively and inquisitive mind, a zany sense of humour, a passion for music and loads of potential. He also had a family who loved him deeply, but our tension-filled environment was bringing us all down.

Then, one afternoon, Henry, our second youngest, got a lift home from school with another mother, Anne. Henry must have mentioned our troubles because she came into the house and asked me what was going on. After I'd finished telling her, she said: 'How about Joey lives at my house for a few weeks, while you and Rob get some counselling and work out what to do?' I was overcome, speechless with gratitude, unable to believe that someone – practically a stranger – was offering to help. At the time, it seemed like a positive step. When Joey came home, Anne asked if he wanted to come and stay with her teenage son in a converted shed in her backyard. He nodded, packed his bags and left. And that's how Joey left home.

The house breathed again, but my boy was gone. For weeks, grief, guilt, relief and love rolled around inside me. I didn't miss all the shouting and door slamming ... but I missed Joey's funny stories and jokes, and I missed *him*. Anne gave us the number of a respected psychologist in town, and Rob and I started a mediation process with Joey. But after the first session, the mediator said she wouldn't be able to work with us. She didn't explain why, but I think her concerns were more about the way Rob and I were behaving as parents rather than how Joey was behaving as a confused teenager.

While Joey was staying at Anne's, she invited me to dinner one night. I watched as her husband threw frozen vegetables into huge pots of boiling water, whacked various frozen pies in and out of the microwave, and piled mountains of food onto people's plates. We ate in front of the television, with the dinner plates balanced on our knees. Joey couldn't stop smiling, and after dinner he and Anne's son did the washing up. Anne's house was chaos, mess everywhere, but it suited Joey. I could see that they genuinely cared for him. But, after two months, when it began to look as though Joey wouldn't be returning home anytime soon, Anne approached a local church on our behalf and asked the minister if any 'empty nesters' in the congregation wanted a boarder. An older couple volunteered to help, and Joey moved in with them. During that time, Joey came around nearly every afternoon, and he often had dinner with us, too. We began to have more good times than bad, and I began to see a brighter future for our family.

Joey was still at high school then, more than bright enough to do further study. But after months of garbage duty, behaviour-level cards, and several long-term suspensions, he left school at the end of Year 9.

'Better to leave now than be expelled next year,' the deputy principal at the time had advised. 'He can always do Year 10 at TAFE.'

It wasn't the right decision. Joey's new friends, in their baggy pants and back-to-front caps, gathered out the front of TAFE each morning, smoking and laughing like they were the lucky ones. Maybe they were, and maybe school would have damaged them further, but after a few weeks, Joey and his friends stopped attending most of their classes. I often see them at the mall these days, slumped on benches near the courthouse or hanging around the toddlers' playground.

If only Joey had been coming to the shed each week, slowly 'getting his shit together' like the others. He'd been to the shed a couple of times with one of his TAFE friends, and I often encouraged him to give it another go, but he wasn't interested.

'I'm a lone wolf,' Joey says whenever I pester him about coming down.

I thought it was time he joined the rest of the pack.

The scent of an idiot

About a dozen boys turn up at the shed each Sunday, and after a few more weeks of filing washers and scrubbing horseshoes, I start getting to know them all. I notice Gazza during a group meeting late one afternoon. He seems more serious than the others, a *real* worker in his baggy overalls, cap pulled down hard over his eyes. Next to him I feel like an impostor in my King Gees, the factory creases still visible, my work boots shiny and new.

Snow has been falling in the high country over the weekend and outside is threatening sleet, but we stand near the open shed doors so the boys can smoke. 'We've got six hundred things started,' says Bernie, his hair ruffling in the wind, 'but we're not finishing anything. I think we need groups – have someone who's shit-hot at welding working with some new fellas. You blokes decide what jobs are most important. The sooner we get started, the sooner we can hook in.'

Bernie throws a piece of chalk over to a boy who begins to write names on the dusty concrete floor. The others stand in a circle around him – choosing group leaders, assistant leaders, offering comments. They decide to have groups of five: two who can weld, two who are handy enough to cut, and one new bloke who can start on easier jobs.

'Crackin' idea,' says Bernie, looking down at the lists. 'Seeing you blokes take a lead on this is really great!'

From behind, I feel a blast of heat from the forge room. I turn to see the fire raging and two boys sitting next to it on upturned milk crates: Thommo, thick-set and moustachioed, who showed me around on my first day, and his mate Freckles, who has the fine features and demeanour of a devious elf. They nod at me with raised eyebrows and guilty smiles.

'What did they throw on the fire?' I ask Gazza, who is busy writing job lists on the whiteboard.

He turns around, lifting the brim of his cap to see. 'Kero,' he mutters disapprovingly. 'Fuckin' idiots.'

*

Most of the Iron Men were recruited from a school welding program that ran the previous year. The local TAFE had asked Bernie, a youth worker known for his unconventional methods, to manage a new welding program for disengaged youth. Bernie agreed and approached the principals of Armidale's two public high schools with a proposal: each could select the group of Year 10 boys who were most in danger of not making it through the year, and he would work with them at TAFE each Friday. The principals readily agreed. For the rest of the year, Bernie taught those boys how to 'fly under the radar' and keep out of trouble at school, while Rocket, the metal engineering teacher, taught them how to weld. That group of boys all made it through Year 10.

One day, as Bernie and I sat together on the concrete ledge outside the shed, I'd asked him what the boys were like when he first met them. He shook his head and grimaced: 'They were the wildest bunch of hoorangs you're likely to come across!'

I laughed at his pained expression. He found his tobacco and rolled a cigarette, his habitual way of settling in for a chat.

'There were some damaged kids in that group,' said Bernie, his voice low. 'It was almost too late to start with them. Hard-core kids on the edge of going inside for violent bashings, already identified as hopeless troublemakers, a lot of them living away from home. For sixteen years they'd heard the only thing that matters is getting a school certificate, and then to be told: "It's all bullshit. You guys aren't going to get there."' Bernie gave a scornful huff. 'The schools hadn't worked on the strengths and dreams of those kids.'

He paused for a moment to light his smoke. 'It was like getting a bag full of wild cats and letting them out in one room where they couldn't escape. The schools kept saying I had to stick with the rules … that the boys weren't allowed to smoke or swear.'

11

Bernie whistled through his teeth. 'For Christ's sake, you send me twenty of your wildest boys – all full-on swearers and smokers and blasphemers – and tell me to enforce the school rules? It was wild!' He grinned, his face alive with the memory. 'We had knives pulled in the welding shed, and just as soon as you'd be finished with the knife incident, the boss man from the college would be yelling, "What the hell is that kid doing up on top of that three-storey building?!" The boys would show up black and blue, on the piss and smoking bongs. Not all of them ended up here at the shed – some did well, some not so well. One of them died, another's in jail.'

'It's hard to believe the boys were like that.' I thought of Thommo with his quiet dignity. 'Was Thommo that wild?'

Bernie rolled his eyes and groaned. 'He was the craziest! He and his mates were riding bikes into poles and dropping garbage bins on each other's heads from the highest roof at school. Whatever someone did that was dangerous, Thommo did something double-dangerous. Thommo wouldn't just jump off the third storey of the building – he'd want to jump through three sheets of glass as well. Taking it to extremes. Crazy self-mutilation stuff.'

We sat quietly for a moment.

'I did a lot of that as a kid myself,' said Bernie. 'Hardly a bone in my body I haven't broken – from having no fear or need for self-preservation. Dealing with those kids rang a lot of bells for me because, all those years ago, I would've been one of those wild cats let out of the bag.'

*

In the makeshift kitchen at the shed, I make a cup of tea to warm my hands and then wander back to join the boys who are still gathered near the door. I notice Freckles has retreated from the fire in the forge and is showing the others a bandage on his arm. Someone says, 'We could all brand our chests: Iron Man Branding!' I sidle up to Bernie to ask what they mean.

'Hey, Freckles,' he calls over. 'Tell Helena about branding.'

Freckles looks a little sheepish, but explains what happened. A few weeks before, he'd heated up a bottle-opener embossed with a turtle and pressed the red-hot end onto his forearm. 'I left it on my skin too long,' he says. Two weeks later, when he finally went to the doctor, he discovered he had a third-degree burn.

'Did you tell the doctor how you did it?' asks Gazza.

'Yeah,' says Freckles, in a 'Why wouldn't I?' tone.

We all laugh.

'Love the fuckin' honesty!' says Bernie, giving Freckles a pat on the back as he walks by, grinning like a proud father because Freckles told the truth, even though branding himself was a stupid thing to do.

Later, when everyone is gone, I talk with Bernie about Gazza. 'He seems keen.'

Bernie reaches into the pocket of his jeans for his tobacco. 'Gazza's a bit older than the others. He's been driving around on Sunday mornings and getting the boys out of bed, taking on the responsibility. He'd be here at six if he could. I'm thinking of giving him a key to the shed. The boys listen to him – he could keep them working.'

'That'd be good for him,' I say, thinking of those serious eyes underneath the peak of his cap. 'He's different from the others.'

'Three or four years ago he would've been like the rest,' says Bernie. 'I don't know his story – he's only been coming along for a few months – but I reckon he was a bit of an idiot.' He clicks his lighter under his rollie, drawing in hard. 'It helps. Idiots respect other idiots. They can smell it – the scent of an idiot.'

What's updog?

A few nights later, washing up after dinner, I hear the click of the side-gate. A dark-haired figure lopes past the window and Rob calls out, 'Joey's here.' My body tenses, my heartbeat quickens. If only I could be more relaxed when Joey comes over, but experience has taught me otherwise. I never know what sort of mood he'll be in. Who will Joey be today, I wonder – Mr Happy, Mr Sad or Mr Angry?

'Hi, Mum!' he says as he comes through the back door. I glance up from the sink. He's smiling broadly, his brown eyes alight with mischief. Mr Happy.

I smile back and relax a little, thinking how handsome he is when he's in a good mood. 'How's things, Joey?'

'Good ... good.' He leans against the kitchen bench and sniffs deeply. 'It smells like updog in here.'

'Hmmm ...' I murmur, keeping my response minimal, wondering what he's up to. Theo comes out of his room, still dressed in his high school uniform. Joey calls his brother over. 'Don't you reckon it smells like updog in here?'

'What's updog?' asks Theo.

'Nuttin', dog,' answers Joey in a thick gangster accent and a big grin. 'What's up wit' you?'

Theo reddens, caught out, while I chuckle over the dishes. Joey can be very funny.

'Want to go for a drive, Mum?'

Night drives have almost become a ritual with Joey and me since he moved out of home. I tell myself it's our quality time, an opportunity for us to talk without the other kids around, but it doesn't usually turn out that way.

'Not really,' I say with a sigh. 'It's been a long day.' But I know two-year-old Freddie is nearly asleep, and Henry is trying to finish his homework. I also know how hard it is for Joey to be quiet. I grab the keys from the top of the fridge. 'Maybe just a short one.'

As I reverse onto the street, Joey plugs his MP3 adaptor into the cassette player. The thumping beat of rap fills the car. The music is so loud people stare as we go past. Each time I turn down the volume, Joey turns it up even louder. I shouldn't have agreed to go out with him. 'Put on a song that doesn't have so much swearing!' I snap. 'I don't want to hear "motherfucker" over and over!'

'Alright, alright,' he says, searching through his songs. 'You don't need to get angry. Let's do a lap around town and check out Hungry Jack's.'

I drive around the block, annoyed with myself. Why do I do this week after week, when my life is already so busy? As we cruise past the back of Hungry Jack's, a local hangout, Joey scans the crowd for someone he knows.

'Stop here a minute,' he says, leaping out to ask the where-abouts of one of his friends. I wait in the car, a faithful servant. When he jumps back in, we drive to an address in Girraween, a housing commission area on the other side of town. I already know this won't be a 'short drive'. Joey doesn't seem to notice when I purse my lips and exhale loudly with frustration.

We stop in front of a brick house. Joey gets out to see if his friend is home. While he's chatting at the door, I remember a phone call with my mother the previous week. She rang to tell me about her friend's grandson, a young man who was often in trouble with the police. 'He joined the army and became a different person,' she said. 'Maybe this would be a good thing for Joey?'

I wasn't sure if I wanted Joey to become a soldier, fighting someone else's war. But the next day I'd looked up the Defence Forces website and read through an impressive list of trade jobs available for army recruits. I rang the recruiting line and asked them to send further information about the training program so that Joey and I could read through the brochures together. The brochures haven't arrived yet, but it's definitely worth a try.

On our drive back to town, I sneak the volume down a notch. 'Oma reckons it might be a good idea for you to join the army.'

Joey looks at me in surprise. 'I've been thinking about doing that already ... I want to be a driver.'

A driver?

'You could learn a trade,' I say, pretending I haven't heard. With a brain like his, he could do anything. 'Telecommunications, or mechanical engineer or systems analyst.'

Joey shakes his head and sighs. 'You remind me of Marge Simpson.' He turns up the music again; end of army conversation. This is how it always is when I bring up something serious.

Later, I drop him at his place. When I found Joey a boarding arrangement in a house only a block away from us, I worried it might be a little too close. In some ways, I was right. He pops around whenever it suits him, wanting food, money, lifts, his clothes washed. Mainly, though, I think he just wants me. For the first year of his life, it was only him and me. I'm sure he'd still prefer it that way – so I could listen to his stories for hours, spend nights driving around town with him, do all his cooking, shopping and washing. I enjoy spending time with Joey, but I have three other children who need my attention as well. Maybe he should have been an only child – we certainly have our best times when it's just the two of us – but that's not how things turned out.

Joey leans over to kiss my cheek before he gets out of the car. 'Bye, Mum, I love you.'

A lucky idiot

The following Sunday, only Simmo, another volunteer youth worker with the Iron Man Welders, is at the shed with Freckles and Thommo. The turn-up is never as good when Bernie is out of town. Stepping over some broken glass near the door, I notice the side window is smashed in, and Freckles is busy welding a security grille to cover it.

I start sweeping up the glass. 'Do you reckon we should smash the rest out? Those jagged edges can be nasty.'

'Good idea,' mumbles Freckles, grabbing an iron bar and handing a hammer to Thommo. They start swinging away at the glass left in the window with great enthusiasm.

Later, when Simmo and I are having a rest in the kitchen while the boys finish the security grille, I ask him: 'Were you an idiot when you were a young bloke?'

Simmo, who is in his late forties and is rugged up in an old footy jumper and a droopy beanie that matches the bags under his eyes, chuckles into his cup of tea. 'Me and my two brothers were all idiots … but I was a lucky idiot.'

'Why's that?'

'Our dad was a school principal, a hard-liner,' he says. 'We moved a lot, and by the time we ended up in Warren, I was thirteen and running amok with my two older brothers. We broke into shops late at night, nicking lollies and cigarettes. We snuck into the goods train a few times, taking whatever we could find, and we went into the church hall and stole boxes of chips.'

Stealing boxes of chips and lollies seemed pretty innocent. In my early teens, I was a small-time thief, too – chocolates from the local milk bar, books from the library, even clothes from small boutiques. Maybe it was something all adolescents went through, a test of nerve.

'And when we moved to Moree,' adds Simmo, rubbing the stubble on his chin, 'it was underage drinking. My brothers got busted for a lot of stuff, and one of them spent time in jail, but I was lucky. I didn't get caught and I ran with a mob with a reasonably sensible side. My late teens though ...' He chuckles again. 'They were pretty wild years. We lived in Sydney for a while, then I went back to Moree, then up to Yamba. In those three years I got into drugs, although in all that time I might have only had acid twice, mushrooms twice, speed half a dozen times and ecstasy three or four times.' Simmo pauses for a breath. 'We smoked pot nonstop ... but I didn't get into heroin.'

'That's alright then!' I say, laughing.

Simmo sits back and folds his arms over his belly, his young idiot self only a gleam in his eye, and grins back at me. 'That's not many drugs, Helena. It's just the way it came out when I said it!'

He didn't need to convince me. In the coastal area where I grew up, smoking dope was a common pastime for teenagers, but I found alcohol an easier way to lose myself. My friends and I used to drink tequila slammers in the local park: lick, sip, suck. We'd be falling over drunk on the way to the pub and still somehow manage to convince the bouncer we were over eighteen.

One of the things that kept him on the right track, says Simmo, was that he always worked. The whole time he was drinking and taking drugs, he had a job.

'But where did that work ethic come from?' I ask, thinking of Joey, who resisted my advice and efforts to get him to finish Year 10 or find a job, and whose work experience consisted of two nights of kitchen-hand duties in a Chinese restaurant.

'I don't know,' admits Simmo, like he's never thought about it. 'To have a car or rent a flat you needed a job, so I suppose it was just to get by. I went from one job to another and didn't particularly care what.'

'What made you pull away from that life? What was the turning point?'

'It was after that year in Yamba,' says Simmo. 'My sister and brother-in-law were going out west to start a business and asked if I wanted to come. I wasn't doing anything else so I went with them. That saved me – not that I was heading for any great crash ...'

'But it was a good move?'

He nods. 'Yeah, it was a good move.'

Over the next week, I thought about this baptism of idiocy. It seemed true enough. Bernie himself came from a stable home but went off the rails in his teens. He reckons he was a bigger idiot than the lot of these Iron Man Welders put together.

'I just didn't fit the system,' he once explained. 'Shithouse at reading and writing, and they're the things society says are most important. As the years go by you start to act the fool, and if you're told you're an idiot enough times, you start acting like one. Relationships with teachers fall apart, and you start to hang around with a smaller and smaller group of like-minded idiots.'

One afternoon recently, while the boys were scoffing a tray of brownies I'd brought along, I asked if there'd been teachers like Bernie at school. 'Hell no!' laughed Gazza, and Thommo said, 'Nah ... no way,' like it was the most ridiculous idea ever.

'Okay, so what's the difference between teachers at school and Bernie?'

Gazza sat back and fiddled with his cap. 'At school I reckon they're on a power trip – a bit of authority and they run with it. Bernie comes down to your level.' Pointing to the ceiling, he added, 'But teachers are up there.'

A few Sundays later, I come home from the shed, filthy dirty, arms aching from scrubbing horseshoes, to find Joey waiting for me with a basket of washing. He hangs in front of the open fridge door and tells me how he saw some of the Iron Men at a party the night before. 'They all like you at the shed, Mum.'

'Probably because of my chocolate brownies,' I joke, but inside I feel warm with acceptance, the same feeling I had earlier when Bernie, after showing me how to use the grinder to file off some nails, told me, 'We'll make you a welder yet!' The shed really does make me happy. And later, as I drag myself off to bed, I wonder if maybe, just maybe, the scent of an idiot lingers on me, too.

A man who had the answers

A small group of volunteers forms the basis of Bernie's grass-roots organisation, BackTrack Youth Works. After I've been at the shed for a couple of months, I'm invited along to my first BackTrack meeting. We sit around Simmo's kitchen table like

King Arthur and his knights at the round table: there's Jayne, Simmo, Sally, Geraldine, Flinty and me. And Bernie, of course: our stand-in king.

Tonight, Bernie's eyes burn bright but look troubled all the same. For the past week he's been busy talking to the media about the Iron Man Welders. Now he's going through a moral dilemma about being seen as the 'boss-man' of BackTrack, the spokesperson with all the answers.

He takes a swig of wine. 'It's hard for me when people ask, "What is it?" Fuck, I don't know.'

At the head of the table, Simmo shifts his half-moon glasses down his nose and moves his chair in closer. His black beanie makes him look like he's about to organise a bank heist. 'BackTrack's a group of people doing shit for youth. I'm here because I like the idea of helping you out,' he says. 'Are you worried it's too Bernie-focused?'

'Yeah.'

Simmo shrugs. 'But I see BackTrack as being Bernie. Some bastard's got to be the leader.'

Bernie runs his fingers through his hair. Although he spent much of his youth as a stockman in Central Australia, his skin is clear and unlined, his face boyish, even though he's approaching forty.

He glances around the table. 'Most of you have known me long enough to know that I'm great at flying off on tangents and having all this passion, but if you lot weren't writing the grant applications or helping out where you can, then it would be nothing – just someone with a lot of passion running around chasing his fuckin' tail.'

Maybe so. But he's the one with all the ideas, the ones that work.

'Can I ask a question?' Sally, Bernie's sister-in-law, looks like she wants more order in this meeting. 'Don't we have a mission statement or vision or something?'

Bernie gives her a wry smile. 'We do that every time we get together, every time we get pissed.'

Sally laughs, shakes her head like she should have known better.

Then Bernie's wife, Jayne, has her say, elbows on the table. A poncho flares over her arms like dark wings and I notice, not for the first time, her robust beauty; she's the sort of woman you'd see peeling potatoes in a Van Gogh painting. 'I'm sure we've answered all these questions before, Bernie. Just keep talking about BackTrack exactly as you have. It's fairly definable – it's us here, in this room. It has been since the beginning.'

Bernie stands, stretches, and goes out into the cold night air, ducking his head as he walks through the back door for a smoke.

*

Not long after Joey left home, I was helping set up for a fete at Henry's primary school. Another mother came over and said Henry and her son had stuck a knife into the tyre of a yellow ute parked in the school car park.

'It's Bernie's ute,' she said, as we examined the tyre. The knife hadn't gone in very far and the tyre looked undamaged, but still – a knife? It wasn't like Henry to do such a thing.

'Who's Bernie?' I'd asked, my face burning with embarrassment.

A woman with dark unruly hair had looked over at me. 'He's my husband.'

She came and stood by the ute with us. I must have stammered out some sort of reply, and I'm not sure why the matter wasn't resolved then and there, but the following Monday, when I dropped Henry at school, I noticed the same yellow ute pull up behind me in the car park, a male driver behind the wheel.

'That must be Bernie,' I said to Henry. 'You need to go and talk to him about what happened.'

I watched in the rear-view mirror as Henry walked over to the driver's side of the ute. A tall, lean man, wearing dark-blue jeans and a cream-coloured shirt, opened the door and got out. I didn't know then that Bernie had once been a stockman, but I remember thinking he looked like a hip cowboy in his jeans and boots, a pair of dark sunglasses pushed back over his curly brown hair.

He knelt down on the dirt in front of Henry, so that he and Henry were face-to-face. They spoke for several minutes. I liked the way Bernie knelt down rather than loomed over – the way he spoke to my son like an equal, even though Henry had stuck a knife in his tyre. Here was a man talking to a boy with respect and I liked it – it was so different from the way Rob and I dealt with the kids. As I watched Bernie kneel before Henry, I realised that I needed to pay more attention to how I spoke to my kids.

The knife business – a silly prank – was never mentioned again, but about a month later, I saw the photo of Bernie and the boys in the newspaper and heard him on the radio. That's when I decided I wanted to do something for BackTrack. Bernie looked like a man who had the answers.

*

Bernie slides open the screen door at Simmo's and a cold gust of night air and cigarette smoke blows in with him. He takes his place at the table, ready to carry on with the BackTrack meeting. The crew falls silent when they see his expression. He tells us he's tired of waiting on a funding application that'll secure him a part-time wage for the next two years. He wants to make a roster and call in some other blokes to help ease the load: 'Otherwise it's just relying on me and …'

'It gets real old,' offers Geraldine with a knowing look. She's a Kamilaroi woman who has worked with Bernie on other youth projects in Armidale.

'Yep,' Bernie says. 'Real old, real quick. And the pressure's on me the whole time. I'm the worst time manager in Australia, and when we get down the shed I go righto, I'll get those three started on that, and then I've got to pick up Tye or someone else, and I skip up there, and then I get back and Simmo's there and I go oh great, Simmo must be working with them on that. But they've drifted off and started fifteen other fuckin' projects, and I go right, Tye, you go and see Simmo and he'll tell you what to do – I've got to go and pick up someone else. I'm a frazzled chook and by the time the day's over I just go what the fuck – we haven't finished anything and we started another thirty things …'

It's true. I've seen how some Sundays are messy and nothing much seems to get finished, but I still reckon Bernie is making great leaps with these boys. And besides, as he often tells me, 'It's not about the fuckin' welding.'

Positive, positive, positive

Armidale is a small university city and, sooner or later, some of the people you see at work, school or even at the supermarket, end up in your social trajectory. Not long after I first meet Bernie and start at the shed, Rob begins playing the ukulele. He joins a folky bush band with Simmo and a few other people, including Jayne, Bernie's wife. Rob is always supportive of me going along to the shed on Sundays, and I'm happy for him to have a new interest. He puts a lot of energy into learning the instrument and spends hours sitting in the garden shed, practising old Johnny Cash numbers. It's good to hear him singing again. When I first met him, he used to play guitar and serenade me with Bob Dylan songs. He's always been a bit of a romantic.

Rob's band members often hold parties, which is a good thing because Rob and I haven't been out much since Freddie's birth. One night, at one of these gatherings, I spot Bernie standing in the shadows of the garden, smoking. I wander over to join him, and we chat about the boys from the shed. Standing next to Bernie, who is about a head taller than me, I have the same 'little sister' feeling that I get with my brothers. Not many people are tall enough to make me feel that way.

When I ask Bernie if the boys at the shed ever say anything about me, he stares at me confused, like he can't work out why I would ask such a question.

'I'm a woman,' I tell him. 'I'm curious.'

'Nah, they've never mentioned you,' he says. 'I suppose that's strange in itself.'

I'd hoped someone would have said something, that I'd made some sort of impact. Maybe the boys are just happy to share their shed with a mother-figure who doesn't hassle them; a Wendy who brings home-baked brownies into their Neverland, who doesn't comment about stained clothes and jeans hanging halfway down their bums, who leaves them alone. If only I could be like that with my own boys.

'Have you seen Joey around on your Streetbeat nights?'

I know that Bernie has come across Joey through his work with Streetbeat, a crime-prevention program for youth in Armidale, where youth workers drive around on Friday and Saturday nights, keeping kids away from the lock-up.

'Yep.' Bernie pauses, like he's not sure if he should say more. 'I think Joey's going through a hard time, Helena. I've seen him pissed a lot.'

I stare at him, shocked. So naive, always wanting to believe my kids are too sensible for drinking and drugs, that they're not having sex or living dangerously. Or maybe I just prefer to pretend something isn't happening rather than face up to the truth, living my life like those three monkeys who see no evil, speak no evil and hear no evil.

'My guess is he's struggling with that transition from boy to man,' continues Bernie. 'Like a lot of the fellas down at the shed. They go along thinking they're men, but they're just little boys strutting around with no fuckin' idea. From what Joey has said, it doesn't sound like he and Rob get along ...'

I nod, suddenly uncomfortable. This conversation is going places I don't want it to.

'Joey's missing out on that significant male role model,' says Bernie, seemingly oblivious to my awkward silence. 'One way of helping him could be to write a list of positives about his father. I can imagine he's got a picture in his head that's mostly nega-tive, you know – "Why isn't he here for me now? Why did he let that happen? Everybody else has got a dad ... mine must be no good." That's probably not the case, but I don't think it helps with any area of your life to be focusing on the negatives. If you keep thinking negative, and soaking negative, and exuding negative, then negative is what you're going to get around you. For right or wrong, there's a positive side to everything. Joey is probably going to be a dad himself at some stage, so I think it's important he gets that positive stuff about his father.'

I slide my hands into my coat pockets, wondering how this conversation had become so deeply personal in such a short time. Bernie and I never talked like this at the shed.

'There are lots of positives about his father.' I struggle to keep my voice steady, glad it's dark so Bernie can't see my tears.

He nods. 'Yep. And it won't hurt Joey to know them because he exudes the negative – it's in his body language, the way he dresses, the music he listens to, the kids he hangs around. Anything down the track that might help him break that cycle ...' Bernie leans over and pats my upper arm. 'Positive, positive, positive, Helena. I'm a big believer in it.'

*

I met Joey's father at a youth hostel in Amsterdam. It's strange for me to call him that – his 'father'. I don't think of him that way. I'm sure Joey does, but we hardly ever talk about him. His name was Khalil. I'd noticed him one night in the hostel cafeteria because he was so handsome with his dark eyes, pale skin and chiselled features. 'I been no good for many years,' he told me, 'but now I am a Christian.' I almost swooned when I heard his husky voice. Fifteen years older than me, his hair already speckled with grey, he dressed in suit pants, collared shirts and ties. He smoked Camel cigarettes and was like a foreign diplomat with a touch of James Bond mystique. We chatted for the rest of the evening and Khalil told me three things: he was a political refugee from Syria, he'd never had a job and he had a drinking problem. I've since developed a theory that people tell you the most important things about themselves in the first conversations you have with them, but, at the time, none of that seemed to matter.

Because of the hostel's lack of space for intimacy, my time with Khalil was based on endless games of backgammon in smoky cafes, on hash joints and shots of *Arak*. My relatives in Holland, who I rarely saw, called me *een rare vogel* – a strange bird – and maybe they were right. Khalil and I talked about travelling to Spain, where he'd lived before, using money from stolen credit cards. I was keen. On one of the few times we slept together, I became pregnant. Khalil talked for hours about what we might call the baby, how we could find a flat to rent in Amsterdam, how we could start a family together. But by then I'd uncovered the truth about his life. Or maybe I just started listening. Khalil had spent years living on government benefits and would probably never find paid work. He owed me a thousand guilders – the equivalent of nearly seven hundred Australian dollars. He'd left the hostel and was renting a small room in the red-light district. He drank too much. 'I'm always trying to make my life better,' he told me in his beautiful accent, lighting yet another cigarette, ordering yet another beer, borrowing yet another ten guilders. Being with him wasn't going to bring me happiness. I knew that. So I booked a flight back to Australia.

Joey was born in Darwin, where I was staying with my sister. He was a home-birth boy, born at sunset while the birds outside sang their evening song – *A baby is born! A baby is born!* Overwhelmed by love, I gazed down in wonder at his dark tufty hair, his rosebud lips, his strong nose and his clearly defined eyebrows. My beautiful boy.

For the rest of the year, I lived with my oldest brother and his family in an Aboriginal community near Katherine. My brother was the principal of the local school, and he offered me a job as a live-in nanny for his two-year-old daughter while his wife went back to teaching. I thought it would be a good place to stop and take a breath, to work out what I wanted for the future.

As for Khalil, he rang three times that first year and sent a postcard: *Together we made little 'Joey'. Together we love him and together we shall be around forever. I love you both. Wishing to see you as soon as possible. Anxious to hear him saying 'Pap'.* Then we lost contact. Eight years later, I received a letter from a friend in Holland. Khalil had been murdered, shot in a sordid Amsterdam street brawl. I wept when I read her words. Joey would never meet him now.

*

At home that night, after talking with Bernie at the party, I sit at the kitchen table and start writing a list of all the lovely things I remember about Joey's father. He was a good man – he just lost his footing along the way.

Dear Joey,

I've been thinking about Khalil lately, and I thought I'd write a list of all the things I liked about him so you have a better idea of who he was. It's a shame he's not alive anymore – I think you would have really liked him. Here's my list:

Khalil …
- *was funny*
- *was handsome with the classical features of a Middle Eastern movie star*
- *loved reciting classical Arabic poetry and literature*
- *loved playing table football – and he was very competitive too!*
- *loved playing backgammon in the brown cafes in Amsterdam*
- *was a loyal friend*

- *loved the Spanish dance music that was popular in Amsterdam at the time – he would clap his hands over his shoulder to the beat of the music*
- *could make delicious baba ganoush – a Lebanese eggplant dip – by blackening the eggplants over the gas burner, and then mixing the smoky flesh with tahini*
- *loved having his hair cut*
- *loved the movie* Down by Law *– especially the scene where the three guys are in the prison cell chanting: 'I scream, you scream, we all scream for ice cream!'*
- *was a deep thinker – often pensive*
- *had a lovely husky voice – when he spoke Arabic it sounded wonderful. Try and listen to people speaking Arabic – it's a beautiful language*
- *was spiritual – his family were from a Christian region of Syria, and when I first met him he was very strong with God*
- *loved going to shawarma bars in Amsterdam and eating freshly made shawarma rolls – which are like Lebanese rolls*
- *always dressed well – he was distinguished and gentlemanly*
- *was a wonderful companion to spend time with*
- *always kept trying to make his life better*
- *was caring and generous*
- *spoke Spanish like he was born there because he lived in Barcelona for several years before Amsterdam – and people used to think he was Spanish, even Spaniards! He loved different languages and was interested in learning.*

I hope this helps you gain a better picture of what he was like. Remember, I've still got the scrapbook I made for you about your first eight years of life. I'm keeping it safe for you, but you can look at it anytime, and we can talk about Khalil whenever you like.

The next morning I walk around to Joey's house with the letter. It's too early to knock so I push the envelope under his door. Throughout the day I imagine him opening the envelope and reading through the list.

Joey rings later that evening. 'I wish I could have met him,' he says.

Sucking lemons

A few days later, Joey comes over with a story about how drunk he was the night before – 'I vomited all over my bedroom floor.'

'I'm not going to help you clean *that* up,' I tell him, trying not to let despair creep into my voice. I lend him the hose, a bucket and some old rags. Later he comes around: tired, belligerent and demanding lemons.

I check the fruit bowl. No lemons. I wish I had some so I could send him on his way. His heavy mood sets my nerves on edge. 'Why lemons?'

'They help with a hangover,' he says, pacing the length of the kitchen.

When I mention the corner store, he says he's already been there.

'Maybe you can buy some at the supermarket?' I suggest.

'I can't walk all that way!' he complains. 'I've got a bad hangover. I already told you that. Why do you *never* listen?'

So, we drive to the supermarket, two blocks away. I buy two lemons. Joey bites through the peel of one and sucks it dry as we drive back to his house.

I park out the front, force a smile. 'Bye, Joey.'

He chucks the remains of the lemon onto the floor near his feet. 'Bye, Mum,' he says, leaning over to kiss my cheek, his breath a mixture of tangy lemon and stale alcohol. 'I love you.'

*

Most of the time, Rob is content to sit back and let me deal with Joey – it's easier that way. He and Joey tend to become antagonistic and confrontational whenever they're together. I always seem to be hustling Joey out of the house in an effort to avoid further conflict. I hate how they muscle up to each other in the doorways, like oversensitive drunks at a pub, shouting rubbish. And I hate how I always intervene and make it worse. We've been trapped in this pattern for a long time now, which is a shame because there were many tender moments between Rob and Joey in those early years.

When Joey was nine months old, we left the Northern Territory and moved to Armidale, high in the New England tablelands, so I could do a teaching degree at the university. I found a room in a share-house with two other women, bought a pushbike with a baby seat on the back, booked Joey in with a friendly family day care mother, and began my studies. I rode my bike to the university each day, and life felt free and full of possibilities.

Around the time of Joey's first birthday, my mother came to visit. While we were having coffee downtown, a bearded man with a wide smile came over to our table. He was from the same small town where I'd grown up, he said, and recognised my mother. She remembered him and his family, and invited him to join us. Rob had a rugged 'bushie' look about him, like he lived on the land. He was thirty-five, ten years older than me, and had gone to school with my siblings. I liked the sound of his voice, the way his lips moved, and the way he kept looking at me. He told us he came to Armidale in his early twenties. At the university he'd studied to become a history teacher, but after three weeks of teaching in a high school in the Northern Territory, he decided it wasn't the life for him. For the next ten years, he had travelled around Australia – living on the dole and occasionally working on building sites – before ending up back in the New England area. Rob spoke proudly of a stone and timber hut he'd built on a scrubby bush block forty kilometres out of Armidale. He'd lived there on his own for six months, but some vandals had recently burnt it down and he'd lost everything. All his books, clothes, photos ... gone. Now he shared a house in town with a philosopher, worked in a truss factory, and had just bought a ticket to India.

Like I said, people tell you everything you need to know in the first conversations you have with them. But at the time, I was concentrating on Rob's lips and thinking how sexy he was, even with his bushy red beard. Before he left, I asked him for his telephone number.

A few weeks later, when one of my housemates had a dinner party, I invited Rob to come along. We sat together on the lounge and talked about our lives and our dreams for the future. I discovered he wrote poetry and enjoyed studying history and philosophy. Books and learning were important to him. He was the only one in his family – third-generation dairy farmers – who had owned a book, and that had been given to him by the Methodist Church. He described a fractured relationship with his parents and said he rarely visited them. As a boy, he was captain of the local football team, and his father used to rip into him from the sidelines and yell: 'Git in there!' and, 'You can do better than that!' Rob ran away from home at seventeen. He was back within a few days after the police were called. He'd spent years going out with a local girl while he was at high school. But when she wanted to get married, he decided to go hitch-hiking around Australia instead. That was his past. As for the future, all he wanted to do was go to India.

The weekend after the dinner party, Rob and I went to see a play at the university theatre. I wore a white puffy coat from Amsterdam and felt like a girl on her first date. When he dropped me home, I asked him to come inside. We drank brandy and kissed by the fire. That was the beginning of our life together.

We only had a month before he went to India. Every day, after finishing work at the truss factory, Rob would come around to help with the evening ritual of feeding, bathing and dressing Joey. 'I don't know how you do all this on your own,' he'd often say. He built a sandpit for Joey in the backyard and fed Joey his porridge in the mornings. When I stayed at Rob's house one night, in his tiny room with a futon bed and a printed cane blind and not much else, I brought Joey in after his bath and Rob had laid the nappy and night clothes out on the bed, just as I always did, and I loved him for that.

Before Rob left for India, I asked him for a copy of a poem he had written called 'Days of My Youth'. I liked it very much, and I've often thought of it over the years:

In the cold-shower Christianity of my youth
when God was all-knowing with a long white beard:
Sunday, between milkings, was for Sunday School and Church,
with great-uncle snoring in the pew behind and great-uncle leading
the choir,
and Sunday dinner with cousins

of roast beef and leaving room for dessert.
Dad said, 'You can get milk out of a bull, but only one squirt',
and I didn't know what he meant.
Corn was cut by hand and the Fergi pulled a sled to the stalls,
and a pocketknife was full of mysteries of Tom Sawyer and Treasure
    and billycarts.

In the spluttering fire of my adolescence,
When God was too difficult to think about:
Rice a Riso seemed exotic and school was full of strangers from ten
    miles away,
and staying over at a mate's place meant a bottle of beer
and being pissed for the first and most ecstatic time.
A girlfriend's pants revealed secrets hardly dreamed of,
but bra-straps were a snap with one hand,
while Mum and Dad fretted and muttered over blow-stains on the
    sheets,
and I chopped the copper-stick of beatings into little pieces
on the woodpile out the back.
Running away from home was easy,
but coming back after three days found Mum on tranquillisers
and Dad in league with the cops.

In the run-free joy of having left school,
when God was Shanka and Going:
The Pacific Highway was the road to the world,
and my thumb the only ticket.
Pot was thirty dollars, and a hundred dollars was a fortune.
The continent was full of me,
life rode in a rucksack,
and the sun could rise anywhere.

Fuckin' 'whatever' isn't an answer

The next time I go along to the shed, Bernie and Simmo round up the boys and we meet in the kitchen to make the final arrangements for a tool-buying trip. A few weeks earlier, the Iron Man Welders had received a five thousand dollar grant to buy new equipment. Since then, the boys had spent hours poring over tool catalogues from Bunnings and other hardware stores, dreaming of what they would buy with the money.

In the kitchen, stained carpet squares cover the concrete floor, matching motley remnants of a lounge suite that belongs at the dump. An old workbench on one side of the room holds an electric jug, an upturned packet of tea bags, a tin of Milo and a ripped bag of sugar. Someone's pouch of tobacco is passed around. As the boys light up, the smoke rests on shafts of afternoon sunlight coming through a barred window.

Bernie wears a vibrant orange polar fleece jumper and stands out like a seedling in a dirt paddock. He tells me they're trying to decide whether to go to Coffs Harbour for an overnight trip, or just make a day-trip to Tamworth, which is only an hour's drive away. Bernie moves across the room to open the window, letting in a blast of cold air, and then takes a seat next to Tye. I'd heard a few things about Tye in recent weeks – he'd been through a lifetime of foster homes, and when he first met Bernie, 'fuck off' was his way of saying 'good morning'.

Whenever I see Bernie and Tye together, it's like seeing father and son: both tall and rangy with their wild brown curls and countryman looks. Tye's face is softer, though, his blue eyes bigger. Simmo once told me there's something about Tye that Bernie recognises in himself.

'Righto,' says Bernie, getting down to business. 'We've got

two options – Coffs Harbour or Tamworth? What do you think, Freckles?'

Freckles looks up from burning the frayed cuff of his jeans with the end of his rollie. 'If we don't take too many people, maybe just a couple of cars, we could go to Coffs.'

'Uh huh,' nods Bernie. 'So how are we going to work out who gets to come and who gets to stay?'

The boys fall silent.

'What do you reckon, Tye?'

'It doesn't worry me,' shrugs Tye. 'Whatever.'

'Fuckin' "whatever" isn't an answer,' says Bernie. 'That's sitting on the fence.'

The rest of us laugh while Tye slides off his beanie and scratches his head. 'I really dunno.'

'I dunno,' repeats Bernie, looking hard at Tye. 'That's reeking of a "whatever" answer as well. A or B? A is Coffs, B is Tamworth.'

We wait. Tye takes a drag on his rollie and blows a dignified line of smoke-rings across the table. 'A.'

Once the others have their say, the boys soon reach a group consensus on Tamworth. 'Okay,' says Bernie. 'We could do it next weekend.'

'I'll be in Queensland,' says Tye. 'Me girlfriend's mum is having a baby.'

'And you're going to deliver it?' jokes Bernie. 'Doctor Tye, eh?'

The other boys chuckle, but I feel a surge of tenderness towards Tye, thinking of all the foster homes he's passed through.

I once asked Bernie where Tye would be if he hadn't become involved with the welding program. Bernie had pressed his palms together and exhaled slowly before answering: 'He'd have a raging drug habit, he'd be extremely violent – mimicking what he saw as a young fella, which wasn't pretty – he'd be bashing women, struggling in a lot of areas, and probably would have spent time in the lock-up.' Bernie looked at me and nodded. 'That's my belief with Tye.'

The talk shifts to a big party the previous night, someone's 18th. Bernie rubs at the corners of his eyes and smothers a yawn. 'I was out driving the Streetbeat car till four in the morning ... that party just went all night!'

'I only had four beers last night,' offers Tye in a low voice.

'Very impressed with that, mate,' says Bernie, suddenly serious. 'That was the most impressive thing I saw all night.'

Gazza taps at the notebook on his lap. 'I think we should get back to this crap. I've gotta head off soon.'

They discuss approximate costs of tools and welders and work out, for the umpteenth time, what they want to buy. Freckles flicks through a tool catalogue. 'How much are you willing to pay for a cordless drill?'

'How much am *I* willing to pay?' Bernie shakes his head. 'How much are *you* blokes willing to pay?'

Again and again, Bernie passes on the responsibility for deciding which tools go on the list. He's like a soccer coach who keeps kicking the ball back, nice and easy, until his players gain confidence.

After Gazza reads through the final list, Tye whistles and says, 'Fuck, we're not going to have much money left after this.'

'We'll have everything then,' says Bernie, and asks Simmo to ring Bunnings in Tamworth. 'See if we can get a discount. Tell 'em these blokes won't steal a heap of shit if they give us a good deal.'

The boys all laugh at that, even Gazza.

They picked the wrong head!

A few days later, reading in bed after a busy day of teaching, shopping and cooking, I hear the back door open. Everyone else in the house is asleep, so it can only be Joey. Urgent footsteps pound up the hallway.

'Mum! Mum!' whispers Joey from my bedroom door. 'I need to show you something!' He leads me to the kitchen and turns on the light. Taking off his cap, he leans forward to show me his head.

'What is it?' I ask, yawning.

'I've got ringworm!' he says anxiously, like it's a life-threatening disease. 'Probably from Tim's dog.' Circular markings dot his scalp, like one of those fields where unexplained patterns appear.

'A friend shaved my head tonight and saw the circles,' says Joey, frantically searching through the medicine cupboard. 'His mum is a nurse and she said we need to put Betadine on it!'

I flick through an old medical book. 'Ringworm isn't anything to do with worms. It's a fungus you pick up from humans, animals or places. That's why it's important to wash your sheets regularly.'

Joey finds the Betadine and dashes into the bathroom. Brown liquid splashes over the sink as he tries to cover his entire scalp with the smelly antiseptic lotion.

I grab one of Freddie's old nappies from the cupboard. 'Put this over you before it drips onto your T-shirt.'

Joey throws the nappy around his shoulders like a cape and narrows his eyes. 'They picked the wrong head! I'm going to sit up all night and wait for them to go.'

'They're *not* worms, Joey,' I tell him, trying not to laugh. 'The marks will be gone in twenty-four hours.' Ignoring the mess in the bathroom, I send him out the door with clean sheets and a pillowcase, along with twenty dollars to buy anti-fungal ointment the next day.

The next morning he staggers up the side of the house with a huge basket of washing and dumps it in my laundry. Before I have time to ask what's going on, he runs back home for another load. 'All my clothes and bedding need to be washed!' says Joey when he returns, desperate to go downtown to buy the anti-fungal ointment.

'Don't forget to come back and help hang out this washing!' I call after him.

Six hot-wash loads later, there's still no sign of Joey, but his quilt covers, sheets, towels, pillowcases, hoodies, jeans and black T-shirts flap about on my clothesline. Thank goodness it's a sunny day. Later, I fold everything neatly back into the baskets and leave them on his front veranda. Joey's housemate, Tim, a divorced man with adult children of his own, opens the door just as I'm struggling up the steps with the second basket. We've become friends over the last few months. He shakes his head in mock-despair at the huge amount of washing at my feet.

I look at Tim, my cheeks burning. 'I know I shouldn't, but sometimes Joey needs help getting organised.'

'Oh, Helena,' he says, like there's no hope for me.

*

Whenever my mother asks: 'How's things with Joey?' I try to answer in a light and positive tone. My parents, especially my father, wouldn't be impressed to know the truth about the heated arguments that Rob and I have with Joey. When my father was a boy in Amsterdam, he grew up with three main rules – obey your parents, respect older people, and be home at six for the evening meal. He doesn't understand why I can't implement this regime in my own life. That's why I don't tell him how things really are at home.

Like most of us, though, my father had his wild times as well – mostly during the years of German occupation in Amsterdam. In those war years, my father was always on the lookout for an opportunity. As a boy of fourteen, along with a legitimate job with a greengrocer, he also had clandestine dealings with skippers from the barges that transported fruit and vegetables to the markets. It was a time of strict rationing, but at night, my father would sneak out on his *bakfiets* – a tricycle with a large wooden tray in the front – and pick up a load of potatoes from one of these skippers to sell later on the black market. 'It made the adrenalin flow through the system,' he once told me. He stole bread and milk from the back of German trucks and wooden decking from ships in the harbour. Like many other desperate citizens, he raided the houses in the deserted Jewish neighbourhood for doors and floorboards, risking his life to bring wood home to his mother. She begged him not to steal, but there was no coal, no food, no money. One time he was discovered and had to go to the children's court, where his mother pleaded with the judge. Her son wasn't really bad, she said, it was just the circumstances. After that, my father never came in contact with the police again.

Due to the strength of his mother, my father's family remained fairly happy during those difficult times. *Sterkte* – strength – is a trait common to the Dutch. As is the ability to be stoic. I wear a pendant that once belonged to my father's mother, an oval-shaped piece of haematite set in gold, which brings to mind the elegance of old-time Europe. People often notice it, especially if they're interested in gemstones. I wear it because it belonged to my oma, and because I want her strength to flow through to me.

I have a photo of her wearing the pendant – she stands by the oven in her tiny kitchen, tea towel in hand. She was always cooking and washing, just like I am.

*

Joey is back the next day, his head still streaked with Betadine.

'Did you find the washing?'

'What?' He looks confused. 'Oh, yeah, thanks.'

He picks up Theo's harmonica from the kitchen bench and blows a few notes. 'I could be one of those guys in the army,' he says, cocking one eyebrow in a charming manner. 'You know, after everyone's fallen asleep around the campfire ... one guy is left quietly playing the harmonica?'

I smile. Joey can be so lovely. 'Yes, that could be you.'

'I'm serious about joining the army, Mum. I might go to Iraq.'

'Maybe peacekeeping in Timor would be better,' I suggest, thinking how Iraq is too close to the action for my liking. The army brochures arrived in the mail the other day, and Joey and I had read through the material together. He got very excited about the exercise program, and said he might even start practising sit-ups and push-ups at home. I don't know if it's foolhardy or rash of me to be encouraging him to join up – I don't want him shooting people or risking his own life – but somehow I can see him in the army. He's always loved following a routine, and perhaps army life would help him become more organised. He was supposed to meet the TAFE counsellor at noon the other day to discuss his attendance. I drove past Joey's house after Freddie's playgroup to check if he'd gone. He answered the door in his pyjamas, unconcerned when I reminded him about the appointment. Instead, barely able to stop laughing, he told me: 'I just realised I've spent the last three months washing my hair with bubble bath.'

I had to laugh, too. Life would be very boring if we all washed our hair with shampoo.

Not gammon

The soft blue sky of New England stretches wide above me as I drive to the shed the Sunday after the boys' shopping trip. When I arrive at the gates, Bernie is heading out in his ute with one of the boys.

'How'd the Tamworth trip go?' I ask.

'It was great!' says Bernie, easing the ute forward. 'Blister will take you around and show you what we bought.'

On the dusty floor of the shed are piles of flattened boxes and plastic wrapping. Blister wanders over, eyes twinkling, quite the gentleman with his dark crew cut, gangster-style moustache and short goatee. He always seems much older than seventeen. We walk around the shed together and he shows me all the new tools, and even remembers how much they all cost. The trip has made a huge impression on him. I suppose it's one thing to have thousands of dollars of donations and talk endlessly in smoky meetings about what to buy, but it's something else to go and spend it on real tools and equipment.

And today, the boys are busy working the whole time – no mucking about with BMX bikes on the piles of dirt out the back or anything like that. Gazza and Thommo make a trolley for the gas tanks for the oxy welder to sit in and the others try out the new tools. When Bernie comes back with food for the barbecue, Blister and Tye cook the meat while I sit in the sun, sorting Bernie's dockets from the previous month. Even with thick socks and heavy boots, my feet still ache from the cold.

Once the paperwork is done, I stand near the barbecue, rubbing my hands together and trying to warm myself with the heat coming from the gas burners. Blister tells me and Tye about his new caravan at the Highlander Caravan Park – ninety dollars a week, electricity and everything included. He loves it. His mum chucked him out of home so he's living in the caravan with his 'missus'.

Tye skilfully flips over some patties. 'That'd be terrific, living in a caravan.'

After lunch, Blister lets Bernie's two border collies, Girl and Lou, off their chains – the dogs are tied up outside the shed whenever Bernie's there. Blister throws a stick to them, over and over, getting the dogs to crouch down and wait each time. Later he feeds the dogs leftovers, dipping the still-hot sausages in their water bowl to make them cool enough to eat.

That afternoon, there isn't time to ask Bernie any more about the tool-buying trip, but as I'm leaving he says, 'Geraldine would be good to talk with.' He laughs, as if remembering something very funny. 'That was a horrible day she had, but we were having the time of our lives.'

I wouldn't have thought Geraldine, one of the BackTrack crew, the type to volunteer for a tool-buying trip. She's a self-confessed 'clothes horse' who straightens her hair and wears high heels. She often seems on the edge of a giggling fit, the laughter held beneath her skin like the bubbles in a bottle of champagne, just waiting for someone to pop the cork.

While Bernie's busy welding with the boys, Geraldine has taken on the wayward girls in the community. She's also a member of Streetbeat night patrol. Geraldine is only short, but Joey, who stands well over six foot, told me how she'd been joking around with him one night at the Streetbeat office, ordering him to commando crawl through the doorway. He said no and a second later found himself on the floor, wondering what the hell had happened. Small, tough and glamorous with a big laugh – that's Geraldine, or Aunty Gel as she's known around town.

The next time I'm over in Girraween, the housing commission area near the university, I stop in at Geraldine's. After she makes cups of tea, we sit on comfy chairs in her lounge room, where knick-knacks are carefully placed on side tables and framed family photos cover every wall. In one corner is the biggest television I have ever seen. Geraldine laughs when she sees my surprised expression. 'I get kids come and sleep over on Friday nights,' she explains. 'I make them a bed on the floor and they watch my big-arse screen … I tell ya, size does matter!'

We talk about the trip to Tamworth. When I mention how Bernie told me it was the greatest fun she ever had, she shakes her head, glossy auburn-tinted hair flying. 'Yeah right!' I watch as she organises her knitting on her lap, trying to picture her in Tamworth with the boys, running up and down the aisles of Bunnings in her high heels. The image doesn't fit. 'It was good of you to help.'

'I'm up for anything really,' she says breezily, counting a few stitches. 'Like most of those boys – they'll come along to anything as long as Bernie's organising it.'

'Why's that?' I ask, curious. I'd never had anything to do with youth workers before starting at the shed and I often wondered what made Bernie's work so special.

Geraldine looks up from her knitting. 'He's just not gammon. He's truthful, honest, moralistic and upright in how he faces the world, and he's not afraid to take on a fight. He's always said his core root is from mother earth, so for him it's about giving back as well. He had people mentor him when he was wild and woolly and they're still in his life. Those boys will be around Bernie forever.'

She goes over to a shelf and finds a photo album, flicking it open to a group photo. 'That's the boys when they started with Bernie at TAFE.'

I laugh – 'What a crew!' Then I notice a picture of a young man standing on his own. 'Who's that?'

'That's my brother,' says Geraldine, staring at the photo. 'He died when he was twenty. He was one of them loose kids – always drinking and smoking – and one night, walking home from a party, he got hit by a car. That was thirteen years ago … he'd be thirty-three now.'

I don't know what to say, it seems such a senseless way to die.

As I'm walking out the door, I remember Joey's Streetbeat story and ask Geraldine if she's ever done any martial arts training.

Her face creases in confusion. 'No. Why?'

I begin to tell her Joey's 'commando crawl' story. Before I've even finished she's giggling, getting louder and louder, holding her stomach, eyes watering.

'I grew up with all boys …' she splutters, then points to herself. 'Small girl – learn how to fight dirty!'

It's funny though, after spending time with Geraldine, she doesn't seem small at all.

Wild country for a wild young fella

A few nights later, as I'm getting ready for bed, I hear the gate click. I hurry to the back door. Joey stands on the patio, looking distressed.

'Mum! *Prison Break* is on and I can't watch it at Tim's because his meditation group is still there!'

'It's nine-thirty, Joey,' I tell him. 'I'm on my way to bed and everyone else is asleep. I don't want the television on now. Sorry.'

'Can you drive me around to Liam's?' he asks. 'I'll watch it at his place.'

I'm tired and I want to say no, but I know that's likely to lead to an angry scene, so I grab the keys from the top of the fridge and walk out to the car in my pyjamas and slippers. We drive to Liam's in silence. Once we arrive, Joey gets out and turns to me angrily.

'I should be able to just watch TV occasionally at your house! You're always putting everything I need onto other people, just like you did when you made me leave home!'

Guilt stabs at my heart. I know I'm intolerant and unreasonable, too set in my routines. And I know other parents wouldn't mind their sons watching television at night – in fact, most teenagers in Armidale are probably tuned into *Prison Break* right now. I really don't understand why I react the way I do. But when Joey comes around unexpectedly, I automatically shift into high alert, which always makes things worse. No wonder he judges me harshly, and I'm sure others in this community do as well. I wish things were different – that Joey could move back home and that our family could live in harmony under one roof. If only he understood how much I love him, how I only want the best for him. But unfortunately, for the time being, the 'best' doesn't include him living at home.

I need to learn how to be a better parent first.

*

Shopping in Armidale's open-air mall one morning, I spot Bernie outside the courthouse. He tells me he's waiting for Thommo – 'He's up on an assault charge.'

'Oh!' I exclaim. 'That's terrible.'

Bernie shakes his head, like he's seen it all before. 'Same sort of crazy shit I did when I was young. He'll probably get off with a caution.'

'I hope so.' I put my shopping bags on the ground and sit on the bench beside him, taking a quick look at the crowd gathering out the front of the courthouse. The Armidale courthouse – an old-style stone building in the centre of town – offers an open-air display of who's in trouble with the law. Like a public playhouse, a Shakespearean drama unfolds here each weekday morning, and I often engage in surreptitious people-watching when I walk past.

Since talking to Geraldine, I'd become curious about Bernie's 'wild and woolly' background. 'By the way,' I say to him now, settling back on the bench, 'you never finished telling me about your idiot days.'

He lifts his eyebrows. 'You really want to know?'

I nod.

'I had a little golden circle just above my head,' he begins, circling a finger over his hair in the shape of a halo. Then he laughs softly and says, 'Well, maybe that's not true. I grew up in Armidale with strict Catholic parents, went to Mass and Catholic schools – all that sort of business.' He pauses to roll a cigarette and waves to someone walking by. 'The rest of my family were fairly academic, but that was never going to be me. I probably spent as much time out of the classroom as in, and the more ancient history, geography and trigonometry I did, the more I didn't want to be there.' He lights up and leans back on the bench. 'I guess a lot of my anger at the time came from being the dumbest in the school – I was always in trouble for smoking and that sort of stuff.'

'Dope?' I ask.

Bernie shakes his head vigorously. 'I never touched dope till I was much older, thank God. Wasn't at a real young age for kicking off with the grog either. It was more just running around wild, looking for thrills.'

With his unruly hair, dark sunglasses, boots and jeans, Bernie could still pass for a thrill seeker. He reminds me of that group of boys who were always outside the principal's office when I was at high school. I'm sure every school has them – they're trouble and make their teachers' lives a nightmare, yet you can't help but admire their daring, their lawlessness.

Bernie left school as soon as he could, a decision which led to his first real 'bust-up' with his family. They wanted him to do Year 12. 'I worked for a year as a travel agent,' he tells me, and I can't help laughing at the idea of him behind a desk.

'Then I ended up in the foothills of the Snowy Mountains,' he says, 'and somehow I crossed tracks with a couple who owned the saddlers – Paul and Annette. No doubt they could see what was going on – a young bloke who thought he knew everything with nowhere to live and very few skills – and they took me in.' A wistful look crosses Bernie's face. 'Must've been tough times for them when I think back, having me there carrying on like a flaming idiot, but for some reason Paul could tolerate all my bullshit.'

Bernie stares down at his boots, quiet for a moment. 'I never had much of a verbal relationship with my own dad. A lot of our talking was around fighting and arguing – not that there weren't good times, and I know my parents love me, but I wasn't understood, and I didn't understand shit myself.'

As we sit in companionable silence, I think about Bernie's words. I wonder what Joey will remember of his troubled years at home, of not being understood.

'It's a tough gig to parent any child,' continues Bernie. 'But it's a smoother transition if there are other older people around to look up to and learn from. I got into horses and dogs through Paul, and he lined me up some work in Victoria where I worked with some of the best horsemen in the industry.'

I watch as he crushes the butt of his cigarette under his boot.

'But I had a passion for wild things, so they sent me off to the Northern Territory, to Newcastle Waters – wild country for a wild young fella! I worked on the outstations, busted a heap of bones, and had a heap of fun – that's where I met Jayne.'

'So how did you become a youth worker?'

'Nuclear science didn't pick me,' says Bernie with a grin. 'Being a policeman or a fireman didn't come and grab me by the collar. But somewhere along the line, the youth work came along, and all of a sudden here's this job I shouldn't have because I didn't have any qualifications. I worked in a youth refuge in Alice Springs, and straight away it was like I'd been doing it my whole life. Youth organisations often use shortcuts – but for me it was always "man-up" and let's fuckin' sort this shit.'

Bernie and Jayne came back to New South Wales to work as house parents for some 'wild lads' on a farm at Tarago, but it wasn't long before they returned to the Territory, where Bernie ended up working with the Warramunga people around Tennant Creek.

'The old fellas sniffed me out and took me out bush,' says Bernie, his voice hushed. 'I'll never know why those proper old men took on a young white fella like me, but I started cruising around with them and they taught me about animals and the bush ... about how things are all connected.' He shakes his head. 'Oh Christ, the things those old men taught me.'

'Like what?'

Bernie whistles under his breath. 'Stuff I probably shouldn't talk about ... but something that would be okay to talk about is whether it's your dreaming how you have a connection with an animal, or how to split dogs and bitches on tracks, how to find animals.' He chuckles to himself. 'White fellas are forever running around chasing things, but those old fellas taught me how to draw things to you, and that's not just with dogs. We do it with the boys at the shed – I call it "visioning on a spiritual level". If I've got a tricky dog or a tricky kid to catch, I see what's going to happen out the front, and then get to it. Doesn't usually happen in a day, but it comes ... eventually.'

Around us, the front of the courthouse is teeming with black-suited lawyers and nervous clients. Everyone is smoking. The drama is about to begin. Time for one last question – 'What else did those old fellas teach you?'

Bernie clears his throat. 'The "uncle" thing, no doubt about that – about the importance of having sensible older people around to show younger people how to grow up.'

Out of the corner of my eye, I see Thommo shambling up the mall. I gather my shopping bags. 'Is that what you are to those boys at the shed? Uncle?'

'Yep,' says Bernie quietly. 'Very similar.'

*

51

Not long after this conversation, I meet with a friend, a psychologist, who has worked with Bernie on various youth programs in Armidale. We talk about his style of youth work. I'm interested to hear her say that because Bernie is self-taught, he hasn't inherited a whole lot of boundaries through doing a university degree – he hasn't become 'bound by his boundaries'.

When I question my friend about this, she explains how there are certain rules involved with having a therapeutic relationship, rules that are in place to avoid the relationship becoming intimate. 'For example,' she says, 'never in a million years would I bring a client to my home, but Bernie breaks that rule.'

So does Geraldine, I think, remembering her big-arse TV and the movie nights.

'He also answers the phone all the time,' my friend adds. 'I wouldn't do that. But something I would do – that other practitioners wouldn't – is if one of my weekly clients was going for a job interview on a Wednesday, I'd ring Wednesday afternoon to see how she went.'

I ask how that's breaking the rules.

'You're not that person's friend, Helena,' she says, giving me a straight look. 'Everyone likes a phone call after they've had a job interview, but am I helping a client if I fill that role, or am I helping them better if I don't fill it? You don't have a thirty-year relationship with your counsellor – that's what you have with a partner or a good friend.'

Afterwards, I think of how Bernie's phone hardly stops ringing, how he gives up his Sundays to spend time with the boys at the shed, and how I have never heard him say the word 'client'.

Joey-in-a-box!

On the night before Joey's 17th birthday, Rob and I decorate the dining room with streamers and balloons and arrange Joey's presents and cards on the table – one of our family birthday traditions. When the kids were younger, we always told them the 'birthday fairies' had been, and even though everyone except Freddie has long stopped believing in fairies, I still like to put up decorations. I also make Joey a 'collage card' – another tradition – from pictures and words from the weekend magazines. *Live your dreams, Joey!* I write on the bottom of the card. *Happy 17th Birthday!!!*

Later, when Rob is asleep, I look through the scrapbook I once made for Joey, which covers the first eight years of his life. I especially wanted him to have a record of our first year together, before we met Rob, in case something happened to me. When I look at it now, the photos of his birth and of happier times with Rob and the other kids leave me feeling a little sad. The book documents the activities Joey used to enjoy – like painting stripes on a cardboard box, climbing inside, and jumping out from the top yelling: 'Joey-in-a-box!', or re-creating Dreamworld's Tower of Terror with his Lego. We had a lot of fun with Joey. In the back pages, I read the first stanza of a poem Rob wrote while I was pregnant with Henry:

> *On a rainy day in December*
> *I think about babies*
> *and how they came to me.*
> *Joey is part of my love with Helena.*
> *He grew as our love grew.*
> *Irascible hero of the backyard, he is my son.*

With the page still open before me, and with Bernie's 'visioning' technique in my mind, I write a positive affirmation for Joey in my journal, my hopes for what the coming year will bring:

Joey is caring, kind and happy. He is busy with work, friends, love and life. Joey is sensible and aware of other people's feelings. He loves and is loved. Joey is great to be around and knows his family loves him. Joey is calm and settled within himself. Joey has all the money he needs. Joey is my beautiful boy.

After I read over the birthday affirmation several times, I close the book.

*

Years ago, when Rob came back from India, he took me to visit his parents, who lived on acreage outside of the small town where we'd both grown up. We swam in their creek that first day – Rob, Joey and me – and in the photos we took I'm impossibly slim and beautiful, and Rob looks impossibly happy and relaxed. Later, up at the house, his mother fussed and made cups of tea. When his father came home from the pub, he joked around with Joey before he and Rob went into the garage, where there was a beer fridge and a transistor radio. I helped Rob's mother prepare dinner. She handed me a bottle of HP sauce, a loaf of sliced white bread and a tub of margarine to put in the centre of the table, all foreign to me. Rob's younger brother and his new girlfriend came over, and she brought her daughter to play with Joey. Everyone welcomed me warmly and I felt part of a real Australian family. But then, at dinner, Rob's mother kept asking why the children weren't eating more, and everyone kept saying, 'Do what you're told!' to the little girl. 'Do what you're told!' said with a rising intonation. I felt uncomfortable each time they said it.

Back in Armidale, Rob wore soft white Indian shirts and a straw hat, and when he cut his beard, he looked like Vincent van Gogh. He enrolled in further study at the university, with the hope of becoming a history lecturer. The following year, when Joey was two, I found a lovely half-house to rent, with its own wisteria-covered veranda and a fireplace in the main bedroom. It seemed like a natural step for Rob to move in with us.

We had good fun in that half-house. On weekends, Rob and Joey spent lots of time together in the backyard, building tree-houses and rock pools. They transformed the laundry into a toolshed and hung a transistor radio on a nail on the wall.

The next winter, our first baby together – Theo – was born beside the fire in our bedroom. My mother called him *het poppetje* because Theo looked like a porcelain doll with his round face and perfect skin. Five months later, Rob and I married in a small ceremony held in the backyard at my parents' house in Sydney. We recited verses from Bob Dylan's 'Wedding Song' as part of our marriage vows, and my father gave a speech in which he said: 'Whatever their road in life will be, it is certain that it will not always be smooth and even. There will be bumps, unforeseen obstacles and setbacks, like in any partnership, but I am sure Helena and Rob have enough common sense and love for each other to conquer any adversity they meet on their way through life.'

When Joey was four and Theo was one, we left Armidale for Brisbane so Rob could finish his PhD in Queensland trade union history. I taught English to migrants four days a week and completed one more year of part-time study in linguistics. Joey went to preschool and Theo started family day care. On weekends, Rob and I took the kids to the beach, or to see the rock-climbers at the Kangaroo Point Cliffs, where Joey, exuberant and inquisitive, asked the climbers lots of questions. At home, Rob fixed a knotted rope around the mango tree in the backyard so Joey could practise his climbing skills.

To boost our income, I also worked in a Turkish restaurant four nights a week. Rob was left parenting for much of the evening, which wasn't easy for him or the kids. Our family life suffered a great deal that year. I remember Joey and Theo crying a lot. When I think of that time now, I don't understand why I was out of the house so much when I had two small children. Even when I became pregnant again, I continued to work two jobs and do part-time study. Rob could have picked up some extra work at night, but we didn't do it that way. I recently heard an interview with Leonard Cohen, in which he admitted that he was 'always escaping' from his intimate others. Maybe that's what I was doing, too. But when Rob started saying: 'Do what you're told!' to Joey, I cut back on my hours and spent more time at home. We needed to carry the load together, and it wasn't long before Henry, a beautiful auburn-haired baby, was born into that house by the river in Brisbane.

*

On the morning of Joey's 17th birthday, Freddie helps me with the 'birth cake' – a rich chocolate sour-cream cake – dipping his spoon into the chocolate icing whenever he thinks I'm not looking. The cake recipe, from an old Women's Weekly cookbook, has about fifteen steps and I make it for Joey's birthday every year. I'd been making the cake on the day he was born.

Later, after buying some last-minute things at the supermarket, I find Joey in the lounge room, watching *The Mummy*, with the volume up loud, all the doors and curtains closed.

I walk over and switch off the television. 'Sorry, Joey, but that movie isn't suitable for Freddie.'

Joey leaps to his feet, his face darkening with anger, and is about to say something about the television, but instead I pull back the curtains and direct his attention to the birthday table – 'Happy birthday, darling!'

Joey holds himself stiff while I hug him, but then his frown disappears as he unwraps the presents. He likes the series of Russian vampire books I bought, and the book from Rob is 'okay', as are the new jeans and Superman T-shirts. Joey loves Superman merchandise – most of his clothes are printed or embossed with Superman logos – and I always look for new T-shirts when I'm shopping. I breathe a sigh of relief once all the presents are opened.

Soon after, wearing one of the new T-shirts and his new jeans – the old clothes thrown in the washing basket – Joey goes downtown to meet his friends, promising to return later for the cake-cutting ceremony when everyone else comes home.

While Freddie is in bed for his afternoon sleep, I make a cup of tea and wonder why the experience of managing Joey's birthday is so fraught with emotion. It hasn't always been that way – we've had some memorable successes over the years – but lately the birthday celebrations haven't gone quite so well. I try to dispel all birthday-related anxiety from my mind, and when Joey arrives back at the house later that afternoon, the six of us gather around his cake like any normal family. As Rob lights the candles, I take photos, aware of expectancy hanging over the table like an unwanted guest. Then, two-year-old Freddie starts to sing – 'Happy birthday to you, happy birthday to you, happy birthday to you, happy birthday to you' – the only words he knows from the song. Tears fill my eyes in this moment of sweetness as I stand in the light of seventeen candles, listening to my youngest boy sing 'Happy Birthday'.

Smiling at Freddie, Joey blows out the candles in one breath and cuts a piece of cake for each of us.

Watch the actions

The next time I roll up at the shed, I find Bernie sitting on the concrete ledge outside the workshop. Inside, I wave to chubby-faced Brendan and spot the looming helmet-headed figure of Jimmy, a tall fellow with a gingery crew cut, working in a welding bay with Simmo. Apart from the three of them, the shed is empty. I stow my bag in the corner and head back outside.

'Where's Gazza?' I ask. 'I've never known him to miss a Sunday.'

'He's sulking,' says Bernie, raising his fists and punching the air a couple of times. 'The boys had a falling out over a girl and they're keeping away from each other for a while.' He shrugs, like he isn't worried. 'Anyway, it's working really well with a smaller group – gives the keen ones a chance to hook in.'

I look at him, not sure if he's trying to convince me or himself. Then I take a seat on the ledge, yearning for some warmth to seep through the heavy clouds. The weather has been freezing cold all week – sleet, snow, rain – with grey skies and the smell of wood-smoke constant on the breeze. One afternoon, I was walking through the park and I noticed the rain on my jacket had lightened. When I held out my hand, an icy snowflake dropped onto my glove. I pushed back the hood of my jacket so the snow could fall on my face. Lovely, soft snow.

'Good to see Brendan so keen.'

Bernie nods and reaches for his tobacco. 'When Brendan first started he was always picking fights with everyone. He'd come from Lismore, was having troubles at high school. But I've never seen a kid respond so well to a few pats on the head. He won a couple of welding competitions we organised and became a changed boy. The prize was a chocolate bar.' Bernie huffs out a laugh, ducking his head as he lights his smoke. 'Willy Wonka knew what he was doing!'

I rub my hands together. 'Maybe the others are just waiting for the cold weather to pass.'

During the afternoon, Jimmy and Brendan work on an order for a portable barbecue, while Simmo and I finish the candleholders. Simmo is frog-voiced from a cold. 'Why don't you go home?' I ask. He says he's here for Bernie.

Afterwards, I clean the 'trophy shelf' – a wide wooden plank about two metres long, fixed at chest height to one of the corrugated iron walls. I'd stood by this makeshift mantelpiece on my first day, examining the photos and objects on display with lengthy consideration, wondering how I'd ever find my place here. The shelf was kept tidy in the beginning, when lots of visitors were coming through, but nearly three months later it's looking shabby. And empty. The photos, most of the glass frames cracked, lie scattered on the table in the kitchen area. The Iron Man Welders' business plan has curled-up edges and the imprint of a dusty boot stamped on it. I look around the empty shed – it's not only the visitors who have stopped coming.

At the end of the day, as I wrap a thick woollen scarf around my neck, Bernie asks the two boys to close up the shed. Simmo and I wait outside, watching the dogs have a run.

Bernie wanders over, looking troubled. 'I think we're losing them.'

Behind me, I hear the boys slide the heavy wooden shaft through the lock of the shed door. Simmo pulls his beanie over his ears, his brow wrinkling in concern. 'Maybe we need to do more personal development with the fellas,' he suggests. 'Have a regular part of the day where we down tools, sit around and chat about shit.'

Bernie nods. 'We've had a couple of chats, but I know that's not enough. Everybody thinks it's the welding that makes the difference, but it's not the fuckin' welding – it's those few minutes you're talking about. Stuff goes on with these kids that you might never hear about. You have to watch the behaviour as well. If you're only listening to the words, you're making a grave mistake. Watch the actions, and when you see those actions change … it's time for something different.'

On the drive home, I think of how Bernie's worries reflect my own. The night before, Joey had called from a telephone box on the north side of town, asking for a lift. I'd found him standing outside a bakery, shivering in the cold. He doesn't dress warmly enough. All his clothes seem to be disappearing. When he slid into the car, I noticed that he was only wearing a hoodie and had tomato sauce stains on his jeans. I lent him a dark-blue fleecy-lined coat from the back of the car – 'Don't give this one away' – and drove him to his friend's flat. Two young men had been sitting on the steps, smoke from their cigarettes curling up into the porch light, and a woman had been standing in the doorway dressed in pyjamas. Inside the flat, through sheer lacy curtains, I saw more people watching television. 'Bye, Mum, I love you,' Joey had said, pulling on the coat and leaning across to give me a kiss.

My throat had tightened. 'I love you too, Joey.'

I drove home, sad about the way things were turning out. Joey's world seemed to have become more desolate since his birthday, or perhaps it was the gloom of a long winter affecting me. In the carport at home I had turned off the motor and sat for a moment in the dark car. I wanted Joey to do well in life – to eat healthy food, to stay clean, to sleep in a bed with fresh sheets and to use his mind in a job he enjoyed. But maybe I was expecting too much from someone who wasn't yet eighteen. At a similar age I was living the party life in Darwin: unemployed, drinking every night, sharing a room at a rundown tourist lodge with several others who didn't look too different from the people outside that flat. Joey's new peer group had accepted him for who he was.

Maybe it's time for me to do that too.

The necromancer of Oz-style aerobics

To be honest, I've never been able to accept Joey for who he is, which is a huge fault on my behalf. He was like a special gift which I never fully appreciated. In the beginning, his eccentricities were charming and a source of pride. He could do complex sums in his head by the time he started school, and his spelling was perfect, even though his handwriting was almost illegible. He wanted to be a magician or a comedian when he grew up, and he told me lots of funny stories about his days at school. He observed life very closely, like a writer, and he was very particular about his appearance. I remember when he was eight, he wore his hair slicked up at the front like John Travolta in *Grease* and he kept a black comb in his pocket. That year, when the school photos arrived, Joey opened the packet and said: 'My hair! What happened to my hair? It's completely flat!' Then he raised his fist. 'Someone will pay for this!' His teacher had to work hard to keep a straight face while she handed out photos to the other kids.

Joey happily went off to primary school each morning with his cool-cat hairdo, often wearing a pair of *Blues Brothers*–style sunglasses that my mother had given him. He loved learning and he settled well into school. His teachers were impressed with the way he zoomed through the reading and writing program, his excellence in maths and spelling, and they acknowledged his cheeky fun-loving nature. From Years 1 to 3, his school reports were overwhelmingly positive. But then, in Year 4, his teachers began saying things like: 'Often disruptive behaviour,' or, 'Joey has a lot to offer, but needs to recognise that others have much to offer, too'.

As he grew older, Joey also became harder to manage at home. He began to lead us on a tumultuous journey through life, and I would swing from despair to elation within minutes. I started to notice his sensitivities – he could smell if ants had been in the sugar, he hated crowds, shopping centres and fireworks, and he never wanted any windows open, even on hot days. When he was seven, I jokingly made him his own business card: *Joey Pastor / Fusspot Extraordinaire / You name it ... I'll complain about it / No job too small.*

During school holidays, when Joey was often at a loose end, I used to send him to cartooning workshops at the State Library. Even as a young child, he was able to convey vivid facial expressions in his drawings, and I think that was because he was so observant. I have all his artworks in a box in a cupboard at home. One of his drawings from that time is a sketch of a confused-looking little boy standing with his hands clasped in front of his body. I still weep whenever I look at it. Joey experienced life so deeply, so intensely, and I don't think I did a very good job of guiding him through those early years.

Because he was the oldest, I didn't realise for a long time

that Joey's reactions to the world were a little unusual. He often teased and provoked the younger boys, and I couldn't leave them alone with him because in less than a minute someone would be screaming. I read parenting books and tried star charts, but nothing ever worked. Joey was like a rare and beautiful orchid that needed certain conditions to thrive, but I just couldn't work out what those conditions were. A friend lent me a book, *Raising Your Spirited Child: A Guide for Parents Whose Child is More Intense, Sensitive, Perceptive, Persistent, and Energetic.* Yes, I thought, that's Joey. The book said many 'spirited' children grew up to be wonderful adults – you just had to get through their childhood first. But that was easier said than done.

By the time Henry was two, Theo was five and Joey was eight, Rob had a constantly furrowed brow and I felt overwhelmed by the challenges of family life. We found a house in a suburb a few miles further out from the city, where the rent was cheaper. Our new home was small, but it had pale pink walls, leadlight windows, and a big tree with a rope swing in the backyard. I kept hoping things would get easier, but they didn't. My friend lent me another book: *How To Talk So Kids Will Listen & Listen So Kids Will Talk*, but it didn't really help either.

We moved again two years later – to a big old Queenslander-style house in the next suburb. Joey and Theo were able to stay on at the same school, which was good, but our rent was much higher and we were soon living beyond our means. Rob had finished his PhD by then, and was writing a book about the history of a Queensland trade union. It was a commissioned book, but he wasn't bringing in a full wage. I managed to find a permanent part-time job as an English language teacher at a Christian high school in an outer Ipswich suburb. On my teaching days, I had to leave the house before seven to catch the train because Rob used the car to take the kids to school and to child care. We needed money, but I think I was escaping again.

Regardless of the complexity of his behaviour, Joey remained very lovable throughout those years, and he won hearts everywhere he went. Towards the end of Year 7, he attended a four-day creative writing camp in the Gold Coast hinterland – an opportunity that came his way after he wrote a wonderful short story called 'The necromancer of Oz-style aerobics'. At the camp, a group of friends gave him the nickname 'Zorro', and at the end of the four days, one of the authors gave him a book with the inscription: *To Zorro, best wishes and* en garde! *If you don't keep writing and drawing I'll come after you.* Joey was bright-eyed as he stepped off the bus, and as we left for home, all his fellow campers were calling out: 'See you later, Zorro!'

The following year, Joey gained entry into a prestigious selective Brisbane high school. His primary school, which had nurtured his eccentricities so well, only had a hundred students; his new high school had two thousand. Joey became one of the 'lost boys'. He didn't want to do any homework and quickly fell behind in such a competitive environment. On school mornings, he'd laze around the house and make excuses, so he wouldn't have to go. Letters came home about unfinished assignments, and I soon discovered he wagged school several days a week. During this time, it became very hard for us to do things together as a family because the kids never stopped fighting with each other. Rob and I were so full of tension and stress – we were always overreacting and making things worse than they really were.

One year, we went to Red Rock for a reunion with my family. On the first day, Joey was sitting in a tree reading. Rob went up to him and accused him of breaking something. Joey exploded with anger, and both his and Rob's behaviour embarrassed me. From that moment, the pretence was over; we were obviously not a happy family. I spent the rest of the week in tears – crying because I couldn't be like my siblings were with their children, or like the other people at the caravan park, who sat around the campsite and played games and relaxed. Over the following days, Joey became mean and cranky with the wind that blew in from the beach. He argued with Rob and me, and fought with his brothers and his cousins. But on the last night of the reunion, the kids organised a talent quest, and Joey did an amazing imperson-ation of Steve Irwin, the crocodile hunter. The rest of my family laughed, but all I could do was cry, full of confused love and pride for my beautiful boy.

Those early adolescent years were very hard for Joey, and for the rest of the family, too. I know Bernie would say: 'No regrets, Helena,' but I feel a lot of sadness about that time because I was often angry rather than supportive. I didn't recognise the beauty of the child – the rare orchid – I had in front of me. Many nights I wept from despair and frustration, but perhaps if I'd just accepted Joey for who he was, and stopped trying to force him to be some-thing that he wasn't, things would have turned out differently.

Can't breathe cake

At the shed the next weekend, the footy commentary booms from the radio but the workshop is empty. In the kitchen, I find Blister and Tye leaning back on plastic chairs, blowing smoke-rings while Sally, Bernie's sister-in-law, rummages through a heap of papers on the table. Thommo is stretched out on the lounge, fast asleep. I say hello and slide a tray of brownies between some overfull ashtrays on the table.

It's a relief to see Sally. Like her sister Jayne, there's something solid and reassuring about her. When we first met I was surprised to learn she was only thirty. Today, with her smiling brown eyes, oval-shaped glasses and hair tied back in a neat bun, she looks fresh and efficient, like Mary Poppins has come to visit. She's trying to get the boys to make job sheets that detail the measurements and steps for each product. 'We can print them up on the biggest sheets of paper,' she says brightly, 'laminate them, and then stick the job sheets on the walls around the shed.'

Next to her, I notice Tye having a coughing fit after stuffing down a brownie.

'Can't breathe cake, mate,' Sally tells him. 'You've got to chew it.' She clears a space on the table. 'We need sign-on sheets as well. Let's make a list of all the boys who've been coming.'

'Some young fellas just turn up for lunch,' grumbles Blister.

I'd noticed how lunch was an important part of Bernie's work. Each Sunday, he went shopping with one of the boys, and later, the others took it in turns to fire up the barbecue, cook the meat, or prepare the chicken and salad.

Tye stops coughing. 'Speaking of lunch ...'

Bernie comes in, car keys jangling. Thommo sits up on the lounge and rubs his eyes, looking around in confusion.

'Not keeping you up, are we?' asks Bernie. He turns to me and Sally. 'A few of the boys are missing. I've just picked up Jimmy, but the manager of the youth refuge reckons Shaun's gone off the rails. He's moved out to a caravan. Brendan's gone too – to Tamworth.' Bernie sighs. 'His dad's a firefighter, and it's his fourth move in a year. No wonder he has problems.'

*

I moved a lot when I was young and it didn't do me any good either. In 1958, when my parents first came to Australia, they lived and worked around the eastern suburbs of Sydney – Rose Bay, Waverley, Bronte, Bondi and Paddington – places that must have seemed like paradise after Amsterdam, a city still in recovery from the war. At first they lived in rat-infested flats with drunken louts for their neighbours, but they quickly built a better life for themselves and their three children. By the time I came along in 1965, my parents owned a corner store in Paddington, and my father worked in two bakeries as well. Like many Europeans, my parents loved the sun, and most of my baby photos show me at the beach, in the arms of one of my siblings. Because I was the youngest by nine years – just like my little Freddie – my family called me '*het kind*'. The child.

'*Waar is het kind?*' they always asked. 'Where is the child?'

My siblings – a brother and sister aged nine, and an older brother of eleven when I was born – began to run wild when I was a baby. 'We were like street kids,' one of them once told me. They rode buses and trains without tickets, begged people on the street for money, and walked around Paddington spitting, swearing, stealing and fighting.

When I was two, my parents bought a bakery business in a small town south of Sydney. The 1880s building, with its shop-front, living quarters and separate bakery out the back, had peeling white paint and a faded *Big Boy* lemonade sign on one wall. Inside, the rooms had boarded-up fireplaces and twelve-foot ceilings. The upstairs section of the bakery house had a long hallway. Every night, before I went to bed, my father would get down on his hands and knees and I would climb onto his back – he would be the 'horsey' and we would go up and down the hallway together. He often played guitar and sang to me as well, songs like 'Oh! Susanna' and 'Polly Wolly Doodle'. We lived in the bakery house for the next nine years, which doesn't seem like much now, but that big old white building is the one solid thing from my childhood I hold on to.

We left the bakery when I was eleven because my father thought he was ready to retire. My parents wanted to send me to an elite boarding school in Sydney – 'We have money enough now!' they said. But I pleaded not to go because I wanted to stay with my best friend. I didn't know then that we would move eight times over the next seven years – to Sydney, to Gunnedah, back to various places in Sydney, and then Bomaderry – or that I would change high schools five times. My teenage years are so full of change and confusion I can't even remember all the places I lived, but with each move, I became progressively wilder. I changed my name several times – to 'Jo' and 'Skye' and 'Jasmine' – started smoking cigarettes, joints and bongs. I drank beer, tequila, my father's sherry and whatever else was on offer. At one stage, we even went back to the bakery, but it wasn't the same. In Gunnedah, where my parents inexplicably bought a motel business, my father almost had a nervous breakdown over the cracks in the concrete driveway, and my mother spent a lot of time lying on the lounge in a darkened room. Meanwhile, I continued to spiral downwards – I was in Year 10, hanging around older boys who smoked and drank too much, who drove cars with loud mufflers, and who weren't the right sort of friends for me.

When I let myself think about that time, which isn't often, I realise I was pretty wild. In fact, Joey's behaviour is *nothing* in comparison to what mine was – he's just loud and argumentative from time to time, not really wild at all. Throughout my teenage years, I acted like an idiot more times than I can remember, which is probably why I'm so comfortable at the shed.

*

That afternoon, Shaun, a lost-looking pup of a boy, comes through the door with his arm in a cast. 'Fell off me bike!' he says, like it's really good news.

While I file washers to fit the pipe needed for the candle-holders, he stands by my side and chats. He's living in a caravan at Pembroke Holiday Park, by himself. 'I've been sitting up late watching horror movies – *Jason X* and *Freddy vs. Jason*!' He starts to describe a scene where Freddy gets his arm chopped off.

I put up my hand to stop him. 'Aaahh! I can't handle that stuff anymore. I had my horror movie stage when I was your age.'

When Blister returns from the grinding room, Shaun races over to show him his arm – 'I'm getting a new cast on Tuesday, a waterproof one.' He scratches inside the plaster with a stick and tells Blister about getting chucked out of the youth refuge. Blister asks him where his folks are.

'Dad's in Perth. Mum's in Moree.'

'How come you don't live with one of them?'

'Mum kicked me out 'cause I was always picking fights with me sister.' Shaun laughs, a crazy cartoon snigger. 'Hee hee hee hee. Got kicked out of the youth refuge for picking fights too.'

He acts like he's proud of it, but I don't think he is. Not really.

'You might get lonely living in a van on your own,' says Blister.

Shaun sniggers again and walks over to show Bernie his cast. Soon Bernie has him holding a length of steel steady with his good arm.

Blister is talkative during the afternoon, more than ever before. He tells me about the caravan park at the other end of town, where he's staying with his girlfriend. He'd rather be in Pembroke, too, but his missus won't let him – 'She thinks I'd always be down here at the welding shed.'

She's probably right.

'I was always fighting with my brothers and my sister,' adds Blister, 'but my mum didn't chuck me out. I left on my own accord. And she always says, "If you're in trouble, you can come back."'

If only I could say that to Joey.

When Bernie stops by the bench where Blister and I are working, I half-jokingly complain: 'It's hard, sticking with the candleholders.'

'Hard sticking with anything,' says Bernie.

Jimmy lopes over in our direction and shows us a jig he's made to twist metal for jobs like fire tools. Bernie twirls the antiquated-looking contraption in his hand and shakes his head in admiration. 'Crackin' idea, Jimmy! So that's what you're dreaming of at night, eh? While those other blokes are dreaming of girls, you're dreaming of jigs!' The boys burst into laughter while Jimmy blushes.

Before I leave, I fetch the brownie tray from the kitchen and offer the last pieces. Tye, holding an oxy welder in one hand, is the first to reach over.

Bernie glances at Tye's lanky figure. 'The amount you eat, you'd think you'd be the size of a hippopotamus. Thanks for the cake, Helena.'

'Yeah, and keep it coming,' someone calls as I walk out the side door.

I turn to see Tye wearing a 'who me?' expression and catch his smile just before he flips down the cover on his welding helmet.

Driving home, I'm almost bursting with happiness. What is it about the shed – a dusty, dirty, noisy place – that lifts my spirits so much? Bernie's a big attraction, of course. He's fun, and the boys obviously love him. I suppose I'm drawn to his wisdom as well. Just as they are.

II

Spring–Summer 2007

Early parenthood

Joey rings to ask if I can give him and his new girlfriend, Melina, a lift. I agree, curious to know more about Melina, who I'd met briefly on the steps of his house in the half-light the previous week. She was tiny, maybe only five foot tall, and looked away when she saw me approaching.

Once in the car – Joey in the front, Melina in the back – Joey says, 'We need to go over to Kentucky Street and pick up Ryan.'

'Who's Ryan?' I ask.

'Melina's baby.'

Melina's baby? My pulse begins to race. Joey's girlfriend is a sole parent? A girlfriend is one thing, but a baby is something else altogether. I glance in the rear-view mirror, and in as casual a tone as I can muster, I say: 'You don't look old enough to have a baby, Melina.'

'She's twenty,' says Joey.

We drive to Kentucky Street, where Melina directs me to a low brick house. A small group of people stand out the front. 'Wait here,' she tells Joey. We watch as she goes inside. A minute later she appears with baby Ryan. He's fast asleep, tufty hair poking out from his fleecy blue blanket. We drive to Melina's flat without speaking. Joey helps her carry the baby inside, and then asks if I can drive him downtown to check his bank balance. On the way, I question him about Melina and the baby. He replies with one-word answers. I prattle on about early parenthood, the loss of freedom – 'I know what it's like, Joey,' I say, parking in front of the automatic teller. 'I had you when I was twenty-four.'

He doesn't comment, but as we head back to Melina's flat, he says, 'Why were you always so hard on me? That's the main problem I have with you and Rob – you were always so hard on me.'

My breath catches in my throat. I can't speak. He's right, of course. We were too hard on him, but the truth of the past rushes towards me like a truck speeding down the wrong side of the road, and all I want to do is swerve and avoid a crash.

*

Sometimes I feel as if I've made a total mess of parenting my kids. Maybe that's because I didn't have a strong example to follow. My parents didn't know what to do with their teenage children either. In my father's self-published life story, he writes: 'It could be argued that offspring not so gifted with too much thinking power are easier to handle, and more apt to listen to parental advice.' When we were living in the bakery house, by the time my three siblings were at high school, any advice my father suggested was looked at with a wary eye. He was a 'New Australian' who spoke with a heavy accent. What did he know about life in this country? Like many migrants, my parents believed education was of prime importance. But in the early 1970s, young people were choosing travelling adventures over university. 'Fruit picking?' my father asked my sister one time, his tone full of scorn. 'Is that what we came to Australia for? So you could go fruit picking?' Those years in the bakery were very difficult for my sister because she wouldn't accept the status quo. 'Why do I have to do everything?' she'd demand of our father. 'Why can't the boys do the washing up?' My sister rolled her own cigarettes and smelled of patchouli oil, and the two of us used to walk the dog along the main street in the evenings. She moved out of home when she was sixteen – she'd had enough of the arguments by then – and went to live with some hippies on the edge of town. I cried a lot when she left.

When Joey and the other boys were growing up in Brisbane, Rob and I really struggled to be effective parents. Our problems were made worse by continuing financial troubles. After he finished writing the trade union history, Rob found it difficult to find reliable academic work. Brisbane was having a massive property boom, and over the nine years we lived in the city, we moved five times because of rising rents. Our last rental house – small, dark and damp – held our unhappiness for just over a year. We had so many arguments while we were there; so much anger and shouting.

I remember one afternoon in that house Joey and Rob had a terrible argument. Rob flew into a rage and Joey lunged at him, both of them yelling at the top of their voices. The younger boys and I screamed for them to stop. A few minutes later, a man from two houses down burst through the front door.

'What's going on?' he asked.

Rob and Joey stepped back, both breathing hard.

'It's okay,' I told the neighbour. 'Things just got a bit out of control.'

Soon after, the police were at the door. They asked Joey if he wanted to press charges. Joey shook his head, his eyes wide and frightened. No.

After the police were gone, the house stood silent with shame. I looked around at the too-small rooms, the cheap carpet, the tatty furniture, the bookshelves made of bricks and planks of wood. I heard my father's voice: 'Is this what we came to Australia for? So *het kind* could end up in a hovel in Brisbane with three kids and no money and the police at the door?'

In the weeks that followed, Rob did an anger management course. I continued to read parenting books. We had yet another session of counselling. Rob and I played backgammon in the evenings, we both cried during BBC bonnet dramas, we had obsessional interests – countries, poets, artists, religions – that we would research and talk about for some weeks before they dissipated, and we tried to keep our marriage alive. Rob could talk about any area of world history, and we often had lively and stimulating conversations. We both tried our best to make things better for our family, but the pressures of life continued to grow.

When Rob got a two-year lecturing contract at a university in Brisbane, we were finally able to secure a home loan. So we moved again – to Ipswich, which was affordable. I thought four degrees hotter wouldn't matter, but it did. The weather was oppressive and unbearable, and we couldn't afford to install air-conditioning. Theo and Henry settled into a local primary school without too much trouble, and Joey continued on at his high school in Brisbane, catching the train into the city each morning with several other students. It wasn't an ideal situation – especially as he was still having trouble at school – but I thought it best to minimise the changes. At first, he would come home with funny stories about the characters he observed on the train, and I remember telling him that he could write a book about all his experiences. But then Joey exploded into puberty and the funny stories stopped. He only wanted to wear black shirts and heavy denim jeans, and he often looked hot and angry. Getting him out of the house in time for the train, or to do anything, became increasingly difficult. I began to research Asperger's syndrome. Today, it seems like every second person has this syndrome, but back then, it was only just starting to be recognised. Joey exhibited nearly all the behavioural traits, so we saw a specialist in Brisbane who, after fifteen minutes, declared that Joey had attention deficit disorder. Joey had responded heartily to a joke, and people with Asperger's syndrome aren't supposed to have a sense of humour. The specialist gave us a script for Ritalin, but I didn't believe medication was the answer. Too many things didn't fit with the diagnosis. We went for further testing, but the results were inconclusive, which left us with nothing.

Meanwhile, we were still having flare-ups with Joey on a daily basis at home, and, on top of everything else, I was pregnant again. Rob kept applying for permanent lecturing positions, yet application after application was rejected. His self-esteem plummeted, but I didn't want to give up hope. He was a good lecturer who gave a lot to his students – he deserved a permanent job. I kept searching for suitable positions in the Higher Education supplement in the newspaper, and I helped him with his applications and job interview skills. At the time, I was teaching four days a week at a TAFE English language centre in south-west Brisbane. Then, two months before the baby was due, Rob was offered a permanent job at the university in Armidale. I burst out crying when I heard the news, the relief was enormous. We were going back to Armidale – where we had once been happy, and where life had been easier.

*

A few days after my drive with Joey and Melina, my father has an operation to remove a cancerous growth from his scalp. When I ring my mother to check how he went, she tells me the operation took three hours.

'Three hours?' I ask in surprise. 'That sounds serious.'

Caught up with a busy life, I often tuned out when my mother talked about my father's medical issues on the phone, but the thought of him lying vulnerable on an operating table for three hours fills me with fear.

Several weeks later, my mother phones again to say my father now needs a course of radiotherapy on the area around the cancerous growth.

'Maybe I'll come up to the Gold Coast soon?' I suggest, concerned for her, but she brushes away my offer of help.

'No, no, I'll be alright.'

We don't ask for help in my family. And we're not accustomed to illness either. When my siblings and I were growing up in the bakery, we weren't allowed to be sick and we rarely missed a day of school. I suppose when my parents were teenagers in Amsterdam, 'sick' didn't get you anywhere. They both survived the *hongerwinter* – the 'Hunger Winter' – of 1944–45, when the Germans stopped all supplies coming into the city, and Amsterdam was without food, gas, electricity and coal for months on end. Over twenty thousand people died from starvation and cold, many of their bodies left on the street. Throughout that winter, everyone was sick, or dying. You had to be tough.

There are a lot worse things than a baby

One night, I take some pizza over to Joey's place and find him and Melina snuggled up on the lounge in front of the television. I stay and watch the rest of *America's Next Top Model* with them, trying to engage them in conversation during the ad breaks, but they're not interested in talking to me. I still don't know much about Melina. She's been very 'closed' and somewhat stormy on the few occasions we've met. It's not that I think she's a bad sort, but I'm worried that one day Joey will come home and tell me that they're having a baby together. I don't want Joey to become a father yet. He's too young.

A week later, Joey comes around and says he's moving in with Melina.

'Are you sure?' I ask, heart pounding with anxiety. Within me, another voice wants to shriek: 'Don't do it, Joey!'

'I know what I'm doing, Mum,' says Joey. He asks if he can leave some of his things with me, for safekeeping. While he's putting his boxes in the shed, the phone rings. Reverse-charge. In the brief pause after the automated message asks whether I want to accept the call, I hear Melina's voice – 'CanyatellJoeyto-ringme' – before the line goes dead.

Joey comes back from the shed. I'm tempted not to say anything, but it doesn't seem right. 'Melina wants you to call her.'

'Was it reverse-charge? I told her not to do that.'

I sigh. The king and queen of reverse-charge calls – they don't even have fifty cents to make a phone call.

When Joey shuffles in with the last of his gear, I ask, 'Where's that blue coat you borrowed the other night?'

He looks at me. 'I traded it for a silver jacket.'

'I said not to give it away – I lent it to you!'

As I rant about the injustice of his behaviour, I wonder at the same time why I care so much about an item of clothing.

After Joey is gone, I sit on the lounge room floor. Next to me is a box full of the stuffed animals and other toys that Joey slept with when he was a baby. He still carts them around with him from place to place. The toys are grubby, in need of a wash. I take them out, one by one: Sleepy Bear, who went with Joey to his family day care mother while I went to university; Sharky, a plastic glow-in-the-dark shark from Sea World; Dino, a stuffed green dinosaur we picked up in a second-hand shop in Brisbane; Dolphin, Little Dino, Rabbit. Tears fall from my eyes. The pain of motherhood, alright. Nothing I do or say seems to make any difference. Helping Joey is like trying to push a big heavy rock uphill – he keeps sliding further back, no matter how hard I try.

I ring a counselling support service and within minutes I'm sobbing, almost inconsolable with grief. It's like Joey has died.

'I want him to find some positive direction in his life,' I weep to the anonymous listener on the other end of the line. After the call, I hug Sleepy Bear to my chest, and imagine Joey surrounded by white light, shining and strong.

*

Driving to the welding shed a fortnight later, with prams still featuring heavily in my thoughts, I notice the poplars lining the highway have grown leaves again. I carry my tray of brownies into the kitchen, waving to Bernie and the boys, welcoming the smell of burning metal in my nostrils. The shed is beginning to feel like home. As I place the brownies on the table, I see Sally's unfinished job sheets lying among the cracked photo frames and tattered tool catalogues. Although the sign-on sheet has made an appearance, drawn up with neat columns and clipped onto a folder, it doesn't look like anyone has been using it.

When Bernie walks into the kitchen, I blurt out my fears about Joey. As always, Bernie remains unfazed. 'There are a lot worse things than a baby,' he says. I suppose he's right, but it still feels like Joey is perched in a billycart at the top of a rise, waiting to go downhill, fast, without any brakes.

We head outside for a moment to escape the noise of the drop-saw. 'Good to see more of the boys here today,' I say, glancing back towards the shed.

Bernie nods and finds his tobacco, looking every bit the yokel in his khaki overalls and checked shirt. 'I had a real good talk with them – just asked a simple question: "Why are we running out of steam?" They came up with about thirty different ideas, but the main thing is they want to muck about on weekends. Maybe we'll move away from Sundays.'

'Fair enough.'

Bernie lights up his smoke and inhales deeply. 'It's the same with all my youth work: I go through patches of thinking, "What the fuck am I doing? I'm sick of this." You bust your arse and they all end up in court. I often think – "Where are we going with this shit?" But then I look at how far these boys have come, and I think, "Nah, we're on the right track. We'll shift in some other direction, but we'll keep at it ..." Whatever's helping this particular group of kids is where we need to go.'

*

Later that week I find Joey asleep at home, curled up like a cat on the sofa. In the laundry are two washing baskets, stuffed with wet clothes and the rest of his possessions. More washing, I sigh, as a mixture of relief and anxiety hits me. When Joey wakes up, he tells me that he and Melina have broken up.

With nowhere to go, Joey sleeps in the spare bed in Theo's room for five nights. It used to be Joey's room, and I probably should have left it that way – so that he had his own space to come back to, even if he wasn't living with us. But Theo and

Henry were sharing – which wasn't working out well – and after Joey had been out of home for six months or so, Theo claimed Joey's old room for himself. Anyway, for Joey, it's moving back home. For me, it isn't. He tries so hard to be 'good', but I'm rigid with tension the whole time. In the end, Theo moves back into Henry's room because Joey sometimes stays up till one or two in the morning playing music. On several occasions, Joey barges out of the bedroom, infuriated because we woke him with our talking over breakfast. I don't want to creep about in my own house. I bite my nails, pick at my skin, pull at my hair – all the old familiar nervous mannerisms. When I eventually tell Joey he can't stay, he says I don't love him. It's not true. I love him very much, but I can't live with him. I wish it could be different, but it just isn't possible.

'Perhaps I'll ask Tim if you can move back to his house?' I suggest.

He scowls. 'There's no way I'm going to live there again.'

'Well, you can't stay here,' I say firmly. 'I'll pay two weeks rent at Tim's to help you catch up ... and cook you dinner some nights.'

Joey stomps out, slamming the back door.

*

In 2004, when Rob was finally offered a permanent job, he and Joey moved back to Armidale five months ahead of the rest of the family. I had a home-birth midwife in Ipswich, and I didn't want to leave six weeks before the birth. I also had to sell the house. So, while I stayed in Ipswich with the younger boys and prepared for the birth, Rob and Joey rented a flat in Armidale. They visited every fortnight. Miraculously, they were getting on better than ever, and, for a while, life seemed much brighter. Our fourth boy, Freddie, was such a gift – a calm, happy baby – and his birth brought the sunshine back into our life. After five months of living apart, I sold the house in Ipswich, and Rob found us a house in Armidale. It was time to be a family again.

Those early months back in Armidale were dream-like. For the first time ever, we had regular, secure income that wasn't going to stop for six weeks over the Christmas holidays. Rob went to work, the children went to school, and I stayed home and looked after our baby. While we were living in Ipswich, I'd started a Masters degree in creative writing, which needed to be completed within eight months. But I didn't feel pressured, and I no longer felt the need to escape either. Joey was enjoying his new high school then and he had made some good friends in Armidale. On the weekends, Rob and I took the younger children to swim in creeks and walk in the bush, like any other normal family. But we soon began to have troubles at home again – that was when Joey started playing loud rap music and shouting a lot. Although our new house was spacious, the layout was impractical and it didn't offer a lot of privacy for a family of six. Sometimes I wonder if any house would have been big enough for all of us to live peacefully together. Rob and one of his friends were able to transform the garage into an extra room, which meant a 'teenage' space for Joey, but his door connected with the dining room, and the walls were thin. When he played his music, it was loud enough to wake the baby, and when we had breakfast, we were loud enough to wake Joey. That was also when I started taking Joey out for night drives. I'd missed out on so much of his life during our five months apart and we had a lot of catching up to do. The drives settled him down and gave us time to talk.

*

After organising things with Tim, I fix up Joey's old bedroom and make the bed with clean sheets. I also buy cereal and milk, razors, a toothbrush and toothpaste. Three days go by with no sign of Joey. He rings on the fourth day, but when I tell him the key for Tim's is in the letterbox, he hangs up.

A few days later, he appears on my doorstep, wearing the same clothes he was in when I last saw him. I find some of his clean clothes and give him a razor. Joey showers with the water pressure turned up so hard the pipes wail. After he's dressed, I hand him the key for Tim's, which I retrieved from the letterbox during the week, and send him on his way, my heart almost breaking in two.

Dog whisperer

At the shed the following Sunday, the workshop is empty but Simmo is in the kitchen. He's kneeling in front of the fridge, sleeves rolled high as he dips a cloth into a bucket of soapy water.

'You're doing a fine job there, Simmo. The state of that fridge has worried me for some time.' I place a tray of brownies on the table, and ask if he's heard any news from Bernie, who has gone to Fraser Island for three weeks, helping a friend trap dingoes.

Simmo wipes his brow. 'He's been offered a full-time job.'

'What?' I ask in surprise. 'I thought he was only going for three weeks.'

'They're asking him to stay on and work there all the time, tagging dingoes. He's a bit of a dog whisperer, old Bernie.'

I stand beside the fridge. How can Bernie go and live on Fraser Island? What will happen to the Iron Man Welders without him? Peering into the empty workshop, I think of the crowd of boys who were here two weeks before. While Simmo continues with the fridge we talk about the future of the project. 'I can't see it surviving long,' I tell him. 'Not without Bernie.'

Tyres crunch over the gravel outside, and soon Gazza and Thommo saunter in. I almost cheer. Thommo looks sick, like he's had a really rough night, but Gazza seems his normal self.

Simmo eases himself up from the floor with a groan, and congratulates Gazza, who has just scored an apprenticeship at the local mine. 'You were only saying the other day you didn't know where you stood,' says Simmo.

'I've just been showing up,' replies Gazza, lifting a brownie off the tray with the edge of a rusty knife. 'Freckles got one as well – for a fitter and turner, so we'll both be doing apprentice-ships out at the mine.'

'You'll have to put in a good word for Thommo,' Simmo says, nodding in Thommo's direction.

I ask Thommo if that's the sort of job he wants.

'Yeah,' he rumbles, not sounding too keen.

Gazza wipes his hands on his work pants. 'Freckles' appren-ticeship is going to be a lot harder. I don't know how he'll go.' He and Thommo snigger together, like a pair of welding-workshop psychics who've already seen the cards that foretell Freckles' downfall.

I reckon he'll prove them wrong. Freckles might act like a misdirected fire-sprite at times, but he's held down a part-time job at McDonald's for years. He'll be alright.

Not long after the branding incident, I'd asked Bernie about Freckles' background. He told me that although Freckles wasn't part of the original Youth Link group, he'd known the others for years and was doing the same sort of stupid things. But he had a strong family network in Armidale, and a lot of older brothers and uncles who tried to keep him on the straight and narrow – 'Every Sunday he goes from here to Grandma's for the big family meal,' Bernie had explained.

I ask Gazza how long his apprenticeship will be.

'Three years,' he says. 'I've already knocked off one year at TAFE. Bernie reckons there'll be a few apprenticeships with the council as well.'

Simmo raises his eyebrows. 'Geez, there'll be no Iron Men left!'

Maybe that'll be a good thing, I think, especially if Bernie takes the job on Fraser Island.

Car doors slam and Freckles, Jimmy and Geraldine walk in, carrying cans of paint, a roller and some paintbrushes. Jimmy turns up the volume on the radio and then burps, long and loud, as he checks out the welding on the bike rack.

'I *love* boys!' laughs Geraldine as she totters back to her car in her high heels. Jimmy gives her a wave and a big smile.

I opt for the job of painting the tool wall with the roller, while Gazza does the edges with the small brush. I also paint two noticeboards in the kitchen, scrub the hand-washing sink in the workshop, and then paint the splashing boards. The paint isn't the right sort for a wet area, but the sink looks clean and sparkling when I finish. I even scour the barbecue utensils until they shine.

I think of Simmo toiling away in the kitchen. What are a couple of clean-freaks like us doing in a place like this?

*

I shouldn't have promised to cook Joey's dinner several times a week. Since he's been back at Tim's, he hasn't bothered to think about his own meals or do any shopping. This isn't unusual behaviour for a seventeen-year-old, of course, and I know I'm still expecting too much from him. But I worry because he no longer has a food arrangement with Tim – he just pays for his room – which means he has a lot of extra money on his hands from his living-away-from-home allowance. I think that extra money is going towards buying alcohol. So, Joey has started dropping around most afternoons to see what I'm cooking. Although we keep trying to have relaxed family dinners, the conversation usually becomes heated and accusatory. I start taking a plate of dinner down to Joey's each evening. We sit together in his kitchen, often with Tim, while Joey eats his meal. One night, Joey tells Tim and me a story about how he and another friend were waiting at a train station in Brisbane when a very long goods train went past: 'All the carriages had BULK MOLASSES written on them,' says Joey, smiling to himself. 'Except for one – it had BULK ASSES!'

Another night, I find Joey listening to a rap CD that a group of local Aboriginal boys have put together. Joey recently started writing rap lyrics, and he has a verse in one of the songs. I sit down and listen to the CD with him. The songs are really good – heavily influenced by American rap, but the lyrics are heartfelt and meaningful. One song is about how the young fathers want the best for their kids – a different life from what they had – but they don't know how to provide it. When I hear Joey's voice on the CD, it sounds deep and resonant – like a man's.

*

A few days later, Joey comes over and I agree to take him for a drive. 'You need to do some washing for me,' he says as he puts on his seatbelt. 'Tim's machine broke down and won't spin. Stop by the house and I'll get the basket.'

Parking out the front of Tim's house, I notice a heap of paper napkins scattered over the street. 'What's all that?'

'They're from KFC. Liam dropped them when he drove me home earlier.'

'Don't you think you should pick them up?'

'It's alright, Mum,' says Joey, shaking his head. 'They're biodegradable!'

While he's inside, I pick up the napkins from the street. When Joey comes back, he's holding a chicken drumstick and his MP3 adaptor.

I pass him one of the paper napkins. 'Use this. I don't want you wiping chicken grease all over the seat. Where's the washing?'

'We'll pick it up later,' he says offhandedly, like we have all the time in the world. 'Have a listen to this.' The car throbs to the sound of Jay-Z's latest hit. When Joey finishes his drumstick, he winds down his window and prepares to throw out the bone.

'Don't!' I yell. 'I'll find a bin.'

Joey chucks the chicken bone onto the street. 'Problem solved.'

As we drive past a block of flats near the university, Joey tells me about a friend who was at the flats with him the previous Friday night. Although Joey got along fine with everyone at the flat, his friend, loud and drunk, created a ruckus and returned the following night in the same state. People in the neighbouring flats complained and called the police. Joey laughs and says the people who rent the flat now have three 'ticks' against them and have to leave.

I look at him. 'That's not funny.'

Joey ignores me and does an impression of one of the things his drunken friend said to the police: 'You think I'm scared of going to jail, man?'

Back at his house, I wait out the front while he gets the washing. He staggers down his front steps with a full basket, and heaves it into the back of the station wagon.

'*Phaw* ... what's that smell!' I complain, holding my nose.

'The clothes have been in the machine for the last three days,' says Joey. 'They might need another wash.'

'Why didn't you hang them on the line days ago?' I ask, the stink of damp and mould catching in my throat.

He shrugs and leans over to kiss my cheek. 'Bye, Mum, I love you.'

*

We wait for Bernie to come back before opening the shed again. About a month later, I spot him out the back of the Armidale Club, looking suntanned and healthy. I'd already heard from Simmo that Bernie didn't take the job. I head over to say hello and ask if I can bum one of his rollies.

Bernie shakes his head. 'I've given up,' he says, 'mainly because I can't stand seeing the boys at the shed smoking my brand of tobacco.'

I congratulate him, noticing how he looks years younger. He's put on weight and his cheeks have filled out. 'How was Fraser Island?'

He inhales deeply, like he's breathing in memories of hot sun, sandy beaches and lush rainforests. 'Great ... I was so tempted to take the job. That's my dreaming – working with dogs, with the earth, trapping dingoes – but I'll stay here for now.'

I remember how Simmo described Bernie as a dog whisperer and a shiver runs over me. But he works magic with the boys, too. And they need him more.

Don't shit in your own nest

At the next BackTrack meeting, the seven of us gather again around Simmo's kitchen table. The night is chilly, reminiscent of winter; Armidale has been hit by a cold snap. Sally and Geraldine discuss a girls' craft program that they've recently started.

'About six girls turned up on the first night,' says Sally. 'I took a suitcase full of wool and we decided to knit beanies. Since then the girls have moved on to scarves and bags. But the problem is things are being five-finger discounted. Someone ...'

'Someone or someones?' asks Bernie, his eyes two specks of blue against the blackness of his beanie and polar fleece jacket.

'Someone.'

'Who?'

'What about the confidentiality thing?' Sally asks. 'No names?'

'That confidentiality shit causes more problems than it solves,' says Bernie, suddenly fired up. 'If you've got something to say, fuckin' say it and we'll keep it in this room here.'

Geraldine, wearing a lurid orange and pink beanie and scarf set, tells us the culprit's name. 'She's taken money out of my car, she's taken stuff out of my office, and she hid that bag of wool that we found under the chair the other day.'

'What would you do if the boys were stealing down at the shed?' Jayne asks Bernie.

He opens his mouth to speak, but Geraldine beats him to it. 'It's only one girl. We're going to have a group meeting with the girls and tell them, "Fuck it. Someone's been shaking stuff."' She looks over to Bernie for confirmation.

Bernie refills his glass of wine. 'Let's go around the table. What would you do and how would you do it?'

'I've got no idea,' says Jayne.

'That's not good enough,' Bernie tells her, the same as he'd tell the boys at the shed. 'That's like a "I dunno" or a "whatever" answer.'

She shrugs. 'Get rid of her?'

'Okay,' says Bernie. 'The next time that girl comes into the room, in front of all them other kids, you're going to say, "You've been stealing stuff – we're kicking you out of this program."'

He stares at Jayne, waiting for her to comment.

She glances around the table, bites her bottom lip. 'Have I just been knocked off the BackTrack crew?'

'Well ...' Bernie holds his palms up to the air. We all laugh, relax a little. 'What about you, Simmo?'

'I'd do a session on stealing,' says Simmo, sitting back in his chair. 'Something like: "We're our own little mob here and we've got this thing going and ..." I don't know. Somehow work your way into it.'

'That's great.' Bernie nods in agreement. 'Stuff like, "When is it okay to steal? When is it not okay to steal? What's one thing you could steal, what's one thing you couldn't steal?"'

Simmo chuckles. 'Who's got a really good way of stealing from Kmart?'

'And where's my fuckin' watch!' jokes Bernie.

When it's her turn, Geraldine looks around in desperation. 'What am I going to do?'

'Have an opinion that's not Bernie's!' says Sally.

'Yeah, come on!' teases Jayne.

'Okay,' sighs Bernie, after everyone has spoken. He's like a tired father sorting out squabbles with his kids. 'If someone's in there stealing shit, I'd be saying, "I got no doubt you mob know who's doing it, and whoever's doing it, they certainly know themselves. But what do *you* guys think we should do?" If we provide them with the opportunity they'll be saying the same things we're saying – it isn't okay. Don't shit in your own nest.'

He drains his glass of wine and finds his tobacco. I notice his plan to give up smoking hasn't lasted long. 'I've got the biggest lot of fuckin' thieves in Armidale down at that shed and there hasn't even been a welding rod stolen 'cause they *own* it – they went out and bought it. I put that trust straight out there. You just keep giving till they don't take it.'

We talk about whether it would be better for the girls if they had their own space to meet, and about giving them the chance to think of a name for themselves.

'When we were working out a logo with the boys,' Bernie says, 'we sat out the back of Hungry Jack's one afternoon and threw around ideas. They suggested things like "Steel Rod Cocks" ... I said yeah, great, that's a good one, put that down, what else? And I suggested we grab onto something already big and out there, you know, like the Big Merino or the Big Banana. One kid came out with Iron Boys Welding. Fuckin' oath. We talked about how we're working with iron, how we're working with boys, or is it men? Iron Man is associated with breakfast cereal – people are familiar with the name. Yep.' Bernie smiles and mentions the boy's name. 'That's when we had him in that TAFE course and he was liftin' everything.'

Simmo laughs. 'Was he the one living at Ebor?'

'No,' says Geraldine. 'Uralla.'

'Thank fuckin' God,' says Bernie as he stands to go outside for a cigarette, 'because the whole of Ebor would have been stolen. Hang on!' He looks down at his hands with an incredulous expression. 'It says on the map there's a town here, but it's been pinched!'

We laugh as he slides open the back door. Sally soon joins him outside while the rest of us finish our drinks and pack up. Driving home after the meeting, I have a giggling fit in the car, thinking of the boys wanting to call themselves 'Steel Rod Cocks'.

It has a certain ring to it, that's for sure.

*

A few days later, I invite Joey to go to the theatre to see *Sweeney Todd* – performed by the local musical society. 'It's my birthday wish,' I tell him when he looks doubtful. 'I think you'll like it.'

At the theatre, we can sit anywhere we want, so I choose seats three rows from the front. Just before the show starts, one of Joey's TAFE teachers walks in. She seems a little surprised to see Joey at a musical society production, but he smiles happily when she sits next to him. *Sweeney Todd* is gory, with lots of blood from Barber Shop throat slicing. When I look over at Joey, he's completely absorbed in the performance.

The boxer

The Armidale Club, a live-music venue, has a theme night featuring music from the sixties and seventies. I sit near the stage with Rob – listening to the songs my siblings used to play on the record player in the bakery house. When I hear 'The Boxer' by Simon & Garfunkel, my thoughts turn to my father, who became a boxer in Holland after the war, while he was doing his bakery apprenticeship. He boxed his first twelve fights in a pair of gym shoes he found at work, and a little saying from the bakery apprentice handbook became his life motto: *Wat je doet, doe het goed*. Whatever you do, do it well.

Later, when he was doing compulsory military service with the Marines in the early 1950s, my father went on to have many boxing successes – Champion of the Netherlands, Military Champ of Europe, and Inter-Allied Champion of the World in the light-heavyweight class. By the time he was chosen for the Dutch boxing team that went to the 1952 Helsinki Olympics, he was planning to leave the Marines and become a professional boxer. But then he had a falling out with his manager and quit. Many of his friends later became professional boxers, but it was enough for my father to know he'd beaten them all in his amateur time.

It wasn't easy for my siblings and me to have a father who was so intent on winning. Intensely competitive, he could turn any game into a combat sport. When he played table tennis with my brothers in the 'big room' at the bakery house, sweat streamed down his face as the ping pong ball flew back and forth across the table. He was the same with poker and Scrabble – he loved to gamble, to win. Even when driving, he always needed to pass other cars, to be the one in front. My mother constantly clutched the seat in fear, asking him to slow down. At traffic lights, he often leapt out of the car to abuse fierce-looking truck drivers who'd edged in front of him. He continued to do this until he was well into his sixties. He thought he could take on anyone and anything, head on, like when he boxed with his reflection in the bathroom mirror each night.

But now he's in hospital – again – recovering from a dislocated hip, which happened three days after his recent hip replacement operation. My father's medical problems seem to be worsening – it's only a couple of months since the three-hour operation on his head. The other week, when my mother rang to tell me my father had gone in for his hip replacement, I was ashamed of myself for completely forgetting he was booked in for the operation. 'Why haven't you rung for fourteen days?' my mother asked. Life is busy.

Three days ago, my mother rang again. After coming home from hospital, my father dislocated his hip getting out of bed in the middle of the night. 'He didn't want to listen to advice about taking it easy,' my mother told me. 'And he didn't want to use his walking stick either.' She had to call an ambulance and now my father has to lie flat on his back for the next ten days. I'd called my mother a few times to see how things were going. She said my father wasn't in pain or discomfort, but she sounded worried.

I look around the room at the Armidale Club. The dance floor is filled with a group of teenagers who've come along with their parents. Some are even dancing with their parents. As I watch them, I feel sad about Joey, unable to imagine him here at the club with me. The teenagers all look as if they have healthy family relationships. I'm sure none of their parents trudge up the street with their dinner each evening. I draw my attention back to the stage, where a young man with a guitar sings Leonard Cohen's 'So Long Marianne', his powerful voice vibrating through my body. On stage, his father plays bass guitar while his mother sings back-up vocals. After the song, she drapes an arm over her son's shoulder –'That's my boy!'

Suddenly tearful, I jump to my feet, in need of fresh air.

'Back in a minute,' I say to Rob, pushing through the crowd to the back of the club. Passing the drinkers at the bar, I catch sight of Tim, Joey's housemate. He follows me outside.

'All these bloody happy teenagers and their parents,' I tell him when he asks why I'm upset. 'I feel like such a failure.'

Tim puts an arm around my shoulder. 'I'm sure they've got problems too, Helena.'

*

'Going to play you some Slim Dusty,' Bernie says, looking over his shoulder with a cheeky grin. 'Get you relaxed and focused on the job.' He sets up an old cassette player on the bench in the kitchen area and walks over to pull open the barred window. 'Crackin' idea or what?'

Apart from several guffaws and raised eyebrows, most of the fellas slumped on the lounge and chairs stay silent. The cloud of smoke hanging over their heads drifts across to the open window. Except for Tye, all the regulars are here today – Gazza, Blister, Thommo, Freckles and Jimmy, and some I haven't seen for months – all busy puffing on rollies and passing around bottles of soft drink. They've been working hard all morning, cutting lengths of steel for a sheep-loading ramp and welding chunky pieces of metal for a bike rack. The shed got so noisy I had to go in search of earplugs. Now I'm happy to sink into a saggy armchair and listen to an interview Bernie and a few of the boys did for the local ABC radio station recently.

'Want to have a listen, fellas?' asks Bernie. 'You can go back to work if you want, but I reckon you'll be sorry.'

From the corner of my eye, I see a slight figure slink off into the workshop with his cap pulled down low. He's not taking any chances.

'Gazza's gone.' Blister nods in the direction of the door.

Lenny, one of Joey's mates who has been coming to the shed for the past month, also wanders away. The others laugh loudly.

'Shame job,' murmurs Bernie.

I want Gazza and Lenny to come back into the kitchen with the rest of us, to listen to the program and feel proud, not embarrassed.

'It played on the breakfast show,' says Bernie. 'A lot of people have been ringing up, saying "That sounds unreal!"' He presses the play button and then walks out to join the other two in the workshop.

A young woman's voice booms into the room: 'If you're someone who has seen the sparks of a grinder or enjoyed the smell of molten metal ...'

The familiar noises of the shed are heard on the player. The boys sneak looks at each other and chuckle nervously.

'... you might be pleased to know the trade of welding and ironmongering is alive and well in Armidale. We had a tour of the Iron Man Welders' shed earlier this week ...'

The woman's voice is backed by sudden laughter from the boys in the kitchen. I'm smiling, too – so strange to hear the world of the shed projected back like this.

I listen as Bernie introduces the reporter to Lenny.

'Tell us your story, Lenny,' she says after he explained how he used a hammer to make a patterned finish on some water bowls. 'You look fairly young – what does the future hold for you?'

'I dunno – banging metal.'

The boys in the kitchen burst into raucous laughter. Now I understand why Lenny left the room. Shame job, alright. But as the interview continues, the boys listen intently, hunching forward on the edge of the lounge with elbows on their knees.

Towards the end of the program, the reporter asks Bernie why the local community supported the project in such a big way. 'People are looking for answers,' he tells her. 'It's a tough business rearing young men: they're dropping out of school, unable to find work, all sorts of alcohol and drug abuse going on. When people start to see young fellas stepping up to the plate, they think, "Well, gee ..." Parents are ringing up, but it comes back to the boys themselves. If they want to do it, we'll help make it happen. For the most part, these kids come from very disadvantaged backgrounds, and I think it's the first time they've realised there's somewhere for them to go in life.'

Near me, one of the boys clears his throat. Looking over, I notice no one laughing now. Not even smiling.

The fishbowl

A few weeks later, I pick up Joey from a friend's place.

'Mum, we need to go to the police station at six o'clock.' Joey is bleary-eyed, unshaven, and as he eases himself into the car, I smell rum. He's probably been awake all night, partying. I was on my way to the shed when he rang to ask for a lift home from his friend's house.

'Why's that?' I ask.

He tells me a complicated tale about being involved in a mishap at a local hotel the other night. His mates told the police about Joey's part in the escapade.

Joey yawns loudly. 'I was in one of the cells at the police station for two hours yesterday. They tried to ring you.'

I take a deep breath, attempting to slow the panic inside. The image of Joey in a cell fills my mind. It isn't right. Joey's not a criminal – he's just been caught doing something stupid, the sort of thing that can happen to anyone when actions come before thoughts. He's drawn to people who live their lives danger- ously – like Sal, always shambling after the mad ones in Jack Kerouac's *On the Road*. Those people are often the most inter- esting, but they also attract the most trouble. 'Clean yourself up,' I tell Joey when I drop him at his house. 'Have a wash, a shave and a sleep. I'll pick you up a bit before six.'

My eyes adjust to the shadows of the workshop after the brightness of the day outside. I catch sight of Tye working alongside Bernie on some shelves designed to fit the window of Jayne's health food shop. He hasn't been to the shed for months because he and Bernie had a falling out. At the Armidale Club the other week, I'd been complaining to Bernie how I was always driving Joey around. He'd told me, 'If there's a glimmer of hope it's leading to something positive, go with it ... but if it becomes a "use", back off.' He'd had the same thing happen with Tye, he said, and had been giving him the cold shoulder – 'But we'll come right again.' It looks like they've sorted the problem.

I wave hello and put my gear in the kitchen. When Tye sees me carrying in a tray of brownies, his eyes widen and he gives me a big smile. At least his appetite hasn't changed. Then Gazza comes over, the brim of his cap pulled down low. He asks me to help him with a job, just as he'd ask any of the boys. Feeling like I've passed some kind of test, I cut lengths of steel in half with the drop-saw, mesmerised by the blade slicing through the metal, sparks flying.

After checking with Bernie about what other jobs need doing, I grab a pair of earmuffs and work at a bench outside, sanding and oiling lengths of timber for the shelves. Jayne's health food shop will be a good place to display smaller products like candleholders and nutcrackers – that's if we ever manage to finish anything.

Later, with an almost desperate desire to see something completed, I work on the nutcrackers. They're made from a metal ring cut from a three-inch pipe, with a threaded bolt which twists down to crush the nut. Blister helps me find a long-forgotten pile of metal rings and I buff them on the grinder until they sparkle. Then I use the bench-drill to make the holes for the bolts.

Each time I pull down the lever, my thoughts turn to police lock-ups and criminal records.

Lost in one of these disturbing daydreams, I jump when Bernie taps me on the shoulder. 'Helena, we're having a short meeting before lunch.'

In the kitchen, the boys have already made themselves comfortable on the old lounges and the air is thick with smoke. Bernie stands near the bench, holding a steaming mug of coffee, upright and stiff-legged in faded jeans and muddy boots, a checked shirt neatly tucked under his belt. He seems a little tense, like he's about to give a presentation, but then he takes a seat at the table next to Tye. 'Let's have a quick chat about making an effort to get stuff on these shelves for Jayne's shop,' he says. 'What things could we finish?'

He's interrupted by someone's mobile phone ringing. Thommo answers the call. I notice his shirt sleeve is shredded, like he's been attacked by a wild animal. The shirt was caught in the grinder earlier.

'It's Jimmy,' he says, 'asking for a lift.' Simmo finds his keys and heads out to pick him up.

'We filled Jimmy's shoes with frangers,' Freckles tells Bernie, an impish gleam in his eye.

Bernie screws up his nose. 'Not used ones?'

'Yeah!'

Simmo soon returns with Jimmy, who swaggers in like a naughty student coming back to class. He greets the other boys with a cocky half-smile. Bernie looks at him. 'You need to finish that bike rack so I can get the fuckin' thing out of here. And we've got the steel for the barbecue edging, so you can get started on that too.'

'Okay,' mumbles Jimmy, the self-satisfied expression fading from his face.

'Freckles, get someone on the fire poker things. Blister and Helena are working on the nutcrackers. Once we get a few finished, we'll put them in cane baskets.' Bernie taps the side of his head. 'Who does the fuckin' thinking around here?'

The boys laugh.

'Tye and me stopped at the Bellingen markets on the way back from the coast last weekend,' continues Bernie, 'and we came away with some new ideas. Tye, go and get that fuckin' round thing from the car.'

Tye comes back with a circular piece of mesh and a light bulb.

'Talk us through the idea, big fella,' says Bernie, nodding at him.

Tye stands by his chair, suddenly shy. 'I forget.'

'Come on – tell us! Put the light bulb in there!'

Tye bends the mesh to form a megaphone-shape, and then holds the light bulb underneath to make a lampshade.

Bernie faces the rest of us, eyes shining. 'What do you think about that? Put a steel plate underneath to make a stand – it's a crackin' idea!'

We stare at him, riveted. My worries about Joey and our visit to the police station are almost forgotten. Bernie is like a man possessed – his enthusiasm flows through the room, and the possibilities for the Iron Man Welders seem endless.

'And who wants to come in tomorrow?' asks Bernie, like he's inviting the boys to a wild party. 'Some of you blokes might get here early.' He looks at Thommo. 'But don't you be using the grinder.'

'And don't be bent,' warns Freckles.

'I haven't smoked dope for eight days now,' says Tye. There's a hush in the room. 'I've just been sitting around people, not even wanting to smoke.'

'You seem to be talking a lot more,' says Bernie. 'And looking at people.'

'I think a lot more about different things ... and I feel more rested,' says Tye, blowing a neat line of smoke-rings into the air.

'That's crackin'.' Bernie closes his diary and pushes his chair away from the table. 'Good to have you back with us too. Tye's doing army reserves now,' he tells the others. 'I've asked him to bring a hand grenade down to the shed next week.' Bernie grabs his welding helmet and strides out to the workshop. A moment later he pops his head around the door and looks at Freckles. 'Frangers in shoes, eh?'

Later, as we sit out the front of the shed eating lunch, I ask Bernie if he knows anything about the incident at the hotel on Friday night. He shakes his head and raises his eyebrows for more information. I briefly mention how Joey was involved and that we have to go to the police station at six for an interview. 'Any advice?'

'Just tell the truth,' says Bernie. 'He'll be much better off and will probably just get a caution.'

Freckles pipes up and says he has three cautions. The next time he'll be charged and sent to a remand centre at Grafton. I wonder if he really understands what it means to be locked up.

One afternoon a few weeks ago, Bernie asked me to interview some of the boys and find out what they'd learnt from the Iron Man Welders' program. Alongside gaining certificates in welding and engineering and learning new skills, I mostly remember them talking about how Bernie and the welding program had helped them personally. Freckles said he'd stopped doing stupid stuff at night and was staying away from the police, Thommo thought he'd become a better person by learning about kindness and how to treat people better, Tye said welding was something to do instead of going out and getting in trouble, and Gazza said he'd learnt how to give everyone a chance. If they'd asked me, I would have said pretty much the same sort of things, except I didn't need help staying out of trouble.

The boys talk about the new police station: a hulking, green-painted brick building on a corner near the centre of town. Bernie finishes his bread roll and asks, 'Any of you blokes been in the fishbowl yet?'

The boys guffaw and make jokes about drunken nights in the lock-up. I don't know what Bernie means by the fishbowl, but I laugh along with the others anyway. I suppose I'll find out soon enough.

*

I have a shower at home before picking up Joey. He looks better – clean-shaven, dressed in baggy jeans and a faded blue hoodie – and on our way to the police station, I mention how Bernie said to tell the truth. Joey nods in reply.

We wait for over an hour in the icy-cold foyer, watching various people come and go before having our initial interview with a fresh-faced blonde policewoman. Then another young police officer, with a muscular build and what looks like a stuck-on mous-tache, takes us to the 'holding area'. He lists Joey's belongings: a cap and a bottle of Coke. On one side of the holding area is a row of perspex-covered cells, each about the size of a telephone box. The fishbowl. I notice how each cell has a curved steel bench. As I look around the room, I'm reminded of places where animals are slaughtered – places easy to hose down afterwards. A toilet at one end of the line of cells has clear perspex on the top and bottom and a clouded area in the middle. I shiver, imagining Joey sitting for two hours in one of these plastic cells. My beautiful boy.

On the counter is a set of scales behind a perspex shield and I ask the police officer what they're for. 'We weigh the drugs in front of people,' he says. I blush from ignorance, out of place in this sterile environment. At least old-style police stations had character. The empty cells in this holding area may have been hosed down and disinfected since the previous night, but I sense layers of wretchedness on these surfaces that will never wash away.

We have our interview with the two police officers in charge of the case. When they ask Joey questions, he slouches in his chair and says things like: 'I didn't really think about it.' He recounts his actions on the day of the incident. As I listen to him describe the amount of alcohol he'd consumed, and how the mishap at the hotel came about, my mood sinks lower and lower. I'd been a heavy drinker in my teens, but a glass of wine or a beer a few nights a week was enough for me now. Rob doesn't drink at all. I find it hard to understand why Joey needs to drink so much, but I guess those tequila slammers seemed like the answer when I was young.

The police give Joey a caution. Three hours have passed by the time we finally walk out the front door. I'm drained, shaking with cold and hunger, and long to be at home eating warm, comforting food. We drive away from the police station in silence. I ask Joey if he wants to come home for dinner, but he's too tired. When I stop out the front of his house I say, with little hope, 'Maybe you should come along to the shed next week ... spend some time with Bernie and the boys.'

'I'll think about it.' He yawns and then leans over to kiss my cheek.

Gotta learn shit for ourselves

The next day, I ring one of my brothers to ask if Joey can visit him in Sydney for a few nights. My brother works as a truancy officer – surely he'll understand how important it is for a male mentor to step in at a time like this. He assures me he'll ring back in a couple of days, but he doesn't. I'm not surprised. We're all busy with our own families and work commitments, and he's no doubt overwhelmed by the needs of the families he's already supporting through his job.

'You make your bed, you lie in it,' my mother always tells me. I think she developed this attitude during the war. My mother was only nine when the Germans took over. Tall and thin, with short dark hair, she was often mistaken for a boy, so she was the one her family sent to the abandoned Jewish neighbourhood to steal whatever she could find. She doesn't like to talk about the war or her family, so I know very little of what went on – only that it wasn't a happy home. By the end of the war, she and her sisters had been without food for so long they developed oedema. My mother was weak and near death when the Americans finally rolled into the city, throwing bars of chocolate from the tanks.

*

At the shed the following Sunday, Bernie pulls up with a couple of new blokes in his ute. I meet Skippa as he steps down from the cab. He's tall and dark-haired, with rounded shoulders and sad eyes.

'Skippa's just been expelled from Year 11,' Bernie tells me, before calling out to the others in the workshop to down tools and head into the kitchen.

The other new bloke is looking at me curiously. As I smile and introduce myself, he reaches forward to shake my hand in an old-fashioned way. 'Nice to meet you, Helena,' he says. 'They call me Marshall.'

Marshall is tall with thick blond hair and a farmer's drawl. As I lead the way into the kitchen, he says he's from Bernie's TAFE group. I can tell he's excited to be at the shed.

Bernie plonks a couple of bottles of soft drink onto the table. The boys wander in and start pouring drinks, rolling cigarettes and talking among themselves.

'I thought we'd see how we're tracking,' says Bernie, once everyone has settled down. 'Have you been going to TAFE, Thommo? Don't fuckin' bullshit me either.'

Thommo flicks a match under the end of his rollie. 'Occasionally.'

'You've only been back a week,' says Bernie. 'How occasional is it?'

'I was there on Wednesday,' says Thommo.

Bernie sighs and turns to Freckles. 'Still feeling good about the apprenticeship at the mine next year?'

'Yep,' says Freckles, pleased with himself. He told me earlier he'll be earning $56,000 by the third year of his apprenticeship. That's a lot of money.

'How about you, Jimmy?' asks Bernie. 'Full-time welding still?'

'Pretty full-time,' admits Jimmy, already turning away, keen for Bernie to move on to the next person. But Bernie leans back on his creaky plastic chair and regards Jimmy with a confused expression. 'You know, Jimmy, at TAFE the other afternoon, I heard your old man saying to Rocket that he'd bring in some forms for you. Surely you're big enough to take in your own forms?'

Jimmy shifts in his seat, and doesn't seem to know what to do with his mouth. 'It's easy for him – he's always at TAFE.'

'So are you. In fact, you're down there more than he is.' Bernie stares at Jimmy, steady and uncompromising. 'Time to man-up. Are you with me? I'm going to check with Rocket and I'll kick your arse if your old man does it.'

Jimmy shakes his head. 'Nah ... Dad took them home and said he'll take them back to TAFE tomorrow.'

'But he's not going to take them,' says Bernie. 'You're going to take them when you go there next.'

It's like watching a showdown between two cowboys, but I already know who's going to shoot straighter and faster. And it's not Jimmy, who sits sulking on the edge of the lounge, his mouth a twisted half-smile.

'Have a thirty-second conversation with your old man,' adds Bernie. 'Take the forms off him and say, "I'm in control of my life."' The others laugh, relieved they're not getting the third degree, but Bernie's expression remains serious. 'Are you picking up what I'm putting down?'

'Yeah,' mutters Jimmy.

'Man-up time,' says Bernie, and I can almost see him sliding a smoking pistol back into its holster. 'Man-up time.'

After checking with the rest of the boys, Bernie asks if they'd mind answering a few questions for a research project he's involved with. The boys organise themselves into two groups: Freckles, Blister, Jimmy and Marshall sit around the table, while Thommo, Gazza and Skippa stay where they are, lined up on the lounge near me. Bernie hands out paper and pens. 'Righto,' he begins, 'what is it that you blokes really give a shit about?'

The boys are silent until Freckles says cautiously: 'Family, friends, full-time job ... getting my head wet?'

The others next to him nearly fall off their chairs laughing. I haven't heard the expression before, but I assume it means having sex. I'm not asking for an explanation, that's for sure.

'You know what you're talking about now,' says Bernie with a smile. He turns towards the despondent figure of Skippa, who sits hunched forward on the lounge. 'What about you, Skippa?'

Skippa shrugs. I wonder if my presence in the room is making the boys inhibited, too shy to say what they really think or feel. I catch Bernie's eye and nod towards the door – 'Maybe I'll go outside?'

'Nah, you stay here.' He crouches down to join the group at the table, who are talking in low voices, laughing from time to time like they're sharing special secrets. 'If getting your head wet is really important to you, put it down,' says Bernie, his voice soft. 'This isn't about bullshit – it's about fair dinkum answers.'

Freckles' group snort and giggle like bashful schoolboys, scraping their chairs across the floor to shift closer together. The silence in the room is broken by their ripples of laughter and comments. I hear Freckles say, 'Enjoying myself,' and next to him, Jimmy nods in agreement, 'Yeah, happiness.'

I look across to the trio on the lounge and wonder how to get them talking. Gazza is supposed to be writing down his group's answers, but his page is blank. It feels like I'm hanging out with the wrong crowd at a party – all the action is happening on the other side of the room.

Bernie fires off another question: 'What makes you happy?'

'Hanging out with mates,' says Freckles, leaning forward to consult with the others in his group. Soon they're spluttering with laughter again.

Bernie, who is now hovering over the lounge like a pesky magpie, asks: 'What makes you happy, Skippa?'

Skippa shrugs. 'Having money.'

Bernie raises his eyebrows. 'Those guys in Hollywood always got more money than they know what to do with,' he says. 'But are they happy?'

Skippa shakes his head and looks across to the other group for support.

'They're just stupid,' answers Jimmy, blowing three perfect smoke-rings into the air.

'Yep,' agrees Bernie. 'But if we say it's not just money, what is it that makes you happy, Skippa, because ...?'

'Doing different shit with friends,' interrupts Freckles.

Bernie ignores him. 'Come on, Skippa, I'm not letting you off the hook.'

I hold my breath, waiting for Skippa to answer. I feel for him. He seems too exposed and vulnerable for this sort of questioning. Like Jimmy and Freckles, I want to protect him.

'Being around people you like,' says Skippa at last, like it's a huge effort.

Seemingly oblivious to Skippa's discomfort, Bernie nods and looks down at his list. 'Next question, if you could change one thing in Armidale, what would you change?'

'Reduce the amount of dickhead cops,' says Jimmy, grinning at the cleverness of his answer.

Bernie looks at Jimmy like he hasn't heard properly. 'Here's your big chance to change something and all you've got is a couple less dickhead cops?' He strides across the room. 'Come on, Skippa, you know I'm picking on you – what's one thing you'd change?'

Maybe Skippa senses the end nearing. He sits up on the lounge and answers straight off. 'Better teachers in school.'

'What about you, Thommo?'

'Less crap.'

'What do you mean? People shitting in the streets or …?'

The boys and I crack up. Even sad-faced Skippa can't help smiling. It's like watching stand-up comedy as Bernie struggles to wrench answers from these boys, forcing them to participate, to *think*.

Thommo shrugs helplessly. 'I dunno.'

Bernie purses his lips and exhales, runs a hand through his hair. 'Righto, last one … if you had a piece of advice for older people, what would that be?'

No quick answers this time. The boys are thinking hard. 'Come on,' says Bernie. 'Older people are telling you guys shit all the time! Here's your one chance to tell them something! What are you telling them oldies, Skippa?'

Skippa shakes his head.

'Gotta learn shit for ourselves,' says Freckles, looking up at Bernie.

'Yep, put that down.' Bernie puts the list of questions away. 'Thanks for that, guys. Okay, let's get back to work.' He and the boys wander off. I notice one lonely brownie on the tray, surrounded by crumbs. No one ever wants to take the last one.

Freckles comes back into the kitchen and searches through the papers on the table for his pencil. I offer him the last brownie.

As he reaches across to the tray, I ask about his branding burn. Freckles rolls up his sleeve, uncovering a mottled, raised oval of skin which vaguely resembles a turtle.

'Will it stay like that forever?'

He nods. 'I could get a skin graft but I'm okay with it looking like this.'

'Do you have any other branding scars?'

'Nah,' says Freckles, shaking his head. 'Lesson learnt the hard way!'

I smile. 'They're probably the best sort of lessons – the ones you remember, anyhow.'

We don't ask for help

A week later, I meet up with a friend from Brisbane at the coast. While I'm away, Rob rings and says, 'You better call your mother. I've just been on the phone with her – I think she needs help.'

I'm a little surprised by his concern. My father is still recovering from his dislocated hip in hospital but, knowing him, he's probably safer there than anywhere else. All the same, I phone my mother. In an offhand way, I mention how I'm close by and that I'd like to visit her at the Gold Coast for a night. She doesn't brush me off this time.

At the house, my mother has pinned a note on the front door with the name of the hospital and my father's room number – 630.

Through the doors of the hospital's main entrance, the air is chilly and smells of disinfectant and hospital-kitchen catering. I walk down corridors and avoid looking sideways at pale old bodies stretched out on hospital beds, tucked in with stiff sheets, finding it difficult to imagine my father in such a place. Sweat drips down my arms, even though it's cold. I arrive at room 630, where an elderly man, who sort of looks like my father, is lying in bed watching television. I stop at the door. Surely my father hasn't changed so much that I can't recognise him? The man stares back at me with a confused expression. My heart thumps wildly.

'Are you okay, love?' asks the man.

As soon as I hear his voice, I know it isn't my father. 'Sorry – wrong room.'

A friendly nurse directs me to room 603. My mother is sitting on a chair by the bed. '*Ach* ... you're here at last,' she says. 'Let's go and get coffee!'

'Hang on.' I lean over to kiss her cheek, forcing back tears. I'm shaken by the sight of my father, old and frail in his pale blue hospital gown. He's lost weight and has a vulnerability I've never seen before. It doesn't suit him. He was a boxer, a big strong man. A few months ago, he'd flexed his arms for the kids and his muscles popped up like Popeye's. I turn to kiss his forehead, controlling the waver in my voice. 'How's the hip, Pup?'

'*Ja*, not so good,' he says with a grimace, his voice weak.

I'm suddenly hit by the realisation that my father might die soon. Even though he's seventy-nine, the thought has never really occurred to me before. I'm not ready. I should have come earlier, should have been supporting Mum. But on the phone she always says, 'Don't come. Your father is okay. I'm alone ... but not lonely!'

We don't ask for help. But my father is *not* okay. Later, when I ask my mother why my brothers haven't come, she can't answer. Sydney is only an hour's flight away.

I stay for a few days, travelling back and forth to the hospital. In between visits, my mother and I walk along the beach, and enjoy fancy cakes and coffee at Pacific Fair. One morning, I notice signs for a surf carnival. All along the promenade, people with white-zinced noses, tattoos and low-slung board shorts or bikinis are busy setting up 'camp' with open-air tents, folding chairs, eskies, bags of ice, cartons of beer and portable barbecues. The smell of barbecued sausages makes me nauseous, and nearly every man I see has a beer in his hand.

'At times I feel like an alien in this country – even though I was born here,' I tell my mother. She agrees. The Dutch don't do hot food on picnics.

When the time comes, I'm reluctant to go back home. It doesn't seem right to leave my father behind in the hospital, to be so far away.

*

Back in Armidale, on the front page of the local newspaper, the free one delivered to every house in town, is a large photo of Bernie. He's wearing a florid green and blue shirt, staring into the camera with a crooked grin. The headline states – 'Top Award for True Believer'. I laugh and read the first few sentences of the article. Bernie's won a New South Wales Premier's Award for his efforts with the Iron Man Welders. Good for him. I look at the photo again. Bernie's tropical-style shirt isn't like anything I've ever seen him wear. Maybe he picked it up during his time on Fraser Island.

I didn't know Bernie had been nominated for the award, and by the puzzled look on his face, I don't think he did either. The article mentions 'Mr Shakeshaft was surprised but beaming about the honour.' I bet he was. He'll be even more surprised when he sees this photo splashed across the front page of the paper. He'll never live it down.

A few days later, I visit Bernie's wife, Jayne, at her health food shop. She's busy serving customers but greets me warmly. I wander around, enjoying the calm atmosphere of her shop, running my hand over one of the metal gum leaves entwined in the decorative railing leading to the upper level – an Iron Man Welders' job.

When Jayne finishes serving, I ask about Bernie's new-found fame ... and about the shirt in the photo.

Jayne laughs. 'Bernie didn't know anything about the Premier's Award – I knew he wouldn't go if I'd told him! I just said we had to go to the ceremony at the town hall to support the people who'd donated money to the Iron Man Welders.' A guilty look crosses her face. 'I bought the shirt in Byron Bay. He's always trusted me with buying his shirts – but not anymore! Anyway, as we walked into the town hall, this man came over and told Bernie that he'd have to go and stand on the stage ...'

Bernie walks into the shop, eyebrows raised at the sound of his name. He shakes his head when he realises what we're talking about. 'Shame job,' he says ruefully. 'When that photographer fella said to go and stand with them three old ladies on the stage, I was thinking he's loopy and he's picking on me because I'm the one in the crazy shirt. Then Jayne said, "He's got no idea." Stop fuckin' around, I told her – what's going on here?'

He sighs. 'I copped it. I wore that shirt to humour Jayne. Now everyone in town is calling it "the shirt award". One girl we picked up the other night on Streetbeat was cackin' herself for about twenty minutes – I've never been so laughed at.'

Bernie looks so comically miserable I can't help myself. I laugh, too. And so does that sneaky earth mother Jayne.

Step up to the plate

The days are getting warmer and Jimmy is sporting a strawberry-blond mohawk. I find him sitting on the old lounge outside the shed, intently smoking a rollie and kicking stones to Bernie's two border collies that are tied up near the door.

'That's a different look for you!' I tell him, laughing.

'Thommo did it after a few drinks on Friday night.' He smirks. 'Mum's not impressed!'

No, I don't imagine she would be.

Dust and gravel spray as Blister pulls up in Bernie's yellow ute, a tattered P-plate stuck to the front fender. The dogs leap to their feet, tails wagging, as Bernie steps down from the passenger side. Thommo emerges from the shed on a remodelled BMX bike, a huge smile on his face. His broad shoulders hunch forward as he struggles to master the chain-link steering wheel which has replaced the handlebars.

Bernie stops in his tracks and laughs out loud. 'Crackin' idea! I can see those being real popular around town!' He shakes his head and wanders into the shed, the rest of us following behind.

Inside, Gazza shows him the bike rack, a contract job for the local credit union, and complains that Thommo, hung-over and ratty from a big night out, did a 'shit job' the Sunday before. The welds are messy and need to be ground back. I help carry the bike rack out to the front of the shed and Gazza and I start filing down the ragged joins.

Blister comes out to lend a hand. He doesn't seem his normal cheerful self, and I noticed earlier that he was walking with a limp. Once the bike rack is done, I find the bag of nutcracker pieces and ask Blister if he wants to help finish them. He dutifully welds bolts onto the inside of the metal rings like he's doing chores for his mother. The nutcrackers only need a coat of spray-paint but Blister isn't interested. He wants to go home.

Bernie asks if I can give Blister a lift to his flat in Girraween. I grab my keys and we head off. To break the silence in the car,

I ask Blister about his limp. He says he hurt his ankle at soccer and it's starting to ache. We hardly speak for the rest of the drive. As we approach the west side of town, he gives directions to his new flat – 'Me and Emma had enough of living in a caravan.' I watch him shuffle down the driveway of the red-brick units.

Back at the shed, Bernie takes me aside. 'Did Blister tell you about Emma?'

I shake my head. 'No.'

'She's got a cyst, and they think it could be cancer.'

'But she's only sixteen … and she's pregnant!'

He nods. 'They're having it checked out this week. From what Blister has told me, it looks like they're preparing them for bad news.'

*

A few days later, Joey and I return to the police station to sort things out about the caution. After we're finished, I drop Joey at his house.

'Wait here a minute,' he says. 'I've got something for you.'

He goes inside and comes back minutes later with a belated birthday card for me. On a white piece of paper, he's drawn an unbalanced set of scales. On the lighter 'up-side' of the scale is a stick-figure with an angular face and a turned-down mouth, wearing a police cap and dark glasses. The figure is surrounded by symbols – a station wagon with an emphasised music note hanging over it, a bank note, a broken bone, a medical cross, and the words 'yell! … argument … fight'. On the heavier side of the scale, outweighing all of the above, are two full-bodied figures – a man with a goatee beard and shaved head wearing a Superman T-shirt, standing with his arm around a woman in a white smock, both of them peaceful and happy.

*

Two Sundays before Christmas, Bernie rings, and says he's heading down to the shed for a couple of hours. I make a batch of brownies and drive over. In the workshop, Bernie is standing at a bench with Blister, organising a heap of metal buttons into piles. He asks if I can pick up all the scrap pieces of metal lying around, and then give the floor a good sweep.

Blister is wearing shorts and thongs – unusual shed-gear – but it looks as if his eyes are twinkling again. He's also had a haircut and trimmed his goatee. I wander over and ask him about Emma.

He flashes me a crooked-teeth smile. 'She's really good. The tests came back clear.' Blister looks down at his thongs. 'Bernie picked me up from downtown today – said it didn't matter what I was wearing. He just wanted me to come over for a while.'

'I'm glad it's worked out so well,' I tell him. 'I was worried for you.'

Once the concrete floor is swept, I take a break on the lounge outside. Blister comes out to where I'm sitting, lighting a cigarette on the way. He pulls up a milk-crate and tells me a little more about Emma and the cyst she had on her ovary.

'The first doctor we went to said if the cyst was cancerous she would only have five weeks to live.' He pauses to take a tight-lipped drag on his smoke. 'But the doctor at the hospital sat down with me and we had a smoke and he explained things without using all them big words – like if you cut the cyst away, even if it was cancerous, it'd be gone with the operation.' Emma had the operation two weeks ago. 'It's been hard at home,' admits Blister. 'I've had to cook all the meals, do all the cleaning, carry Emma to the shower and to the toilet, but now she's getting stronger.'

The baby is fine and Emma is over three months pregnant. Blister reckons the baby is a boy because of the way it's kicking.

I laugh. 'You sound like a proud father already!'

Blister finds a piece of scrap metal to throw to the dogs. 'We're going to wait three or four years before having another kid because if it's a boy and it's like I was ...' He raises his eyebrows, suggesting hard times ahead.

'What were you like?'

'I had ADD.'

'Really?' I'm surprised. 'You don't seem that way.'

To me, Blister has always been the gentleman of the shed, the 'care-taker'. He's the one who shows an interest in the young fellas when most of the others can't be bothered.

He nods. 'I've got the adult version of it now, but I was always in trouble when I was little. These days I only get aggressive if I'm drunk and someone disses Emma or my mum or my little brother. I don't mind if they diss me ... but not them.' He crushes the butt of his cigarette under his thong. 'We couldn't find out what sex the baby is because it turned its back to the screen.'

Bernie wanders out from the shed. 'Blister, when you two are finished yarning I want you to give Helena a lesson in welding. Give her my helmet.'

A thrill runs through me ... welding! In the storeroom, Blister finds some leather gloves for me and Bernie's blue welding helmet.

'It's a good one,' he says, handing it over. 'Take care of it.'

After putting on a leather welding jacket and some strap-on leather pieces for leg and feet protection, Blister hooks up the welder. While he scouts around for scrap metal to practise with, I stand by the bench trying to stay calm, even though my heart is beating wildly. Me – welding?

When we're ready to start, I place Bernie's helmet over my head like I'm getting ready for a space mission. Blister squeezes the trigger on the welding gun and taps it on the metal bench.

Everything goes dark. A sudden shot of panic makes my throat turn dry. I swallow, wondering if I've momentarily blacked out. The only thing left in this night-time world is a small flash of green. Then the green flash disappears and it's light again. Through the helmet-visor, I see Blister leaning over pieces of metal at the end of the bench, lining up the copper wire of the welding gun. He lifts the visor of his helmet – 'You have to line it up really well because it's hard to see when you start welding.'

I connect the brief and confusing darkness with the trigger on Blister's welding gun. 'I didn't know everything went dark!' I tell him.

He laughs and flips his visor back down.

I never expected a welding lesson to be so intimate – it's like Blister and I are the only two people left in this dark world, with just a small green light to guide us through. Maybe this is why the boys enjoy welding so much. It really is an escape. And Blister is the perfect teacher. He shows me how to hold the welding gun steady, draw straight lines, do a tack – all the things I've heard about for months. My welds are jerky and messy, but at the end of the lesson he's full of compliments. 'That's a good weld here,' he says, pointing to a join, ignoring the hole I burnt through the pipe when I was supposed to be attaching it to a flat piece of metal. He could just as easily say: 'That's a shit weld.' But he doesn't.

As we walk outside to join the others, with me holding my 'welding trophy', we pass the bike rack which still needs re-welding. Blister stoops down, checks the joins and shakes his head in disgust. 'Shit welds.'

Outside, Bernie is sitting with Freckles and Jimmy on the concrete ledge. I take a seat and listen in on their conversation, noticing Jimmy has swapped his mohawk for a stubbly crew cut. A late-afternoon breeze stirs the leaves in the gums along the side fence, and the dogs from next door bark as Lou and Girl chase after sticks that Blister throws for them.

The week before, Bernie organised a competition to design a pamphlet holder. Jimmy's entry was judged the winner and now Bernie hands over the fifty dollars prize money. 'Get some credit for your phone,' he says in a quiet voice. 'Before you just go and drink it all.'

'Mum's buying me credit.'

'Don't worry about your mum. You do it. And step up to the plate, or I'm going to have a talk with your mother.'

'What's she going to do?' scoffs Jimmy.

'Wait and see. I'll put some things in place you won't like.'

'And I'll go, "Mum ... get fucked."' Jimmy laughs like he's said something funny, but no one else joins in.

'Hey, not to your mother,' says Bernie in a low voice.

Unconcerned, Jimmy says that he tells his mother to get fucked when she needs to be told to get fucked.

'Is there another way you could address it?' asks Bernie. 'As opposed to talking to her like she's one of your mates at the pub?'

'She tells *me* to get fucked,' says Jimmy, looking to Freckles and Blister for support. They both stare at the ground.

'I'm not talking about what she does,' continues Bernie. 'I'm talking about when you tell her to get fucked, like you tell Freckles to get fucked when you're at the pub. Is there another way?'

The three boys are silent, deep in thought.

'Get off my back?' offers Freckles.

Jimmy shakes his head. 'If I'm going to say, "Get off my back," it comes out as, "Mum, fuck off!"'

Bernie asks Freckles what he does when he feels like telling his mum to get fucked.

'Walk off.'

'That's what I do too.' Jimmy leans over to spit into the trench next to the concrete ledge. 'But Mum follows me and keeps jabbering shit in my ear.'

'What I'm interested in, Jimmy,' sighs Bernie, 'is whether it's possible for you to try saying, "You're in my space. I'm happy to sit down and talk about it, but following me around is making me really cranky."'

'I've tried that.'

'I'm coming up with a plan for you, and it's going to involve not telling your mother to get fucked.'

Bernie crosses his legs and stares at Jimmy with narrowed eyes. 'We liked you better with the mohawk, mate.'

Not my fault

Three days before Christmas, I hear knocking at the front door, and then at the window. I check the clock – four in the morning. I jump out of bed, heart thumping, imagining the worst – accident, death, disaster. My legs shake as I open the door, Rob behind me. A police officer stands on the doorstep, his torch shining down. I quickly scan the porch, but he's on his own. I'm sure there have to be two if the news is really bad.

'Do you have a son named Joey Pastor?'

I nod, too scared to speak. The police officer says Joey is at the police station. He's been charged with another offence and because he's only seventeen, a parent needs to be involved.

I don't want to go to the police station at four in the morning. I don't want to see Joey in one of those perspex cells, to have that image hanging in my head over Christmas.

'Can you go?' I ask Rob. 'Bring Joey back here.'

Rob pulls on some clothes and goes to the police station. He soon returns, alone. 'Joey told me to fuck off ... he didn't want me there.'

He takes me in his arms and holds me close. 'They'll let him out in the morning, Helena, when he's sobered up.'

I lie in bed for hours, unable to sleep, drifting off briefly before daylight.

The following afternoon, Joey comes around in clothes that smell of alcohol and cigarettes. 'What's going on?' I ask. 'Do you *want* to spend Christmas in a juvenile detention centre?'

'The police overreacted,' he replies. 'It's not my fault.'

'It never is.'

He flops onto the lounge and tells me about the misadventure he had with his friend Tobias the previous night. Joey has been cautioned again and put on bail. He has to be home at nine every night, either at Tim's or at our house.

My son on bail. His second caution. You only get three.

Joey stands up, ready to go. 'I need you to drive me somewhere.'

'I can't do that,' I tell him. 'I'm going to a friend's house to sing Christmas carols.'

Singing is the last thing I feel like, but Freddie has been looking forward to it all day. 'You'll have to walk.'

'It'll only take five minutes,' he insists, his voice rising.

I shake my head. 'Sorry.' I know that no drive with him ever takes five minutes.

Joey curses loudly and storms through the lounge room, knocking against the telephone table and a bookcase on his way past. *Crash!* The phone falls to the ground, glass tinkles, books scatter over the carpet. He doesn't care. The front door slams shut. *Bang!* I kneel on the floor amid the rubble. In my hand is a framed photo of Joey and Theo, aged six and three. They're perched on a rock at the Brisbane Botanic Gardens, their faces laughing and happy behind the broken glass. Tears roll down my cheeks. Crying won't help fix this mess. I wipe my eyes, pick up the bookcase, replace all the books and then wrap the broken glass in newspaper.

Later, as I pick up the phone, I notice the number display doesn't work and the plastic covering is cracked. What does it matter? I don't care if the phone never rings again.

*

On the night of the BackTrack Christmas party, the sky fills with heavy clouds and rain blows down in sheets. I enjoy summer storms in Armidale, but driving out of town to Bernie and Jayne's place, I have to be careful the car doesn't slide off the muddy road. I park as close as possible to the front door, then dash across the grass with my bag and a bottle of wine. Inside, I catch my breath and look around the room. On the hearth, a small Norfolk pine sits in a bucket, its crisp scent infusing the room. The tree is decorated with tinsel and coloured balls, a pile of presents underneath.

Bernie is in the kitchen, looking clean and fresh in a blue and white football jersey. As I place my cheese and biscuits on the table, Jayne walks in from the back veranda and hugs me warmly. She hands me a parcel from under the tree – 'Merry Christmas, Helena!' Under a layer of red cellophane and gold ribbon is a box of Turkish Delight, my favourite sweet-treat from her shop, and ... a nutcracker with its own wooden stand!

'Who finished it off?' I ask Bernie.

'Who do you reckon?'

Taking a macadamia nut from a bowl on the table, I place it on the metal ring, twisting the bolt down onto the nut until the shell cracks. It works perfectly.

We join the others on the back veranda. The rain has eased, leaving the chill of a New England summer's night. In the distance I make out the misty shape of Dumaresq Dam – once the water supply of Armidale – with the platypus-like hump of Mt Duval looming large behind. A pack of black-and-white dogs run past the back steps, heading towards the horse sheds, their fur flattened from the rain. Bernie calls them back with a sharp order and then says to Simmo, 'Let's set up the gas barbie on the veranda.'

Flinty, another youth worker from the BackTrack crew, helps bring the barbecue up the steps. He nods hello in his solemn way, the plaited strings of his Nepalese beanie framing his wispy beard, his hair pulled back in a ponytail. I listen in as he and Bernie discuss their plan to take the boys camping at a friend's bush property near Ebor.

'I want to take them rabbiting,' says Bernie. 'Do some killing.' Noticing my expression, he adds, 'So they see where meat comes from. It's one thing to put a piece of steak or a sausage on the barbie, but it's another to think: what animal gave its life so I can have life?'

Bernie mentions a time when he and Jayne were house parents on a farm near Goulburn with a group of boys who were 'too wild' to go into mainstream anything. 'We used to go rabbiting at night and try and catch them by hand,' he tells me. 'It was months before those boys finally bagged a rabbit, but the build-up was all about how they were going to kill that fuckin' rabbit.

They'd have punch-ups through the day, sorting out the pecking order as to who got to do it.'

I smile, picturing the scene.

'They had no idea how they were going to kill it, except that they were going to *smash* it and *whack* it.' Bernie lifts his arm to demonstrate. 'I eventually taught them how to sneak out around the spotlight to chase the rabbit back towards the light, and it wasn't long before they had a rabbit. But all of a sudden they had a frightened little animal with its life at stake – trying to get away and biting and scratching them – and they were passing it around like a hot potato. I didn't show them how to hold the rabbit, that was for a later lesson, but I grabbed it and said, "Scottie, you're the man ... come and kill this rabbit."' Bernie shook his head. 'Those boys were in tears, couldn't kill it between the six of them. They ended up letting the rabbit go. It didn't mean a whole lot to me at the time, but I realise now it was a good lesson on how we kill things. That's why it's good to get those boys out bush ... they spend all day shooting things on their computers, but give them a real gun and tell them to shoot a rabbit – most of them choke.'

Bernie's story reminds me of a story my father once told me. In the third floor apartment where he lived in Amsterdam, they often 'grew' a rabbit in the attic. The slaughtering of the animal was an event of much importance. Usually it was done by an uncle, but on this particular occasion, my father's father was going to kill the rabbit himself. After ten minutes in the attic, he came downstairs, looking rather pale.

'*Is het gebeurd?*' his children asked. Is it done?

They raced upstairs to find the rabbit still running around the room, with a rope around its neck.

My opa – known for being a big, strong, tough man – had tried to hang it.

When the food is ready, we head out to the backyard, where we drag in a few sawn-off logs and sit around the fire to eat. Soon the rain clouds disappear, leaving the sky full of stars. The meat is the best I've ever tasted – organic fillet steaks from Jayne's shop, marinated and cooked to perfection. So different from the beef patties and sausages served up for lunch at the shed.

After the meal, the dogs snuffle about for scraps while we talk about what's in store for the New Year. Bernie tells us that Blister has just scored a painting apprenticeship with a local fellow.

'Beauty!' says Jayne, raising her glass. 'Another BackTrack success!'

Bernie doesn't look so sure. 'His missus doesn't want him to do it. She's in tears and they've just had a big barney. She wants him home.'

'They like being at home with their blokes,' adds Geraldine. 'Doing nothing.'

'She needs to get her own life,' says Bernie with a heavy sigh. 'They're just kids ... with a long history of living with unemployment.'

Later, just before I leave, I remember my nutcracker, still lying on the table inside. As I make my way around the fire, Bernie leans back and asks if I want to come along to Ebor with him and Flinty. 'I'll think it over,' I tell him with a surprised laugh. 'But I don't think rabbiting is really my thing.'

'You won't know until you try it.' Bernie's tone is light, but his eyes are serious. 'Might be time to step up to the plate, Helena.'

'Maybe,' I say, as I open the door to the kitchen. I know I won't go rabbiting, but his comment leaves me thinking of the challenges I do need to face – like fixing things between Joey and me.

Just out walking

On the afternoon of Christmas Eve, Joey rings and asks me to pick him up from a friend's place. 'I've bought presents for everyone,' he says happily. 'I need you to help me wrap them.'

Once he's in the car and we're on our way home, we stop to save a small turtle stranded in the middle of the road near the university. Joey carries it gingerly over to show me.

'It really stinks!' he says.

He's right – the smell is overwhelming. Even after he leaves it in the bushes, his fingers still reek of smelly turtle.

Joey wipes his hands on the car seat. 'Imagine how bad a skunk would be!'

We laugh.

At home, I help wrap his presents – rap CDs for Theo and Henry and a fancy Super Soaker water gun for Freddie. After dinner, we all sit around the tree, opening gifts and being nice to each other. Later, Rob and the older kids play poker, a Christmas tradition from my own family, while I put Freddie to bed and clean up.

Then, just before nine, Joey goes back to Tim's, in time for the bail conditions.

*

In the early hours of the morning, four days after Christmas, two police officers are at the door with torches and serious expressions.

'We're looking for Joey,' one of them says. 'He was seen down-town at midnight.'

Joey is still on bail. What was he doing out at midnight?

'He hasn't been here today,' I say, my mouth instantly dry. 'But I'll check.'

I find Joey asleep in Theo's room, stretched out on the spare bed in his boxer shorts. He must have come in the back door without me hearing.

'Joey,' I whisper. 'The police are here.'

He wakes, rubs his eyes, and pulls on some clothes.

The police take Joey away.

'I couldn't sleep,' he tells me before he leaves. 'I was just out walking.'

Now he's breached his bail conditions and will go before a magistrate in the Children's Court the next morning. The magistrate will decide whether to send Joey to a juvenile detention centre in Grafton or increase his bail conditions.

I lie awake for the rest of the night, imagining Joey sitting on a curved steel bench in the fishbowl. Over the past week, I'd begun to think things were improving, especially after Joey came around one night and told me he'd been invited to a youth camp in Jindabyne. He asked for money to pay the deposit and said the camp was organised by a local Christian group. I gave Joey the cheque straight away, happy he was doing something positive.

As dawn breaks, I hear birds twittering in the bamboo outside my bedroom window. I suddenly feel very scared. 'Please don't let Joey get locked up,' I whisper. 'I want him to go camping with the Christians.'

The next morning, before I leave for the police station, I ring one of Rob's friends, a former parole officer, and ask him what he thinks will happen.

'Because it's Joey's first breach, and because he wasn't out drinking or being stupid, he'll probably just get his bail conditions increased,' he says. But then he adds, 'You never know what a judge will decide, though.' Rob's friend also mentions how juvenile detention centres are dark, hard places, where young boys are often raped and become someone's 'bitch'.

I close my eyes, blocking out his words. This isn't going to happen. Joey will stay in Armidale and this will only be a lesson. Like Bernie says to the boys at the shed: 'First time is learning. Second time is stupid.'

*

I meet Don, the Legal Aid solicitor, in the icy foyer of the police station. He's a large, bumbling man, whose words rush from his mouth with the hint of a stutter. I find his awkwardness strangely reassuring. Joey is still inside the police station and I haven't been able to see him.

'He's fine,' Don tells me. 'The police bought him breakfast from Macca's!'

Out on the footpath, where we can talk in private, Don chain-smokes, holding each cigarette between his thumb and first finger. 'The most likely scenario is that the magistrate will change the bail conditions,' he says. 'But there's no guarantee.'

Then Don looks at his watch. 'The police will bring Joey over to the courthouse shortly. I must warn you, Helena ... he'll be handcuffed.'

I nod, struggling to maintain control. How had I become part of the public drama at the local courthouse?

Inside the courtroom, I sit on an uncomfortable wooden pew, droplets of sweat sliding down my arms. The police bring Joey through the doors – he's wearing silver handcuffs around his wrists.

He was just out walking, I want to protest. He couldn't sleep. He's a good boy.

The magistrate listens as the details of Joey's offence are read aloud. I keep my eyes on the back of Joey's stubbly scalp as he stands before the judge. I listen while Don explains to the court how this is Joey's first breach of bail, how he has a family who cares for him, how his mother is sitting in the courtroom.

Confused by the legal terminology, I soon lose track of what's happening. It takes a while for me to realise the judge's decision is to increase the bail conditions – Joey is to reside with us, his family, in our home; he is not to be absent from home between 8 p.m. and 8 a.m.; he is to present himself to police for curfew checks; he is to obey all reasonable directions from his mother; he is not to consume alcohol or drugs not prescribed by a doctor; and he is to next appear in the Children's Court on 10 January.

I stand, my legs almost crumpling with relief.

*

We have our annual New Year's Eve party, but no one arrives till after nine. By then I feel like a friendless pariah. When the first guests finally walk through the door, disappointment flashes across their faces. Others trickle in, but my confidence is gone. The anxiety of waiting for people to arrive is too much after the courtroom events of the previous day. Joey – happily settled back in Theo's room – and the other kids watch movies together. Rob and a couple of his friends stand around a fire near the back shed, playing musical instruments. Inside the house, the other guests and I sit at the wooden table and chat. My nutcracker is in hot demand, people get drunk. I don't need to do much – just listen, occasionally laugh, and wish for it to be over.

Later, while I'm out the front saying goodbye to the last guests, Joey dashes past and sprints down the street. 'Joey!' I call. 'Where are you going?'

He returns a minute later with his mate, Lenny, who lurches drunkenly in front of me. 'He needs a bandage,' says Joey. 'He's hurt.'

Lenny's arm is badly gashed, blood everywhere. Saliva fills my mouth. 'Maybe we should call an ambulance?'

'Nah, no ambulance,' slurs Lenny. 'I'm right – jus' need a bandage.'

'He's walked all this way looking for help,' says Joey when he sees the worried look on my face. 'He can't be that bad.' We wash Lenny's arm under the tap, while Rob finds a bandage in the first aid kit. The cut is deep and will definitely need stitches.

Lenny doesn't want to stay at our house, he doesn't want to go to hospital, and he doesn't want to go home either – 'I promised Mum I wouldn't get into trouble,' he says over and over. As Rob and I talk about what to do, Lenny becomes agitated, worried that we're trying to take him to hospital. Joey takes him aside and softly reasons with him until he agrees to go to another friend's house with Rob, but only if Joey travels with them in the car.

I clear the table and wash up, hoping the police won't turn up while they're gone. When Joey comes back, he stands by the bench in the kitchen and talks and talks – about how Lenny told him he lost his mates while he was out, and three drunken guys had attacked him and thrown him up against a window, which smashed.

I kiss Joey goodnight, thinking how much older he suddenly seems. 'I'm proud of the way you behaved tonight,' I tell him. 'You were a good friend – calm and caring.'

He nods. 'I'm glad I couldn't go out tonight, Mum … I'm glad I stayed home.'

Afterwards I think about alcohol and the havoc it wreaks. Lenny could have died if the glass had slashed his wrist; he could be lying near the window now, bleeding to death on the street. It happens.

The other day, when I'd driven Joey over to Lenny's house, Lenny was getting out of a car with some awful-looking men who had bottles of grog under their arms. One of them said, 'What the fuck are we doing standing out here?' and Lenny told him to shut up and stop being rude because 'Joey's mum is in the car.' Lenny cares about things like that.

'Keep Lenny safe,' I plead in the still of the night. 'Please.'

III

Summer–Autumn 2008

You only want me out of the house

Having Joey home isn't easy. The house is crowded, tension builds. I sleep badly, waiting for the police to come knocking, which they do in the early hours of most mornings to check if Joey is home. Each time they come, I have to wake Joey and bring him to the front door. Rob and I begin to transform into nuclear reactors again. I start shouting at the children over small things, and each day Rob fronts up to Joey with his chest puffed out like a cranky rooster. He starts telling me I have to *force* Joey to get a job, *force* him to be more responsible, *force* the court to change the bail conditions. When Rob speaks this way, I grit my teeth. I'm tempted to snap back and blame him for everything, but I know that's not fair. We need to work through this together – learn how to be less adversarial and more loving with each other, but most especially with Joey.

A welcome break comes when Rob takes the three younger kids down south for a week's holiday at the beach with his family. I'm supposed to go, too, but I have to stay in Armidale because of Joey's bail conditions and his upcoming court appearance.

While Joey is out visiting friends one afternoon, I submit his court form and visit various people to ask if they can write reference letters. I want him to have the best possible chance of staying out of a juvenile detention centre. Because Joey doesn't have any formal clothes, I buy him a pair of black pants, a pin-striped shirt and some black lace-up shoes. He tries on the outfit that night.

'You look like you're going to a wedding!' I say, smiling at how handsome he looks. 'That'll be a useful outfit for job interviews in the future as well.'

Later, when I mention it's likely the bail conditions will be changed so he can go back to Tim's house, Joey turns on me. 'You don't love me. You only want me out of the house.'

'That's not true,' I tell him. But I know from his perspective, it probably seems that way.

What I want is to heal my relationship with Joey and to be a better parent for him. I also want him to go on the camp to Jindabyne, and to move back to Tim's so the pressure eases at home.

The phone rings. It's Tim, asking if I'd like him to come down to the court in the morning.

'Thanks,' I say, touched by his concern. 'That'd be great.'

He's a good man.

The next morning, while Joey is in the bathroom, I ring Don, the solicitor, and reiterate the importance of changing the bail conditions. He says he'll see what he can do.

We wait outside the court for three hours. When Tim arrives, Joey looks surprised, but greets him politely. Lenny's mother, her face worn and drawn, is also waiting outside the courthouse. Lenny is up for an alcohol-related incident. I stop and talk to his mum for a few minutes, and wish them both a positive outcome.

When Joey's name is called, we file into the courtroom. The court date for the charge is put back to a later date, but apart from that, things go as well as can be expected. The judge changes the bail conditions so Joey can go back to Tim's house. He's also allowed to go on the camp to Jindabyne.

I leave court a much calmer woman.

This old-school fella called Maslow

Bernie and a few of the boys are heading out to the shed – the first day back this year. 'Did you hear the news about Gazza?' asks Bernie when he rings. 'He lost his job and his apprenticeship.'

'Gazza?' I ask. 'What happened?'

'He didn't turn up to work for five days and didn't have a good enough reason,' says Bernie with a sigh. 'He's also broken up with his girlfriend and has to find a new place to live. I need to find out what's going on with him.'

'You think he'll be okay?'

'Not sure,' answers Bernie. 'He's one of those quiet ones who doesn't give much away. There's some sort of family stuff going on that I can't work out – him and his older brother are always knocking the dust and shit off each other every time they have a drink. I don't know what it is ... but it's the quiet ones you have to watch.'

I'm the first at the shed, so I wait out the front until Gazza arrives to unlock the gate. He opens the side door of the shed and we walk into the workshop together.

133

'Bernie told me what happened with the job,' I say, looking sideways at Gazza. 'Are you sad about losing the apprenticeship?'

He shrugs. 'I was at first but now I'm just looking ahead.'

Good for him. First time is learning. Second time is stupid.

As Gazza and I heave the wooden roller-door across its runner, Bernie pulls up in the ute with Skippa, Blister and Marshall. Then Jimmy and Thommo arrive, nursing takeaway coffees and hangovers. They head straight for the kitchen. Jimmy doesn't look too much the worse for wear, but Thommo, still in his clothes from the night before, seems strangely fragile and smaller than usual. He puts his skate shoes on the table to use as a pillow. I notice his feet are bare and dirty, the frayed ends of his too-long jeans crusted with dried mud. He looks broken. Bernie once told me that he thought Thommo had a 'real sad quiet' about him – and it's very much evident today.

'Was Tye at this party last night?' asks Bernie.

'We weren't at a party,' says Jimmy. 'We were at the pub.' He glances across at Thommo. 'Where'd we go? The Kilda, the Wicklow, back to the Kilda again.'

'Good to hear you're doing some exercise – you're a health freak, Jimmy.' Bernie rubs his chin and looks across at the boys. 'I don't know … you blokes are all over it this morning.'

After making a coffee, Bernie takes a seat at the table. 'How's the start to the New Year, Thommo? Feeling good or bad about it? One to five – one is shit, five is great.'

Thommo lifts his head off his skate-shoe pillow. 'Two and a half.'

'If there was something you could do to get off to a better start, what would that be?'

'I dunno,' says Thommo. 'Just getting things sorted.'

Bernie turns to the others. 'What do you blokes think Thommo needs to work on?'

'He needs a house,' says Gazza. 'He needs to sleep properly instead of going from house to house.'

Bernie asks the boys if they've heard of Maslow's hierarchy of needs. They shake their heads.

'This old-school fella called Maslow came up with this thing like a pyramid,' explains Bernie, 'and it's about being happy and sending your life in a certain direction. He reckons until you get shit like accommodation, safety and food sorted, nothing else matters. It seems to me that this basic stuff is what Thommo needs to sort out first.'

After some encouragement from Bernie, the boys offer further thoughts on what Thommo needs to work on to improve his life. Bernie nods at their suggestions and then turns back to Thommo. 'How do those things sound to you? Get your licence, back off the piss, work on your sleeping habits and accommodation?' He pauses. 'Which one do you reckon is the most important?'

'Accommodation,' rumbles Thommo, half-asleep. He lays his head back on the skate shoes.

Bernie wipes a hand across his forehead and sighs. 'Doesn't look like we'll get much work done here today, so I'm going to sit with each of you – one-on-one – and work out what you need to make a priority in your life. I want to see some fuckin' rock and roll for you blokes this year.'

Before we finish, Bernie tells the boys he's looking for some helpers for a dog jumping event at the Armidale Show in a couple of months. 'It'll involve a bit of training,' he says, 'and learning my way of working. The last thing I want on the night is a pack of uncontrollable dogs.'

Most of the boys are keen to be involved. Jimmy seems especially interested, and asks Bernie if he can bring in his blue heeler next week – 'She's a good little jumper,' he says with pride. Gazza isn't interested. During the afternoon, the boys rig up a basic dog jump out of a steel frame with planks of wood that slot in to make the jump higher each time. The same model they use at the show. I busy myself cutting lengths of pipe for the next lot of nutcrackers, while Bernie and Thommo drive off to get lunch. They soon return with loaves of white bread, chips, a container of gravy, a cooked chicken and two bottles of Coke. I join the others in the kitchen, feeling like a real worker – filthy dirty, eating chips and gravy on white bread and loving it.

After lunch, Bernie backs the ute until it's flush with the doors of the shed. He places the metal dog jump near the back, so the dogs will land in the tray of the ute. 'That's how they do it at the show,' he says. 'So the dogs don't have far to jump down.'

Bernie has his two border collies, Girl and Lou, and also Sammy – a kelpie pup he's training for a farmer. Jimmy holds Sammy on the lead while Bernie goes through his training methods, which mostly involve hand movements for sit, down, up and stay. Each time the dogs do the right thing, Bernie pats them heartily and croons: 'Good dog!'

After the demonstration, Marshall is the first to step forward, but when he has trouble getting Girl to sit, Bernie comes over to lend a hand. 'You need to be thinking in your head what you want the dog to do, Marshall.'

'I'm no good at this,' grumbles Marshall, ready to throw down the dog's lead.

'The minute you start thinking that, it's over,' says Bernie. 'You're in control of the dog, Marshall. That's what you've got to be thinking.'

Marshall straightens up and gives Girl the hand movement for 'sit' with a look of fierce concentration. This time the dog sits down. Then Marshall readies himself and the dog for the jump. When she makes it over the wall, I cheer and clap.

Blister has worked with the dogs before, but even he has trouble getting Lou to jump.

'Say it with enthusiasm,' instructs Bernie from the side. 'That dog needs to think jumping over that thing is the best fun in the whole world!'

The boys feed the dogs titbits of leftover chicken for encouragement. Gazza and I sit on upturned milk-crates and watch. Joey would like this, I think to myself. He's always loved animals. Maybe the dogs will be the way to get him to give the shed another go. Just before they finish, Bernie comes over to see if Gazza has changed his mind about having a go. Gazza shakes his head – 'Nah.'

'Do you train the dogs for the show every year, Bernie?' I ask.

'Never done it before,' he says with a grin. 'That's why we're going to smash it this time. Not even going to be drunk when we get down there.'

Later, as the boys pack up the metal jump, I join Bernie outside while he has a smoke.

'Time for something different?' I ask, raising my eyebrows.

He nods and tells me how he first brought in a heap of border collie pups when he was working with that wild group of boys at TAFE. The pups belonged to a friend who had a farm out at Ebor. Bernie asked the boys to help him train them.

'It was the first time I saw that group of hoorangs settle down,' says Bernie with a chuckle. 'I taught them how to understand dog language and we just flew into it every week. That's when we started working on: "How do we get things done in a non-violent way as opposed to a violent way?"'

His eyes light up, like he's remembering something very funny.

'Around that time,' says Bernie, 'I was down the street with Tye one night. A bikie dude – who looked like he might just bash you for looking at him – was across the road wrestling with this thumping big pit bull. The dog was pulling on the lead out in front of him, so Tye went straight across the road and said, "I'll tell you what's wrong with your dog, mate!" I was trying to hide – you don't start telling people how to handle their dogs – but Tye's over there telling him, "The reason why he's pulling out there in front means he thinks he's the top dog." And then he's motioning for me to come over. The bloke was saying, "You won't fix this dog … he's done this for three years," but Tye says, "Nah, mate, we'll fix this in five minutes." So there we were, in the middle of the night, with this big bloody fella covered in tattoos, and we got that dog to walk behind in a handful of minutes. Later I told Tye if he ever fuckin' did that again, I'd kill him. Don't worry about the dog biting him – I'd bite him!'

One big smile

Joey's bus for Jindabyne leaves at midnight. I'm still awake at quarter to twelve, so I walk around the corner to Tim's house to see how things are going. One of the Christian youth leaders is waiting in a car parked out the front. Joey meets me on the steps of the front veranda with a backpack slung over one shoulder.

'Mum! We're just going to the bus station.'

'I thought I'd come and say goodbye,' I tell him. I give him a quick hug. 'Have a wonderful time, Joey.' Then I hurry back home, before he can see my tears.

I miss Joey terribly while he's away. I don't understand our relationship. I wish we could love each other easily, without all the dramas and the arguing. When he rings from Jindabyne a few days later, Joey sounds happy. He's having fun and making lots of new friends. This camp may be a turning point – Joey might come back to Armidale ready to finish Year 10 and move ahead in life. After his phone call, I try to enjoy the break. At least for this week I don't have to worry about Joey sticking to his bail conditions. But even though I go to bed early, I don't sleep well.

The day before Joey arrives home, I go around to Tim's with fresh sheets and make Joey's bed, tucking in the corners neatly and arranging all his soft toys around the pillow. Tim has his neighbours over for drinks, and I accept his offer to stay and have a glass of red wine. Later that night, I ring Joey. He's on the bus to Armidale, he says. I won't need to pick him up because the camp leaders will drop him home. Without thinking, I mention his bed is made up with fresh sheets.

'Why did you do that?' he snaps in a whisper. 'You know I don't want you in my room!'

I hold the phone away from my ear and take several deep breaths. The wine, combined with my lack of sleep, has weakened my defences.

I swallow hard. 'I did it because I love you, Joey. I thought you'd like to sleep on a clean bed after being on a bus all day and night.'

He hangs up on me.

A short while later, he rings back and apologises. 'I just don't want you going near my room, Mum.'

The next afternoon, I hear the gate click and then a knock on the window.

'Joey!' I marvel at the difference in his appearance as he walks in through the back door. His face, normally so pale, is full of colour and life. 'It's so good to see you!'

Joey laughs and leans back against the kitchen bench – 'The camp was great!' He tells me about all the people he met, the fun times he had. Later, he puts on a DVD which has the highlights of the week's activities – sail boating, drama nights, crazy flour and water fights. It's incredible to see Joey's beaming face featuring throughout – participating in everything.

'I had a lot of fun on the camp, Mum,' he says, cocking one eyebrow in a charming manner. When I next look over at him, his face is one big smile.

My beautiful boy.

When he was growing up, Joey was always reluctant to try new things, especially organised activities, but he often enjoyed himself once he overcame his initial fear. I spent a lot of time asking other parents for ideas, or searching notice-boards and newspapers for sporting activities. Nothing really worked – probably because Joey wasn't a 'group' person – but I kept trying to find something to capture his interest. Then, as a gangly and gawky thirteen-year-old, he became a mad keen breakdancer. Every Saturday, he caught the bus into the city for dance lessons in the Ritz Ballroom at the Cunnington Dance Studio in Brisbane. The old couple who worked in the soft-drink bar looked as if they had been there forever, and you could *feel* the history of dance in that studio. Joey and his dance group – the BodyRock Crew, a group of guys aged from eleven to twenty – were in three performances for Youth Week that year. The first performance came at a time when Joey had been rather troublesome at home, but when I saw him doing his solo on stage at the Ithaca Skate Park, my heart surged with love for him. The BodyRock Crew also danced in the Queen Street Mall one night, and their final show was at the South Bank Piazza in front of a large crowd who cheered loudly. After the performance, Theo and Henry stood in awe of their big brother, and Rob and I were brimming with pride.

Fully loaded

'That's a good dog!'

The Armidale show is less than a month away now and training has begun in earnest for the dog jumping event. Earlier, Bernie thought it was going to be a 'no-show' day, but it wasn't long before Blister arrived in his I'M SOTALLY TOBER T-shirt, followed by Marshall, Gazza, Jimmy, Skippa and Thommo. Jimmy brought in his blue heeler bitch, Vickie, and Thommo brought his girlfriend, Amber.

Thommo's wearing the same tattered jeans and black T-shirt. Although his clothes don't look as if they've been washed since I last saw him, he's had a shave and a haircut and the circles under his eyes are gone. While the others help Bernie set up the jump, Thommo waits with his arms crossed over his chest, like he's hugging himself. His girlfriend stands to one side, holding Sammy's lead, the kelpie pup now known as 'The Five Thousand Dollar Dog'. It's strange to see a young woman in the shed, especially one dressed in a baby-doll mini-dress with shoestring straps and white platform sandals.

Bernie strides around in his old blue singlet, jeans and boots. With three border collies, the kelpie pup and a blue heeler, the shed has a definite 'outback' atmosphere today. Bernie borrowed the third border collie – a lively dog called Banjo – from Simmo. I notice Skippa is having trouble controlling Banjo. 'You gotta read the dog, Skippa,' calls Bernie from the side. 'Give him enough slack on the lead to let him do what he needs to do. You need to know what works best for your dog.'

I smile at his words. The dogs are just like the boys. Bernie uses the same methods in his youth work.

On the next attempt, Banjo flies over the top without touching the plank. Skippa walks past, grinning.

Bernie lines his tape measure against the jump. 'Just over six foot. Seven foot two is the record.' He takes Lou by the collar and runs up with her. When Lou scrambles at the top and falls back down, Bernie catches her and pats her head softly. 'Good dog!' He looks over at the boys. 'Shit, we're in trouble – that's about as high as that dog can jump.'

He calls Girl over, looking at her, then at the jump. 'Hey, Girl. Can you jump that high or can't you?' He turns back to the boys again. 'At this sort of height, if you don't "see" the dog jump over it in your head, the dog won't do it. I don't know why it works that way ... but it's pretty fuckin' accurate.' Bernie stands on the platform behind the jump and encourages Girl. With a bit of help from Thommo, the dog manages to make it over the top.

After the training session, Jimmy's dog does a poo near the side of the shed. The kelpie pup strains at the lead, aching to reach it. 'That dog would eat shit off a shovel, I reckon,' laughs Bernie. 'Jimmy, your dog ... you clean the shit.'

*

A few days later, Joey rings, excitement in his voice. 'I went to dog jumping, Mum. I worked with Lou and she jumped higher than ever before!'

'That's great news, Joey!'

'Bernie said I might be able to get an amendment to my bail conditions so I can go to Ebor and camp with the others and learn more training.'

It's encouraging to hear Joey's enthusiasm about the dogs, and if this was going to work, I needed to pull back from the shed. Joey didn't need his mother hanging around watching from the sidelines. Bernie has clearly tapped into something special by bringing in the dogs, and Joey's not the only one who's been drawn to the shed lately. Aboriginal boys have been coming along in droves. Bernie's had to scout for extra dogs – mainly border collies – from all over Armidale. After an article about the dog jumping program was featured in the local newspaper, people started turning up at the shed, offering to lend Bernie any dog with a spring in its step.

Simmo hosts a gathering for the BackTrack crew and their families the following weekend. Flinty and Bernie are busy barbecuing steaks and sausages when Rob and I arrive with Henry and Freddie.

'Joey told me about dog jumping,' I tell them. 'It's a miracle!'

Bernie laughs. 'He's fully loaded now. He rang *me* today to check what time it was on.'

A major shift has occurred – not only with Joey, but with me, too. I'd spoken to him earlier and he'd mentioned dog training was on that afternoon. Around three, I rang to see if he was going, but heard the engaged signal on his phone. On the internet, I thought. At about six, he'll probably remember – 'Dog jumping!'

I almost walked around and knocked on his door, but stopped myself. Joey needed to remember, not me. If he missed out, so be it. But later, curious, I drove past the shed. The dog jump was set up around the side and about a dozen boys stood holding dogs on leads. When I saw Joey in the crowd, an enormous weight lifted from me. I didn't need to take on the responsibility for this one.

I ask Bernie how Joey ended up with Lou.

'The dogs are picking the boys,' says Bernie, turning over sausages. 'No doubt about it. That's a bit of the magic.'

'But how do they pick them?'

'They follow the boys around, smell out the personality – find what they're looking for. The boys don't even know it's going on.' He smiles. 'I've had many fun hours seeing those dogs sort out the boys. When we started, I thought the boys would all want the dog that jumped the highest, but they don't give a shit about which dog wins.'

He reaches for a bottle of red, fills his glass and then offers the bottle to me. 'The dogs are bringing out the soft side in the boys. I often see them sitting and patting the dogs.' Bernie looks at me and chuckles. 'You wouldn't see them showing that sort of attention to their mothers. It's a good way for them to let out some sort of emotion – and the dogs are always highly sensitive to whether they're having a good or a bad day.'

Just as Bernie is, I think to myself.

'Joey reckons Lou is the smallest and cleverest dog.'

'Yep, that's her,' says Bernie. 'Way smart dog, but Christ, she drives me bananas.' He laughs and rolls his eyes in exasperation. 'If we're doing jumping, she's the one that pulls up and goes, "Jump the fuckin' wall yourself."'

I laugh and take a sip of wine. 'I've been meaning to ask … how do you stop a dog pulling on the lead?'

144

'Those old fellas in Tennant Creek taught me how to do that,' replies Bernie. 'But they don't have collars or leads.' He puts down his tongs and turns to face me. 'It's about understanding how the dog works in the pack. There are only two types of dogs – you're either a leader or a follower – and there's only ever one leader, but lots of followers. So, with dogs, it's really fuckin' simple … if you're a leader, you're out the front, and anytime a dog is pulling on a lead, he's challenging you.'

Bernie moves away from the barbecue and lights up a smoke before he continues. 'At the shed, I'm teaching the boys how to be a leader with the dog – even if they're not natural leaders. When we walk the dogs as a pack, all the boys walk out in front, all the dogs behind. That's the way it is. From time to time, I might need to pull a dog into place if he's challenging the leadership, but if the boys are calm and assertive, the dog will understand his role. If the dog challenges that role, it's not acceptable. For example, if the dog pulls off in front, then the boy changes direction. He doesn't need to grab the dog or flog it with a stick … he just goes, no, I'm the leader. The dog will only challenge when the boy lets his guard down.'

'Is it the same with you and the boys?' I ask him. 'Are you the leader?'

'Absolutely,' says Bernie without hesitation. 'I'm the pack leader. Not negotiable. And I'll do that as nicely or as hard as I need to, and if the boys are challenging me and don't like it? Fuck off and find another pack. Go back to jail. That's when it's hard – when they come out of jail. Constantly challenging, falling behind, same as what the dogs do. Well, fuck off.'

Bernie looks at me. 'The interesting thing is that they keep coming back. Why? Because we're giving them something they're not getting anywhere else.'

Over dinner, the conversation turns to the popularity of the dog training program. 'It's going properly silly,' Bernie tells us. 'Everywhere I go in town, Aboriginal kids are asking, "Can I come down the shed ... even just help with it?" I've never run anything that draws the countryman kids like this ... Flinty's been picking them up at school, and they're all waiting out the front for him. Those boys are showing up, eh?'

Flinty nods. 'Couple of carloads.'

I'd noticed how Bernie had a good connection with the Aboriginal boys at the shed. For a while, I thought he must have been Aboriginal himself. But when I'd asked him about it, he had shaken his head. 'Nah, I'm just a simple pup who's been invited into their business.' Bernie's voice became soft and low as he explained his relationship with Aboriginal culture.

'It's because of the respect and the trust I give out,' he said, 'and from being in the right place at the right time and doing the right things.' He looked at me then. 'To have Aboriginal people give me permission to work with young fellas, to have them say: "That's alright – you can do that" ...' Bernie paused for a moment, '... that's probably the most humbling experience of anything in my life.'

Crowd-pleaser

On the day of Joey's next court appearance, Bernie arrives at the courthouse while Joey and I are talking to the solicitor outside. Don tells us that he's discovered a probationary constable was responsible for charging Joey and Tobias on the night they were arrested. 'The police don't have a real case,' says Don, 'and because they haven't bothered to put in their brief, we have to wait another couple of weeks.'

Today, Don will ask the magistrate to make a further change to the bail conditions so Joey can go with Bernie and the dog jumping crew to rural shows in the New England area. We also need to work out a date for the next hearing. Joey's co-offender, Tobias, is now at the juvenile detention centre in Grafton. He had since breached his bail and had been denied a second chance on it and had to wait out his court date in custody. He'll have to be brought over on the day of the hearing.

Bernie has come along to say he'll take responsibility for Joey if they change the bail conditions. He wants to see Joey do well, too. Don nods and hurries off to talk with another client, calling over his shoulder that he'll be back when Joey's name is called. I notice Joey is wearing worn-out sneakers with his black pants, and that his shirt is hanging out.

'We'll get him to tuck his shirt in before we go inside,' says Bernie when he sees the look on my face. He turns to Joey. 'I'll give you some hints on courtroom etiquette, too – I got in a lot of trouble being cheeky to magistrates.'

Bernie pulls out his tobacco and rolls a smoke. 'I once had a run-in with the highway patrol in the Snowy Mountains, when they pulled me up for drink driving years ago. I was just over the limit but I acted like a smart-arse and it was one of my early lessons ...' He looks at Joey. 'Don't be a smart-arse with the police. They stuck a heap of stuff on me – dangerous driving, all that sort of shit. I was angry about it, but that's the reality of what goes on ... there's a time to be smart, and a time not to be,' he says as he lights up. 'You certainly don't joke with magistrates in the court – while everybody else might find it highly amusing, the judges are the ones who make the rules.'

Joey yawns and stretches his arms over his head. 'I'm getting bored of waiting.'

Bernie shakes his head and sighs. 'Joey ... shut the fuck up.'

Soon enough Joey's name is called and we troop inside. I sit near the front, with Bernie next to me. Before I can work out what's going on, everyone stands, ready to leave the courtroom. The magistrate has said no to any changes. Joey's bail conditions remain the same. My faith in justice is shaken and I'm angry, especially with the judge who was dismissive and arrogant. He barely looked at the reference Bernie wrote for Joey.

Joey's face is downcast as we leave the courtroom.

'I'm pissed off as well,' says Bernie, once we're outside. 'But when it comes down to it, Joey, we're all here because you did something wrong. If you hadn't breached your bail in that first week, the judge would have probably been more lenient.'

He's right. And things could be so much worse. One of Joey's other friends was waiting outside the court for an 'aggravated break and enter' charge. I was sad to see him there – he always had a big smile for me and seemed really friendly. Now he's facing nine months in a juvenile detention centre and he's only sixteen – just a young bloke who did something crazy without thinking of the consequences.

I thank Bernie for his support.

'Joey will be okay, Helena,' he says, giving me a reassuring pat on the arm. 'He should learn something from this. See you at the show tomorrow night.'

*

The grandstand is full and the crowd three-deep around the fence by the time Bernie drives into the showground, pulling a trailer-load of dogs behind his yellow ute. People cheer. My throat tightens when Joey clambers down with the others. As I watch Bernie and the others unload, I think of how he's brought these boys from the edge of society to centre stage. Thommo, Tye, Blister, Freckles and Jimmy assemble the jumping wall, mature with responsibility. Over the last weeks, as more and more Aboriginal kids have taken on dogs, these old-school Iron Man Welders have stepped up to help Bernie with the program. Joey and a heap of young boys stand holding their dogs with confidence, somehow managing to contain their excitement. Skippa, no longer the sad-eyed boy from months ago, struggles with Banjo, who barks and barks.

All of a sudden, six police officers, dressed like a riot squad, come swooping along the showground fence with a sniffer dog. They force the dog to brush up against people's legs. From where I'm sitting, it looks as if the police are targeting the Aboriginal boys lined up along the fence, just inside the ring. The boys, focused on their dogs, seem unaware of the police passing behind. The sniffer dog moves on. I shake my head, baffled. Why would the police search for drugs at a time like this, while young people are engaged in a positive activity, some of them for the first time ever? What if the police had led someone away just when the event was about to start?

The dog jumping begins. The ringmaster makes good-natured jokes about the dogs, quickly locking into their different personalities: Geordie, as always, is super eager; Zorro flies over the jump without a care in the world; Lou has a relaxed and nonchalant style; and King, a wiry brown farm dog, is an instant crowd-pleaser who loves the attention. Everyone cheers and claps loudly when each dog comes to its limit and is led away from the competition. Bernie stands to the side, stepping in only when the dogs baulk at the jump. The boys have everything under control. Along with the rest of the crowd, I whoop with pleasure when each dog makes it over the plank as the jump gets higher and higher.

When Zorro, the champion jumper, finally reaches his limit, the crowd gives the entire dog jumping team a standing ovation. All around, people are smiling. Some, like me, have tears in their eyes. In the ring, the boys and their dogs gather around Bernie as he speaks to them intently. Afterwards, when the jump is dismantled and the dogs are loaded back into the trailer, Bernie comes over to where the rest of the BackTrack crew are sitting. We congratulate him for masterminding the 'feel good' event of the show. Bernie nods and looks back to the boys, who are still standing around the ute in the centre of the showground.

'What did *they* say about it?' I ask.

'They loved it,' he says. 'Look at the actions – that's more important than the words. They're sticking around and talking about it for over half an hour … It wasn't a hassle finding anyone today. They were ringing *me*.'

*

Two days later, I see Simmo downtown. 'Did you hear the news?' he asks. 'Banjo died yesterday.'

'Oh!' I immediately think of Skippa and what a difference that crazy dog made to his life. Skippa's eyes were shining with happiness at the showground the other night. He couldn't keep the smile off his face, even though Banjo was never an easy dog to manage. Joey always said Lou was the best behaved dog, and that Banjo was the naughtiest because he was always barking. Bernie used to place his hand over Banjo's snout and make a growling noise in the back of his throat – dog language. Banjo would look ashamed for a few minutes, but would soon start barking again.

'The vet reckons he ate rat poison,' adds Simmo. 'Two of the lads came over from the high school this morning in their break. They weren't even sure if it was my place, but they introduced themselves and told me how sad they were about Banjo.'

At home, there's a message from Bernie on the answering machine: 'Not sure if you've heard ... Simmo's dog died. We're having a smoking ceremony for him out at my place after dog jumping this afternoon. I'm trying to find Joey.'

When I phone Joey to tell him about Banjo, he takes a sharp breath. 'Oh! – I'll ring Bernie straight away.'

I can't make it to the ceremony that afternoon. But the next day, when I see Bernie shopping in Coles, he tells me how important it was for the boys to go through the ritual process. 'Handling death is something we do very poorly in Western culture,' he says with a wry smile, throwing tins of spaghetti and baked beans into his trolley. 'But that mob in Tennant Creek taught me how going through a process like a smoking ceremony can help. It doesn't make death any easier, but it helps to handle it.'

This is my dog

Don, the solicitor, calls with some good news. He's just heard a case in court for Tobias, the co-offender who was charged with the same offence as Joey. 'The police withdrew the charge,' says Don. 'Tobias got a two-year good behaviour bond and no criminal charge.' Because Tobias has been in trouble with the police before, this bodes well for Joey's first offence. We're due back in court the next day. I want Joey off bail so he can go with the dog jumping team to Walcha.

I'd driven Joey around to Tobias's house the previous week. Tobias had just been released from the juvenile detention centre. He stood out on the street by the car, talking to Joey through the window. I listened to Tobias tell Joey stories about his time inside, making it all seem like a grand adventure.

Sometimes I worry about Joey's friendship with Tobias. Perhaps I should be putting more energy into helping Joey join the Defence Forces, where he can earn good money, finish Year 10, get a driver's licence ... and get away from Armidale for a while. It's been hard work trying to get him to fill in all the application forms. But that afternoon, as I waited in the car for Joey and Tobias to finish their conversation, a long-haired toddler came out of the house, calling for Tobias. I couldn't work out if it was a boy or a girl, but I watched as the child tugged on Tobias's jeans, wanting to be picked up. Tobias hoisted the toddler onto his hip and held the baby with such tenderness that I was ashamed of myself for having judgemental thoughts about him. Tobias is probably a kid who's been labelled his whole life, and here I was, doing the same.

The next morning, Joey and I are outside the court by nine. We don't have to wait long this time. When his name is called, Joey slouches into the courtroom, hands in his pockets. 'Take your hands out of your pockets when you stand before me,' bellows the judge. 'Don't cross your arms either.'

It's like being back in school. The judge demands respect, yet treats the solicitors and the other people in the courtroom rudely. But at least he has bothered to read Joey's references. Don informs the court how Joey has been to the Christian youth camp, how he's been involved with dog jumping, how his mother is in the courtroom. After considering the paperwork and the reference letters, the judge says Joey can come off bail. Because it's his first offence, he gets a twelve-month good behaviour bond and is to report to Juvenile Justice each week. My held-in breath escapes as I realise Joey won't have a criminal record.

He's free.

Outside, I thank Don for his efforts and say goodbye to Joey. Walking home, emotionally spent, I remember Bernie's words from the previous court session, and wonder if Joey really has learnt something from this experience.

A few hours later, Joey comes around while Freddie and I are eating lunch. Joey, still in his 'court clothes', is holding a rope tied to Lou.

'This is my dog,' he tells Freddie, and then turns to me, his face open and light. 'I talked to Bernie about buying Lou. He asked me how much I reckoned she was worth. I said, a hundred and fifty? He said, "Try again." Two hundred and fifty? "Try again." Five hundred? "Try again." He said she's worth around a thousand dollars ... but I could pay for Lou by mowing Bernie's lawn.'

'That'd be a great thing to do,' I say, pleased to hear him so excited.

We head into the backyard so Lou can be off the lead. Once Joey unties the rope, Lou runs straight over to Freddie's clam-shaped swimming pool and submerges herself in the water. Joey and Freddie laugh and laugh while I grab my camera from inside. I take photos of Joey kneeling down with Lou, his arm around the dog's neck.

*

Over the Easter weekend, Rob takes Henry to a folk festival in Grafton for two nights. While they're away, Bernie and Jayne host a BackTrack get-together. It's a perfect evening – the sky full of stars and the first chill of autumn in the air. Bernie sits on a rolled-up swag and tells me the barbecue is Jimmy's latest design – 'It's got swing-around hotplates and everything!'

'Good old Jimmy!' I laugh. 'How is everything at the shed?' I haven't been there since the dog training began.

'Triple J want to come up for the Wool Expo and follow us around for the day,' says Bernie, rolling a smoke. He stokes the fire and uses the end of a burning stick to light up. 'Parents are coming over to the shed to watch their kids training the dogs.' He shakes his head, like he can't believe it. 'Getting those country-man kids engaged in anything is really difficult, but we had fifteen boys at the shed last week. I was the only one supervising. Came home, went to bed and freaked out.'

I feel a sudden pang of guilt, but I don't want to help out at the shed while Joey is involved with the dogs.

'We got Skippa a welding apprenticeship through the week as well,' he adds. 'Now we're almost down to no boys from that original mob. We've been *too* successful.'

Jimmy is the only Iron Man Welder left.

'Hanging around like a cobweb,' sighs Bernie. 'Funny how Jimmy is doing dog work with all the Aboriginal boys – he's often the only white fella when we go places.' He chuckles. 'Around that Sorry Day time, when all the old prejudices were coming up, Jimmy was saying things like: "My dad's car window was bashed in 1979 and it had to be Kooris because they were in town." Maybe this is his lesson.' Bernie yawns and stretches his arms out wide. 'It's taken me a few weeks to realise I can't hang on to those other boys forever. They've all got jobs now – even

Blister – but we need to stick with him because he's got the baby coming soon.' We talk about how we can help Blister and Emma with some meals, help them find a house, and encourage Blister to stop smoking inside.

Before I go home, Bernie takes me aside. 'I saw Joey wandering around last night. He was sober, said he couldn't sleep. Something's going on with him, Helena, and I'm trying to figure out just what it is.'

*

The following weekend, Joey comes around in a bad mood. When I ask about the dogs, he says he doesn't want to be involved anymore, that it's all boring. He argues with Theo, argues with Freddie, and argues with me. Then he breaks a sword Theo made at school and knocks the television over. I'm a shaking wreck by the time he storms out the door. This is too much, especially with Rob teaching at a weekend school in Sydney.

I don't know what has caused this change in Joey's behaviour, especially when things seemed to be going so well. I still swing from despair to elation with him, and I still don't know how to deal with his anger when he explodes like this. But I do know I need to toughen up. Things have to change. Cooking his meals, driving him around, giving him money when he's broke – none of it is improving his life, or helping to send him in the right direction.

The next day, when my head is clear, I write Joey a letter. I tell him that it feels like we've gone back in time to when he first left home, to when he was being really angry. For the moment, because I don't want him coming around and arguing with everyone, I suggest that we have a break from house visits and look at doing some mediation so we can build up positive times again. We could go to the movies once a week, or something like that. I also explain that I'm not doing the dinners anymore, or supplying him with breakfast cereal or milk – he needs to budget his money so he doesn't run out. Finally, I remind him that I love him, and that I want to improve our relationship.

At Joey's house, I knock on the door, nervous but determined to see this through. He comes out in his boxer shorts, rubbing sleep from his eyes. He reads the letter while I stand on his doorstep. Then he rips it up and throws it at my feet.

A few days later, my mother rings from Wollongong, where she and my father have gone to buy a unit. They've wanted to move away from the Gold Coast for years, and recently decided on Wollongong as an option for the future. But things aren't going well.

'I don't think it's a good idea to move,' she says, her voice wavering. 'We need to be close to your father's doctors. He still hasn't recovered from his hip replacement.'

'It might be better down there,' I tell her. My brothers live nearby and would be much closer. 'You're so far away from everyone on the Gold Coast.'

My mother soon regains her composure. She's overwhelmed from making all the decisions. Because my father is taking strong pain medication, he isn't his normal self. My brothers are supposed to be helping them find a unit, but when I ask about them, my mother sniffs. 'They are so busy with work ... we hardly see them.'

After their stay in Wollongong, where my father barely leaves the hotel room because of the pain in his hip, my parents decide to stay on the Gold Coast. On their return, they buy a second floor unit in a complex at Broadbeach Waters, the same neighbourhood they've lived in for years.

Fixing some shit

Joey comes around at seven in the morning to borrow a carton of milk. 'I haven't got any money for the next ten days,' he says. I'm just sending him on his way with the milk and half a box of breakfast cereal when Rob comes into the kitchen. Within seconds he and Joey are involved in a heated exchange and Rob tells Joey he is not to come to the house again.

'Fuck you,' roars Joey.

Theo and Henry run to their bedrooms while Freddie clings to my leg. I silently curse Rob as I try and hustle Joey out the door – 'Let's sort this out later.' Joey stands fuming for a moment and then stomps up the side path, slamming the side gate so hard the house rattles.

I turn to Rob and say, 'He was just here to borrow some milk … why did you have to make a big scene?'

As I stoop to pick up Freddie, I think of the letter I gave Joey a few weeks back – the one he ripped up and threw at my feet. So much for my resolutions – I'd slipped back to old habits again.

The next morning, I go around to Joey's to give him his TAFE enrolment form that needs to be returned, and also an article about online stockbroking that he might be interested in. While I wait on his doorstep, Joey goes inside and comes back with a folded piece of paper – 'A letter for you' – and then closes the door in my face.

That afternoon, while Freddie is having his nap, I make a cup of tea and read Joey's letter. In the letter, Joey describes how things are from his perspective: how the problems between us have gone on for too long, how he thinks I put Rob before him, and how he feels pushed away from his home and his family. My heart aches when Joey compares himself to a friend who is alright to have around for a little while, but then you get sick of them and want them to leave. He ends the letter with an ultimatum: he's not prepared to come around or talk to me until I have sorted my priorities and I am able to show some understanding of the way things are for him.

I refold the letter and place it back in the envelope. Joey's words are confronting, disturbing and painful to read, but he's right. The chasm between him and the rest of the family – and particularly the arguments between him and Rob – have gone on for too many years. But I don't like ultimatums, and I'm not going to choose between him and Rob. And I'm not going to be like a dog with her tail between her legs either. Later that night, when the kids are asleep, Rob and I talk about the flare-up he had with Joey. We both want to make things better for Joey, and Rob says he will try and set up a mediation session for the two of them.

A week later, Rob comes home from work and tells me he's arranged a mediation session. Joey has agreed to come along. I look at Rob, impressed that he's made an effort to improve his relationship with Joey. He's stepped up to the plate, and I need to do that, too. 'You won't need to be involved at this stage,' he tells me, and explains why it's better to address the issues separately for now.

On the day of their first mediation appointment, Joey doesn't show. Rob meets with the Family Support counsellor on his own to discuss the issues he's most concerned about. He books an appointment for the same time the following week, with the hope that Joey will appear.

That afternoon, Joey rings. He tells me that Bernie has been over at his place and they've had a chat.

'We're not calling it "mediation",' says Joey. 'We're calling it "fixing some shit" and I'll give it a go next week. Bernie is going to be my support person.'

I'm glad Joey is keen to go ahead. Things need to be resolved between all of us.

'I also told Bernie about joining the army,' adds Joey. 'He thinks it's a great idea.'

*

On the weekend, I take Freddie to see the dog jumping display at Central Park, where a huge crowd is gathered under the trees, cheering loudly each time a dog makes it over the jump. At the end of the show, I wander over and thank Bernie for helping Joey see the benefits of mediation.

'You'll need to be involved too, Helena,' he says, in a voice that means business. 'Not this week, but next time.'

I nod.

After we talk a little more about the mediation process, Bernie asks me what Joey was like as a two-year-old.

I look at him, surprised by his question. Whenever I think of Joey as a young child I become choked with emotion. We did our best, and Rob was a loving step-father when Joey was a toddler. We always tried hard, but we made so many mistakes as Joey got older and his behaviour became more challenging. Maybe it's the way Rob and I behave as parents under pressure, or maybe it's just me – I don't know, but I've always wanted Joey to feel loved and part of the family.

'I need some time to think about that,' I tell Bernie.

By the time Joey was two, we were living in our fifth share-house in Armidale. I'd already established a pattern of moves and disruption that would continue for the next thirteen years. But I was young – only twenty-four when I had him – and I knew very little about parenting. I didn't understand the importance of stability. For a large part of that year, Joey and I were still on our own; Rob had returned from India, and we were seeing each other regularly, but he was living in university accommodation while he finished his honours degree.

I was in the second year of my undergraduate degree, but I managed to fit full-time study into three and a half days. Joey went to his family day care mother four days a week. He loved *Thomas the Tank Engine*, playing with his trucks and bulldozers in the sandpit, feeding the ducks in the pond, farm machinery, fire engines, ambulances, cats, dogs, horses, going high on the swings at the park and sliding down slippery dips. I didn't have a car, so we went everywhere by pushbike. Joey sat close behind me in his bike-seat, talking and pointing to things that grabbed his attention. He was highly observant, even then. He loved climbing trees and going up ladders. Sometimes he could be as dark as a storm cloud, but then his whole face would light up when he smiled.

At the end of each semester, we travelled down to Sydney on the train to stay with my parents. My father would mind Joey so my mother and I could go out for coffee or go shopping in peace. Joey often had tantrums in the supermarket and crowds unsettled him, so it wasn't easy to take him with us. I think it started to dawn on me that year that Joey was a bit different from the other children I saw around me. He was much more complex. My brother and his wife, who also lived in Sydney, had a daughter the same age. Whenever we went to the beach, they lazed around on towels while their daughter sat quietly by, watching sand sift through her fingers. Meanwhile, I ran around chasing after Joey – who was here, there and everywhere. He had a lot of energy for mischief.

He was always asking questions. I thought he needed *more* – so, later in the year, I took him out of his family day care arrangement and enrolled him in a structured learning program at the university child care centre. It was a mistake. Really, when I think back on that time, I can see that Joey needed *less* – less disruption, less rushing out the door in the mornings, less comparisons with other children, less stress. The only thing he needed more of was unconditional love.

From time to time, I see toddlers, usually boys, struggling with their mother or father in the supermarket. They are notice-ably louder and more intense than other children, and they remind me of Joey when he was young. The parents always look troubled and weary, and I often want to reach out and tell them things like: 'Don't worry ... you're doing a good job ... rest as much as you can.'

*

Joey's 18th birthday is approaching. I'm not sure what to do, espe-cially since things are still a little strained between us. Bernie once told me that 'uncles sometimes need to be forced into their job', so I email my brothers and suggest it might be beneficial for them to reconnect with Joey as he enters adulthood.

My middle brother rings and says Joey can come down for three nights. Joey will then catch the train from Sydney to visit my older brother, who lives further down the coast. The two of them have already worked out suitable dates.

'Thanks ... thanks so much,' I say. 'I'll get his ticket tomorrow.'

For his birthday, I'll buy Joey a train ticket and some sports shoes, jeans, T-shirts and socks – new clothes for a new man. I'm also going to take him away to the coast for the weekend. It's been far too long since we had a holiday together.

IV

Winter–Spring 2008

Jail is the fucked-est environment

On the morning of Joey's birthday shopping trip, he opens the door dressed in his boxer shorts, rubbing sleep from his eyes. Why can't he be ready for once, I think, before going back home to have a cup of tea. By the time I return to Joey's, he's invited his friend Tobias to come shopping with us. He's also asked Tobias to come along on our coast trip. I'm a little disappointed, but I guess I didn't make it clear that I wanted it to be just him and me when I described it as: 'I'm going out of town for a few days – do you want to come along?' I thought the shopping and the trip to the coast might be a chance for some mother–son bonding, but perhaps it'll make things easier with Tobias coming along.

Our first stop is the railway station, where I buy Joey's return ticket to Sydney. Then we drive downtown. 'Where do you want to buy shoes?' I ask. Joey suggests a sports store near where we've parked. As we go inside I notice one of the shop assistants looking warily at Tobias and Joey. Because of her attitude, I'm inclined to leave the store straight away, but I know Joey won't want me making a fuss. While one of the shop assistants helps Joey with his shoes, Tobias browses through the athletic-brand clothing, casually hanging a couple of jackets and T-shirts over his arm.

I watch him go into the change room. The shop assistant looks up from tying Joey's laces and calls out to another assistant who is tidying racks at the back of the shop. She walks over and they exchange glances. The other woman moves across to stand near the change room, looking as if she's poised to kick in the door at any moment. Joey is happily oblivious to what's going on, but I feel like I'm watching a suspense thriller.

Tobias comes out of the change room, holding one of the T-shirts. He waits at the counter with his wallet in his hand.

Don't do it, I want to yell. They think you're a thief.

As I pay for Joey's shoes, I burn with injustice. This shop doesn't deserve our money.

As we head outside, we bump straight into two beefy-looking police officers.

'Tobias!' they say.

A sense of shame creeps over my skin as the police talk to Joey and Tobias. I feel like white trash – even though I haven't done anything.

'There was a break-in at a house on Brown Street about half an hour ago,' says one of the police officers. 'Two white boys and an Aboriginal boy.' The police officer suddenly notices me. 'Are you with …?'

'Yes,' I tell him curtly. 'We've been shopping, and before that we were at the train station.'

The police officer nods and turns back to Tobias and Joey. He mentions the name of a local boy and asks if they've seen him around.

'I saw him at dog jumping last Wednesday,' says Joey, but doesn't offer any further information.

The police look as if they're making up their minds about something. 'Okay then,' one of them says. They leave.

We walk back to the car, Joey and Tobias excitedly discussing who might have done the break-in. I follow behind, considering Tobias. I don't really know much about him. He's polite and well-mannered whenever I'm around, and I always enjoy his witty sense of humour, but he has an 'edge' that unsettles me. Maybe the police are right to be suspicious, but I don't like the way they questioned Joey and Tobias on the street.

For the rest of the morning, it seems that people stare at Joey and Tobias with suspicion in their eyes. At the newly built shopping plaza, Joey waits with Tobias on a seat while I do some browsing on my own. Walking up to them later, I realise they stand out like a pair of roughnecks with their hooded jackets and low slung jeans.

*

Recently, when Bernie and I were discussing the problem he had securing funding for BackTrack, he'd expressed his frustration at not being able to access much money until *after* a kid had been locked up. 'Then you get the money,' he said, lifting his shoulders in bewilderment. 'But by that time it's already fucked because once they lock a kid up, there's an eighty per cent likelihood that kid will be locked up again, and again, and again – no matter what interventions you put in when they come out. And once kids have been locked up, they come out different.'

'I've noticed that,' I told him. 'They seem to have a sort of hardness about them.'

'Yep,' agreed Bernie. 'It's the jail-talk, which is all about covering your arse when you're boxed into a corner. And for the Joeys of the world, kids who have been to jail have got street-cred because they've been in a place where you gotta watch your back – where you swap stuff for smokes and the whole credit line

runs on matches and Tally-Ho papers and drugs. Juvenile detention isn't so bad, but in the big houses, people are just bombed
out of their fuckin' heads from stuff they make themselves to
whatever else they can get.'

He shook his head at me. 'Jail is the fucked-est environment,
Helena.'

*

I'd planned to leave early for the coast, but it's mid-afternoon by
the time Joey and Tobias are ready. 'It'll be almost dark by the
time we arrive,' I grumble. On the way, we stop for a break at
Ebor Falls, and as we admire the view from the lookout platform,
Tobias lights the stub of a rollie he has in his pocket and shares
it with Joey. People stare at them because they stick out like a
pair of hoodlums, just like at the shopping centre. A minute later,
when I notice Tobias about to throw the butt on the ground, I tell
him, 'You can't do that … this is a National Park.'

Joey shoots me a dark look, like he thinks I'm being a prig, but
I don't care.

Back in the car, we listen to rap – a little bit of Wu-Tang Clan
and Busta Rhymes, and a little bit of Flo Rida and Lil Wayne.
Joey and Tobias sing along with the lyrics and discuss the rappers'
lives. Tobias shares Joey's passion for hip hop, and they often
have lengthy discussions about the lyrics and meanings of the
songs. Just before Grafton, we pass a sign for the juvenile detention centre where Tobias had been held. He asks me if we can
drive in so he can pick up a painting he left behind.

'Maybe on the way back,' I say.

We arrive at the cabins on sunset. Despite the cold, I take
Joey and Tobias down to the beach for a quick swim, hoping to
wash away the sense of squalor clinging to my skin. We search

for crabs along the shoreline, and then eat dinner at the local fish and chip shop – normal holiday stuff – but for some reason, when I look at Joey and Tobias, sitting at the table in their hooded jackets, I long to be elsewhere.

On the walk back to the cabin, I call my mother from a public telephone box. My father is going into hospital again the next day to have an arthroscopy on his knee – a simple one-day opera- tion – and because we're only an hour and a half away from the Gold Coast, I ask if we can pop up and visit them.

'I could take Pup home from the hospital,' I suggest, 'while Joey and his friend cruise around Surfers Paradise for a couple of hours.'

'No, you can't come,' my mother says. 'I can't have it right now.'

She's worried about my father, I know that, but it still feels like a rejection.

The next day, instead of driving to the Gold Coast, I take Joey and Tobias to Chinaman's Beach and show them my way of body surfing. Although the water is chilly, the sun provides enough warmth for us to swim. Joey and Tobias stay in the water for ages, long after I've gotten out, having the best time ever. I take photos of them afterwards, bare-chested buddies with huge grins, arms draped over each other's shoulders.

Lone wolf

Back in Armidale, I ring my mother to see how my father's arthroscopy went.

'He'll be in hospital for another week,' she tells me. 'The doctors found an infection under his kneecap.' The doctors have already removed his kneecap and he's booked in for a knee replacement the next day.

I'm unsettled after the call. My father went into hospital for an arthroscopy. Now he's having a knee replacement? To think of him undergoing a major operation, when he still hasn't fully recovered from the hip replacement, worries me. He isn't strong enough. Besides, they're moving into their new unit in fourteen days and have advertised a garage sale at their place on the weekend. I pour myself a glass of wine and lie down by the fire to rest.

The phone rings. It's my sister, who lives in Bali. She's heard about my father's knee and says she's coming over to help my mother with the move.

'That's a relief,' I reply. 'I thought I'd have to do it.'

'Pup's immune system has really disintegrated from the antibiotics they gave him after the hip operation,' my sister says.

She sounds like she's making the trip to be with my father one last time.

My siblings and I have always called our father 'Pup' – not 'Dad'. Perhaps 'Pup' is an abbreviation of the Dutch word for father – 'Papa'. In any case, I can't imagine him being called anything else. I can't imagine him not being around, either.

*

On the Sunday after Joey catches the train to visit my brother in Sydney, Bernie calls and asks me to pick up Blister. 'No worries,' I tell him, happy to be asked. I've been avoiding the shed since Joey joined the dog jumping crew, so today will be a good opportunity to catch up with what's been happening.

I spot Blister waiting out the front of his flat. When he sees me pull up, he looks disappointed. He was probably hoping Bernie was coming to get him.

On the way to the shed, I ask about Emma's pregnancy.

'It's a girl,' he says with a shy smile. 'We found out on the last ultrasound.'

'I thought you said it was going to be a boy!'

'I was hoping for a boy,' he admits. 'We're going to move into my brother's house soon. It's right next to Mum's place in Girraween.'

I swing through the gates at the shed and park the car. 'You'll get lots of help with your mum next door.'

Bernie and a group of boys and dogs are standing outside the doors. As we walk over to join them, I ask Blister how he's going with his painting apprenticeship.

'It was boring,' says Blister. 'I quit.'

Bernie gives him a sideways glance. He calls out to Skippa. 'Hey, Skippa! Does welding get boring?'

Skippa nods.

'And that's welding!' says Bernie, his tone incredulous. After we talk about different jobs we've had, Bernie mentions a time he worked as a drilling assistant – 'I was earning two thousand dollars a week,' he explains, 'but it was the most boring job I ever had. The boss only ever spoke about ten words and most of them started with "c" and were preceded by "useless". I lasted six months.'

The boys ask Bernie what he does now.

'I'm a youth worker,' he says, giving me a quick grin.

The boys don't seem to realise. What do they think Bernie is doing out here each weekend?

A black poodle is tied up with the border collies and kelpies. Bernie's minding it for a friend and, although it has a name, he calls it 'Poodle'.

'Poodle thinks it's a person in a dog's body and doesn't under-stand why we can't see that,' he says. 'It's used to eating with humans, sitting on the lounge, sleeping on its owner's bed. Poodle got quite a shock when I put it in the kennel with all the other dogs.'

He's interrupted by the sound of growling. The poodle is trying to mount Jimmy's dog, Vickie, a tail-less blue heeler that always looks as if she's about to bite someone's head off.

'Watch,' says Bernie, unconcerned. 'Vickie's given him one warning. She's growling but still playful. When that stump stops wagging ... Poodle better look out!'

Shortly, two older men and a middle-aged woman pull up at the shed. Bernie goes over to talk to them. After a few minutes, he calls for the boys to join him.

'These folks have come from Inverell,' he says. 'They're keen to have a look around the shed and talk with you blokes 'cause they're thinking of starting a similar sort of thing.'

'We've already started a "Men's Shed" for the older men in the community,' explains one of the visitors. 'They retire from work and feel lost, like the world doesn't have a place for them anymore.'

'Sort of like welders,' says Bernie.

'Yes,' agrees the man, chuckling. 'We hope to encourage young people to come along as well, so they can learn skills and gain knowledge from the older men.'

Bernie asks Blister and Jimmy to show the people from Inverell around the shed. I listen in as they show off the equipment and some of the 'arty' stuff they've been working on lately. Jimmy has made a Ned Kelly sculpture, decorative iron flowers for the garden, a fancy bench and a table.

'The manager of the credit union bought the Ned Kelly one,' says Jimmy proudly. 'He's going to put it on display.'

After the visitors have gone, we head outside and sit on upturned milk-crates in the late afternoon sun.

'That was good to see those people meeting you blokes,' says Bernie. 'They're pretty interested in what we're doing.' He leans forward and rests his elbows on his knees. 'We're getting lots of positive feedback about the arty stuff from people in town ... you know how much Ned Kelly went for? Two hundred dollars!'

'Two hundred and sixty,' says Jimmy. 'And we got an order for another one.'

'Yep, we got orders for dragonflies, flowers ... I'm thinking we'll restart the girls' program soon. Maybe they can hook in with some of this arty stuff as well.' He looks around at the boys. 'If you lot were in charge of the girls' program, what activities would you set up for them?'

'Washing up,' says Jimmy.

Bernie sighs. 'Jimmy, how the fuck are you going to teach someone how to wash up? First you have to have some idea of the concept!'

Jimmy laughs. 'I know how to use a dishwasher!' Then he says, 'Hey, I've got a Queensland joke.'

'Righto,' says Bernie. 'Here we go.'

'What do you put on a big dick?'

'Big condom,' says Blister.

I can see the answer isn't important. Jimmy is busting to get to the punchline.

'What do you put on a small dick?' he asks, smirking.

The others suggest small condoms. Soft condoms? I focus on the sand piles at the back of the yard, wondering how to make a getaway.

Jimmy shakes his head and grins. 'A maroon jersey.'

The boys laugh and laugh while I sit on my milk-crate, not knowing where to look.

*

On the morning of his 18th birthday, Joey catches the train back to Armidale. Apart from checking that he'd arrived safely, I'd avoided ringing my brothers because I wanted to give Joey some space. But today, before I make his birthday cake, I phone my middle brother to see how the visit went.

'We really enjoyed having Joey come to stay,' he tells me. 'Lots of laughs and good times – he's quite a poker player!'

When I ring my other brother, his wife answers the phone. 'We didn't see quite enough of Joey,' she says, her voice warm and loving, 'he should have stayed longer.' I hear my brother in the background, keen to take the phone.

He comes on the line and says, 'I want to tell you what a wonderful young man Joey is, Helena. You and Rob have brought him up well … and he's full of good values.'

I hold the phone and weep. Crazy. Someone in my family is finally telling me we've done a good job and all I can do is cry. I'm glad Joey had a good time with them, that they love him as uncles. Maybe they'll invite him down more often now.

While I mix the ingredients for the chocolate sour-cream cake, I think about the past eighteen years. How can it be so long ago that I gave birth to my beautiful baby with the rosebud lips? Once the cake is in the oven, I make Joey's collage card. The central photo is of a howling wolf at sunset, with a golden red and orange map of the world in the background, and on the back I write: *Dear Joey. Congratulations on your 18th – you may think you're a 'lone wolf' but LOTS of people love you very much, most of all me! Love Mum.*

Later, I pick up Joey from the train station. When I rang his mobile earlier in the day, he'd said he wanted me to wait in the car, not on the platform – 'Too embarrassing' – so I sit in the car and watch him approach, backpack slung over his shoulder. My son, the traveller. He opens the door of the car.

'Good to see you, Joey!' I tell him, hugging him tight. 'Happy birthday!'

At home, we stand around the birth cake, and in the flickering light of eighteen candles we sing 'Happy Birthday' – just five of us this time. Joey's train was delayed in Sydney and Freddie is already asleep. Joey is shining with happiness, just like he was after the camp at Jindabyne. He talks and talks about how funny his uncles were, about what a great time he had with his cousins, and how much he loved their cats, which are friendly and sociable.

He shows us his birthday cards, the new silver and black cap one of my brothers bought for him – 'It was fifty dollars!' – and then Joey gives me a copy of a lovely photo of him standing between his uncles.

My beautiful boy.

Thank goodness your father isn't here!

My father is still in hospital without a kneecap because the doctors are waiting for him to get stronger before operating. My mother cries on the phone whenever I ring to see how things are going.

'I think I need help,' she admits. Boxes need to be packed for the move, and the garage sale is on the weekend. 'Your sister can't come until the end of the month,' adds Mum, bursting into tears.

'I'll come,' I tell her.

The following weekend, Henry and I drive up to the Gold Coast. We find my mother in high spirits, busily preparing for the garage sale. She sends Henry around the back to fetch the heavy plants, and asks me to carry the outdoor furniture. When I ask if we can go and see Pup at the hospital, she waves her hand impatiently – '*Ach*! We'll go and see him tomorrow. I've had enough of that hospital!'

At the garage sale the next morning, she keeps saying things like, 'Thank goodness your father isn't here!' as we sell paintings and plants for one or two dollars, and when we drive off to the beach at eleven, we leave the unsold items on the driveway with a big sign: 'ALL FREE – PLEASE TAKE AWAY!'

'Your father would have been sitting there till it was dark,' my mother laughs, snapping on her seatbelt. 'Don't tell him how cheap we sold everything!'

We visit Pup that afternoon. I'm shocked to find him looking much worse than last time, and I hide my concern as I bend down to kiss his forehead. His right leg is covered in bandages, and as he shifts himself into a more comfortable position, he grimaces with pain. I'm suddenly filled with rage at the hospital staff, especially the doctors. *Is this what you do to someone who's nearly eighty? Take their fucking kneecap out so they can't walk?*

Somewhere along the line, someone has stuffed up.

My father is still dignified, even in his blue pyjamas, but he's clearly not doing too well in this round. I find it difficult to see him so vulnerable. Making an excuse to go to the bathroom, I stand with my hands on the edge of the basin, taking deep fortifying breaths. In the mirror, my face looks pale and frightened. *Come on, Helena*, I tell myself. *You need to be strong.*

When I come back into the room, my mother is feeding mandarins to my father, segment by segment. He has no appetite, but at her insistence he obediently sucks out the juice, spitting the pith into her hand.

For the next hour, Henry and I sit beside Pup's bed. We tell him about the garage sale, carefully omitting any mention of the outdoor furniture left on the driveway.

'Everything sold by eleven?' he asks with surprise.

We nod.

When he queries me on how much we sold the plants for, I change the subject – 'I was packing a few boxes last night, Pup, and I found your classical guitar book in the study. Maybe I'll get a friend to record your favourite pieces onto a CD, so you can listen to it while you're here.'

I show him the book, expecting him to tell me which ones are his favourites, but he can't. His mind is too foggy from the pain medication.

*

Not long after I get back from the Gold Coast, I escape to the shed, where the kitchen is smoky and cold. Skippa, in his cap and work shirt, sits brooding on the lounge. On one side of him is Freckles, who runs the flame of a silver lighter over the tip of his thumb. You can tell he's a man with money now. On the other side of Skippa is Jimmy, hung-over and yawning from a big night at the pub. Thommo stumbles in, looking younger and fresh-faced without his moustache. Earlier, I'd noticed Freckles, Jimmy and Thommo wandering off to the sand piles in the wasteland behind the shed. They'd walked in ten minutes later, their eyes glassy, sneaking looks at each other and giggling. It wasn't long before Bernie stopped what he was doing and took the three boys aside for what looked like a serious discussion. They knew they weren't supposed to smoke dope at the shed.

On the kitchen table, someone has written: *Freckles licks shitty cocks.*

Bernie comes into the room, tugging a Russian-style sheepskin beanie down over his ears. He pulls up a chair and says hello, steam escaping with his breath. Skippa, who recently began his first year as an apprentice welder, is ready to quit. Bernie's interested in hearing what the other boys think he should do.

'Stick it out,' says Freckles. 'So you end up with a trade.'

'It's harder to find another apprenticeship if you just quit and look for somewhere else,' agrees Jimmy. 'A lot of employers don't want first year – they want you past that point.'

'I don't know if I can hack it,' says Skippa, folding his arms against his chest. The main problem is his boss, a huge man, who is notorious for yelling at his workers.

'He'd scare the shit out of me if I was working there,' admits Bernie. 'Having a seven-foot Brahmin bull screaming at ya … but you could get a boss like that at Hungry Jack's and after three years all you've got is hamburgers.' He picks up a piece of metal from the table and twirls it in his hand. 'Have you ever heard anyone thank him, Skippa?'

The boys look at him, confused.

A cunning expression crosses Bernie's face.

'What I'd be doing,' he explains, 'is saying: "Thanks for the input, Boss. I'm picking up that we're slow, lazy and we're fuckin' up all the jobs. I'm going to work on those three things today and be the best employee you've ever had! How about we get back to work?"'

Everyone bursts out laughing, slapping their legs and guffawing.

'Could you have a crack at that?'

'He'd probably tell me to fuck up,' says Skippa with a shy grin.

'Maybe … but if you just do the same as everyone else, nothing will change. If he sacks you, so be it – "Thanks for sacking me, Boss" – and tell him I said to do it. You'll be smiling for the rest of the day. If he can't work out how to get the best out of his workers, that's his problem, not yours.'

Bernie's strategy sounds like fun, but three days later, when I see him down at the mall, he tells me Skippa quit his job.

'All that yelling and screaming from his boss really pushes his buttons for some reason,' he says thoughtfully. 'Skippa's one of those quiet ones – his dad died when he was very young, he's Aboriginal but not very black, that sort of thing.' Bernie's eyes meet mine. 'There's a lot of shit underneath the surface with that kid … but he'll be right. Skippa will come through this.'

*

'We need to have faith the doctors know what they're doing,' my older brother tells me on the phone the following week. 'Pup will be alright.'

I'm not so sure. Neither of my brothers has been to see Pup yet. They don't seem to be taking it seriously, no matter how many times I say, 'Pup is really sick.' The idea of Pup dying scares me. I want him to make it through this awful hospital stage he's been in for so long. Earlier, I'd been speaking to my mother, and asked if my brothers were coming to help with the move. 'They can only come for two nights each,' she said, bursting into tears, 'and that's after the move.'

'I'll come,' I told her, wondering how I'd go with another six-hour drive so soon. 'Take some of your homeopathic calm pills.'

Later that night, I email my sister to check the date that she's arriving. She emails back and says she can't take leave from work for another month or so. I stare at the computer. I obviously haven't been going about this the right way. I send my three siblings an email saying that our father is in a really bad way. Our mother needs help and I can't do it all. Then I go for a long walk, up and down the steep hills around the graveyard on the south side of town.

When I get back, Joey is in the kitchen. 'Hey, Mum … can you shave my head?'

Dealing with a whole mess of hair is the last thing I want to do, but perhaps I can use it to my advantage: 'Only if you promise to ring the army and find out more about the application process.'

He nods.

Once his head is done, Joey rings the Defence Forces recruitment line. I sweep hair into the dustpan and listen as he tells someone he wants to be a driver. Less than a minute later, the call is finished. 'The person on the phone said maybe I should think about getting my driver's licence first if I want to be a driver,' says Joey.

'What?' It could take Joey years to get his licence. After Joey leaves, I ring the Defence Forces recruiting office and lodge a complaint.

Before bed that night, I check to see if my email had any effect. Yes. My brothers have changed their minds. One will stay with Mum for a week before the move, and the other will stay the week after. My sister has arranged time off work, and will book her flight the next day. Perhaps I will go up again the following week if my mother still needs support.

The boxing cabinet

A few days later, a truck-load of my parents' old furniture arrives. They've given it to me because they're buying new things for the unit. Rob is away at a two-day conference in Sydney, so the house is in chaos as I try to find a place for everything. I ring Mum later to let her know the furniture arrived safely, and when I ask about my father, she becomes teary.

'It's okay,' I tell her. 'Crying is good.'

'Your father isn't improving,' she sobs. 'He's getting worse.'

'We need to have faith he'll get through this.' I repeat my brother's words, even though I don't really believe them. Because she doesn't drive, my mother is travelling back and forth to the hospital by public transport every day. It's all becoming too much for her. My middle brother is arriving at the Gold Coast on Sunday evening, five days away.

For the rest of the week, each time the phone rings, I fear my mother will tell me my father is dead. When I phone Pup's hospital room, he speaks in Dutch for most of the call. I don't know how to deal with this – we've been shielded from death because the extended family all live in Holland and have been remarkably healthy. I've only been to one funeral.

Then, on Friday morning, after dropping Freddie at preschool, I listen to a message from Mum on the answering machine: 'I've got bad news for you ...' she begins. I hear her crying before she hangs up.

I immediately phone my father's hospital room to see if he's still alive.

'*Ja?*' he answers in his weakened voice.

'Just wanted to say hello.' My hand grips the receiver so hard it hurts. 'I love you, Pup.'

I ring Mum on her mobile. She's walking around the hospital grounds, trying to bring herself under control. 'I'm coming up this afternoon,' I tell her. 'It's too hard for you to be on your own like this.'

After calling Rob at work, I arrange for a friend to pick up Freddie from his preschool, throw my swag in the car and leave. Six hours later, I arrive at the Gold Coast. My mother makes me a cup of strong sweet coffee before we visit my father. At the hospital, as we walk down the corridor, she hands me a pair of dark sunglasses, the sort movie stars wear.

'So he can't see us crying,' she explains.

Once we enter the room, I understand the need for the glasses. My father is propped up in bed, looking pale and skeletal. My mother's composure in the room is admirable – *sterkte* – but she keeps her sunglasses on the whole time. Meanwhile, I struggle and make excuses to go to the bathroom.

The doctors have found a shadow on my father's lung which may be a serious cancer, or it may be the imprint of lymphoma cancer he's had for twenty years. They'll do more tests after the weekend.

On Sunday, my brother arrives from Sydney. His flight doesn't come in until after six, but he's keen to see Pup straight away. I drive him to the hospital while Mum makes dinner.

'Expect the worst,' I tell my brother as we walk down the corridor to our father's room. But Pup is alert and clear, sitting up in bed eating dinner and watching the football. He says his leg is feeling much better.

My brother brings a positive and cheery energy into the room. I sit back on a chair in the corner and watch him talk to Pup about the football. He's stepped up to the plate better than me. Mum and I had slid into negativity, brought on from exhaustion and worry. Maybe Pup needs male company, not two snivelling females in dark sunglasses who run into the bathroom twenty times during every visit. I'll return to Armidale tomorrow – let my brother do his share while I rest and focus on my own life.

My older brother is coming up next to take over. Then my sister will be here.

After dinner, I pack the car, ready for the trip home. Mum has prepared boxes of unwanted household items for me to take back to Armidale – towels, blankets, cutlery and books. She also tells me to take my father's boxing cabinet.

'Why are you giving me that?' I ask in surprise.

My father's boxing medals and trophies have always been kept in a glass-fronted wooden cabinet which one of his bakery bosses made for him out of an old cupboard. Over the years, in our various houses, this cabinet always hung on the wall in the lounge room where we watched television. I never thought it anything out of the ordinary. But now the cabinet is like a precious relic from the past. I'm reluctant to take it.

My mother says she doesn't want the cabinet in the new unit. 'It wouldn't look good there,' she tells me, waving her hand. 'You take it to your house, Helena.'

My brother and I carry the cabinet out to the car. As we place the wooden box onto a piece of stained carpet in the back of the station wagon, I assure my brother I'm not claiming ownership. Together we tuck towels and blankets around the cabinet, to keep it safe.

Driving home the next day, I keep thinking about the cargo in the back of the car, and about my father's rich and varied life. He's been an Olympic boxing champion, a successful baker, an energetic tennis player, a bridge champion, a classical guitarist, a harmonica player, a yodeller, a card shark and a mad Scrabble fiend. He and my mother have loved each other for over fifty years.

Pup is old, I tell myself. He's had a good life. Whatever happens now is okay.

*

A few days after I get back to Armidale, the news comes through. My father isn't going to live for another ten or fifteen years. 'Maybe a couple of months,' says my older brother on the phone. 'More likely weeks.'

I knew the news wasn't going to be good. Pup has deteriorated so much over the last few weeks. But still, I can't comprehend how he isn't going to be here anymore. My brother talked to Pup about what the doctors said. 'He's still with it enough to understand,' says my brother, his voice breaking. 'He shed one tear ... and then asked about everyone else. He was so stoic.'

Of course.

After the call, I kneel on the floor and sob. Later, I ring the hospital.

When my father answers, I swallow hard and then take a deep breath. 'Pup, I'm very sad.'

'*Ja,*' he says in a thin wispy voice. 'What can you do? Everyone is sad.'

'I love you.' I've said this more times over the last couple of weeks than I have in forty years. 'I'm really going to miss you ... and I'm coming up again as soon as I can.'

He sighs. '*Ach*! – so much travelling.'

That afternoon, I drop in at the shed. Jimmy is there with some new blokes. He tells me Bernie is at the hardware store. I wander around, looking at the iron flowers and dragonflies the boys have been making.

Bernie arrives, looking like a stranger in his dark sunglasses and a red and black shirt. When he sees my face, Bernie takes me around to the side of the shed, away from the boys and the noise. He rolls two thin cigarettes while I tell him about Pup.

'I'm scared of this death business,' I say to Bernie, lighting up with shaking hands. 'But I'm thinking of taking Joey with me to the Gold Coast next weekend.'

Bernie's eyes are intent and serious. 'Yep,' he agrees, 'if you can do it, let Joey be around him as much as possible. It's good for a young bloke to be around death.'

The high-pitched shrill of the drop-saw pierces the air.

'Death isn't something that's really talked about in our culture – certainly not with boys,' continues Bernie. 'One time I was at this funeral for a young fella who died. When they started carrying the casket down the aisle of the church, this other kid sitting in front of me, who I knew to be a good mate, had tears streaming down his face. His dad whacked him across the ear and told him to get his shit together.' Bernie shakes his head. 'Death scares the shit out of young fellas. All that stuff about not showing your emotions and not talking about things, not crying ... when all that's muddled in front of you it's hard to go through a grieving process. But you may as well not be frightened of something that's going to happen at some stage.' He looks at me. 'It's about how you deal with it in two parts, Helena – in your head and in your heart, or in your spirit.'

'I'm having trouble with the head part.'

Bernie nods in understanding. 'The boys freaked out when Banjo died. Those boys still talk about that dog and that cere-mony we had out at my place. A couple of them, whenever they come out, ask, "Can we go down and have a look at the grave?" And we talk about things like: Where do you think he is now? Do you see him in any other of these dogs? If you could do one more thing with him, what would you do?'

'I miss the shed.' I stub out my cigarette and find my car keys. 'All these trips to the Gold Coast.'

'We'll be here when you get back.'

*

On the phone, my mother is talking about palliative-care options. That's how she wants to do it. I'd hoped my father would be able to die at home, but my mother can't manage him because he's unable to walk and has lost all his strength. Even though he's skinny, he's still big. She and my brother have almost finished packing up the house, and are visiting Pup several times a day.

'*Ja*, last night it was a nightmare,' she says with a heavy sigh. 'Pooing and peeing. Your father doesn't care – he's past it. The hospital is going to transfer him to M Ward, palliative care.'

M Ward sounds like the final solution, the place they send people with no hope, like in those scary movies about psychiatric wards. I don't know how to cope with something as big as this, but at the end of the week I'm driving up to the Gold Coast with Joey.

So brave

The six-hour drive with Joey goes well. Not too much rap, no arguing, and Joey even sleeps for a few hours. While he's asleep, and the car is quiet, my mind wanders back to other times, long ago, that Joey and his grandparents shared. Joey was four months old when I first took him to meet them in Sydney. I felt anxious on the flight from Darwin – it hadn't been easy for Mum and Pup to accept that *het kind* was a sole parent. I knew I'd disappointed them, but my parents loved Joey from the moment they saw him. My father ate dinner in front of the television with Joey on his lap, and whenever Joey cried, my father croaked, '*Ja, ja* ...' in his gravelly voice. My mother bought crocheted blankets and jump-suits and covered Joey's face with kisses.

As he grew older, Joey and I had many holidays in Manly with my parents. My father often took Joey to the local park, and when Joey fell over or did something silly, my father would say, 'Bung!' Joey enjoyed riding a little red pedal-car that was kept for the grandchildren to use. He and my father went all over Manly together – Joey in his red car and Pup walking along beside him.

One night, Joey slipped in the bath and cut his chin open. My father and I took him to the medical centre and comforted Joey while a doctor stitched him up. Joey screamed the whole time we were there. All I wanted to do was run out of the room, but Pup held him down, calmly repeating, '*Ja, ja* ... it's okay, Joey. It's okay.'

When Joey and I reach the Gold Coast, I find it strange to drive past the turn-off to my parents' old house. So many changes. The day before, my mother moved into her new unit, a 1970s high-rise at Broadbeach, just down the road from where they used to live. Mum buzzes us in, and is waiting outside the lift when it opens on her floor. She looks tiny, hunched over with grief.

'Your father is very bad,' she says, her face solemn. 'We need to go to the hospital. The doctor said if the family want to see him, they should see him now.'

We drive to the hospital, my hands white on the steering wheel. Mum wears her enormous sunglasses. Joey sits silently in the back, looking stunned. I park the car and we march purposefully towards my father's room, fear building with every step. But Pup is okay. He's noticeably thinner and dis-oriented, but he's okay. He's still Pup. Not as bad or as scary as I'd thought. I kiss his forehead and hold his hand, tears filling my eyes. I need to be strong. I'm here to support my mother, but this hospital turns me into a weakling as soon as I walk through its doors.

'Don't make a drama of it, Helena,' says my father in his feeble voice.

I laugh through my tears. That's so like him. How can he be dying? I suddenly remember Joey, sitting quietly on a chair in the corner of the room, and motion for him to come closer to the bed, to touch his grandfather.

I take photos, the saddest photos I've ever taken of Joey and his grandparents. I rest my head on my father's shoulder. We talk about normal things, like Pup learning the guitar at fourteen, what Amsterdam was like after the war, the new unit. But soon Pup becomes confused.

'What is going on here?' he asks Mum, like it's a perfectly reasonable question.

Mum takes Joey to the hospital cafe to buy lollies. 'For the stress,' she whispers as they leave. Joey looks pale.

I don't know what to do or say when they're gone. While my father naps, I walk up and down the corridors, taking deep breaths. My mother and Joey return with a bag of liquorice allsorts. We all have one, but my father can't finish his, can't chew it hard enough. My mother takes it out of his mouth and pops it into hers. They hold hands. Pup says he dreamed about police stations and his old bridge partners.

'Do you ever dream about me?' jokes my mother.

My father becomes tired. He wants to lie down with the lights out. I don't like leaving him there – he should be coming home with us.

'So brave,' a nurse comments when we pass the desk. 'He's been in pain for a long time. Never complains.'

'Only to me,' says my mother, making a face. My father has been very cranky with her over the past week. I suppose he has to take it out on someone. We drive away from the hospital, the three of us crying – a car full of tears.

'He was so peaceful tonight,' says Mum, finding her tissues. I buy a bottle of wine on the way home. Maybe Pup will die tonight – the nurses said he'll be at peace. They've given him strong medication so he can't feel anything, but this doesn't seem right to me. I want the old Pup back – the one who has the strength to go back into the ring.

My mother's second floor unit is bare of furniture – she's still waiting for the new lounge and dining room suite to arrive. On the balcony are a wooden table and three matching chairs. She has a new bed in her room and an old single bed in the spare bedroom. 'Joey can sleep there,' I say, 'and I'll sleep in my swag.' I open the wine and we sit on the balcony, overlooking a lush tropical garden lit up by a string of soft yellow lights.

The phone calls begin. My sister is coming in twelve days. She's asked Pup to hold on till then. 'He's given up the fight,' Mum tells her. 'The doctor says he's had enough.' Later, when I hear my mother talking to our Dutch relatives on the phone, I notice she ends every call with the words: '*Ja ... sterkte*'. Strength.

Facing hard times with strength and courage is important in Dutch culture. My parents' generation learnt about *sterkte* during the war years, but it's probably something I need to cultivate within myself, especially in the weeks ahead.

After the call, Mum turns to me and says, 'I show you later what my new Duster Buster does.' She's been in a shopping frenzy for weeks – I guess it's her way of coping.

The phone rings again, one of my mother's closest friends on the Gold Coast. Her friend's niece works in a funeral home at Beenleigh, and she wants to talk about pre-paid funerals.

'He's got all that weird talk about police stations,' says Mum, changing the subject. 'But he was lying with his hands crossed over his chest when we left – very peaceful.'

Joey sits at the end of the table, eating cheese and crackers. We've barely had time to talk since we arrived. I wonder how he's feeling. I don't think he had any idea how sick Pup had become. In the morning, Joey is catching the train to Brisbane to stay with an old school friend. I know Bernie said it's good for him to be around death as much as possible, but Joey will see his opa again when he returns.

After the phone call with her friend, my mother starts coughing. She coughs so much she can't take in a breath. I race into the kitchen and search through the rubbish for the paper bag some mushrooms came in.

'Breathe into the bag,' I instruct, trying not to panic.

I hold her shoulders until her breathing returns to normal.

Sterkte

Before Joey goes to Brisbane, the three of us walk silently down the hospital corridor to Pup's room, accompanied by the now-familiar feelings of apprehension and dread. Through the open door of Pup's room, I catch a glimpse of him trying to pull himself out of bed.

Mum rushes to his side. 'What are you doing?'

'*Ja*,' says Pup, sounding cranky. 'I've been waiting so long for the nurse. *Ik moet plassen.*'

My heart sinks. Pup needs to pee. I'm not ready for this.

'We'll help you,' says Mum. My father collapses back onto the pillows, and I go around to the other side of the bed. Without the sheet covering him, I see for the first time his stick-like legs, his shrunken stomach, his bony ribcage. We pull down his pyjama pants and Mum undoes his adult nappy. My breath dries in my throat. This is too hard. *Sterkte*, I tell myself sternly. Oh, Pup. But somehow he manages to look dignified, even like this.

I notice Joey on the chair in the corner, rubbing the palms of his hands over his face, like a ringside attendant who can't bear to see anymore. As soon as Pup is lying comfortably again, I wave Joey over to join us. With tears streaming down his cheeks, Joey sits by the side of the bed with his head bowed and holds his grandfather's hand.

Joey is still weeping as we head back to the car. 'People don't change so much from day to day,' he says. 'When I took the photos yesterday, Opa didn't look so bad. But today ...' He wipes his eyes with his sleeve. 'He used to play Scrabble and now he can't do anything.'

On the way to the railway station, I talk to Joey about all the things his opa did in his life – 'He was always a high achiever.'

Joey begins crying again. 'The only time I saw Opa smile was when he asked me about joining the army.'

'He wants to see you do well in life, Joey – he's always been so proud of you.'

The next day is my mother's 78th birthday. In the morning, the phone rings – too early for birthday wishes. 'It's the hospital,' I say, passing her the phone.

This is it. My father is dead. I watch my mother's face. But a look of relief smooths her frown and she laughs heartily before saying: '*Ja*, thank you for letting us know ... we'll come in later.'

'What is it?' I ask when she hangs up.

'Your father has a black eye,' she replies. 'The nurse doesn't know how it happened, but she didn't want us to be alarmed when we visit him today.'

'We're past being "alarmed",' I say. 'A black eye is nothing.'

At my father's bedside later, Mum jokes that he must have dreamed he was back in the boxing ring last night, swinging wild punches. Although I laugh along with my mother, my insides are aching at the sight of my father. He's sitting lifelessly on the bed, his eye black and bruised, the shape of his bones showing through his skin.

On the way back from yet another visit to the bathroom, I spot a birthday card lying on the floor – one of my brothers must have bought it the previous week. I show it to my mother, and she asks Pup to write something for her birthday. He always wrote beautiful messages in her cards. My father holds the card upside down for a while. When I realise he's not capable of writing anything, I take the pen from his fingers.

'You tell me what you want to say, Pup, and I'll write it down.'

This is what he tells me:

Dear Sonja,

It is the end of the line, but I love you always. We have a lifetime behind us, more happy times than sad. They were not always easy along the way, and we had high mountains to climb, especially in the last few years health-wise. One has to expect that.

I love you.

Lots of love and happiness on your birthday, and I just like to say, I would do it all again.

Tony

After Mum reads it back to him, she rushes into the bathroom. I prop the card on the bedside table, thinking how lucky my mother was to meet my father in Amsterdam all those years ago – to find a man who brought light into her life, and who still loves her so much, even after fifty-four years of marriage.

The pain of him dying, of him slipping away from her, must be unbearable for them both. I want death to come quickly now. Although we keep telling Pup to wait for my sister to arrive, I don't think he will.

The saddest songs

At the unit, my mother has boxes of new cutlery, plates, glasses and towels lined up along the wall in the lounge room. Any spare time she has away from the hospital, she goes shopping. But she isn't ready to open any of the boxes yet. When I look around the room, I think how strange it is to be in a place where my father has never lived, where he will never live.

'He wasn't interested,' my mother says when I ask her what Pup thought about the place. 'When we came for the inspection, he just stared out the window.' She was the one who made the decision to buy it. I'd been feeling sad about them leaving the old house, which had so many memories of Scrabble games and swims in the pool and glasses of champagne on the patio, but I like the new unit. It's fresh and sunny. I even like the way it has no furniture. The unit feels temporary, like the space Pup is in.

Later, my mother takes me down to the car park underneath the building, where my father's silver Holden sedan is parked near a small storage shed. Pup loved that car – it's a powerful model with mag wheels and everything, and with a slight touch of the accelerator, he was able to zoom in and out of lanes in the traffic. I'll be taking over ownership of the car soon, but we still need it to travel back and forth to the hospital. I stand back as my mother opens the shed. Apart from a few photos and a recently bought guitar, still on its stand in the empty lounge room above us, my mother wants me to have all my father's possessions.

Holding on to his belongings is too painful for her.

The next morning, we pick up Joey from the train station, and the three of us stop in at the hospital for one final visit before Joey and I drive back to Armidale. My middle brother is returning later in the day to help Mum through the next few days.

Pup looks terrible but is still stoic in his blue-striped pyjamas. I realise my father is approaching death the same way he approached those fierce-looking truck drivers who used to offend him all those years ago. Mum and I thought Pup was crazy for leaping out of the car and shaking his fist at truck drivers who'd muscled into his lane. But now I admire his courage. I know this will be the last time I see him. I hold his hand and clip his fingernails, kiss his forehead, tell him I love him and say goodbye.

I cry the whole way home, too afraid to ring Rob en route as I normally do because I'm sure he'll tell me Pup is dead and how will I be able to drive after that? At a little petrol station at

Mallanganee, I stop and check the oil level. Joey stays asleep in the car as a woman comes out to help me.

'Are you moving?' she asks, with a glance at my battered station wagon, packed with boxes of my father's clothing and paperwork, his old guitar, a television, a spare mattress and my swag. With Joey slumped against the window, and my reddened eyes, we must look like a couple of desperados escaping to a new life.

'No,' I tell her. 'My father is dying.'

The woman hugs me, one of those rare moments of kindness from strangers, and says, 'I've got some books from the Bible that might help you.'

'That's okay.' I manage a smile. 'I know he's going to a good place.'

Joey sleeps all the way to Glen Innes. When we stop at KFC, I wait in the car while he buys some takeaway food. Back in his seat, he looks over at me and says, 'That was real hard seeing Opa at the hospital, but I'm glad I did it. I think I was closer to him than the other grandkids.'

'You spent a lot of time with Opa when you were young.'

He chuckles and opens a box of chicken nuggets. 'He used to take me to the park a lot, and when I fell over, he'd always say "Bung!" It was such a funny word. I'd be in pain but still laughing.'

Then Joey takes out his MP3 player and asks if he can play some music by Nas. 'This is meaningful rap,' he says, 'used to convey a real deep message, not like the usual stuff I play for you. The whole album by Nas – *God's Son* – is about loss.' Joey shakes his head and sighs. 'That damn song where he says goodbye to his mother is probably one of the saddest songs I've ever heard – "If heaven was a mile away,"' he sings, '"would I pack up my bags and leave this world behind?"'

I glance across at Joey, impressed. He's busy dipping a chicken nugget into a container of sweet chilli sauce. After he licks his fingers clean, he searches through his music for a song called 'Thugz Mansion', a collaboration Nas did with Tupac Shakur, and says, 'Leonardo DiCaprio named Nas as the greatest poet of our generation.'

'Hmmm,' I murmur when the song finishes. 'I think I'd like to hear more of his music. You've got good taste, Joey.'

As soon as we arrive home, I ring my mother.

'Your father was much better in the afternoon,' she says. 'He perked up with your brother's arrival … but I won't be surprised if we get a call in the night.' Her voice is light, almost gay. Perhaps she's in shock. When she mentions that Pup was worried about some bottles of grog hidden in the bakery house, she laughs heartily: '*Ja* … I told him we found the bottles and you drank them all!'

The next day, my guitar-playing friend gives me the CD of classical music he's recorded from my father's Carulli method book, the one Pup had as a fourteen-year-old boy in Amsterdam when he first started learning guitar. When I listen to the CD at home, I burst into tears. The pieces are so familiar – it's like Pup is sitting in the lounge room with me, playing his guitar. I make four copies of the CD. I post one to the Gold Coast, priority paid, and send the other three to my siblings. Then I take Pup's old guitar to the local music store, and ask them to give it a clean and polish and a new set of strings. Later, when I pick it up, the guitar shines like new. I splash out and buy a hard-cover guitar case which looks like it belongs to a rock and roll band. With a satisfied smile, I lay my father's guitar on the green velvet lining. Pup would have a fit if he knew how much money I'd spent. I've never been good with money. Not like him.

*

My father becomes increasingly disoriented. The nurses prepare to move him to M Ward – palliative care. One day, when my mother and brother turn up at the hospital, they discover Pup halfway off the bed. Dishevelled and confused, he keeps saying – '*Afgelopen!*' which means: 'This is the end – no more.'

'Pup wants to go home,' my brother says when I ring the hospital room later. 'He's had enough.' My brother also tells me my father now has two black eyes.

'Two?' I ask.

Low blood platelets are causing the bruising. Pup's body is shutting down.

'Can I speak to him?'

My father's laboured breathing comes on the line. 'Have a listen to this, Pup,' I say, holding the receiver up to the stereo and playing one of the pieces from the CD. The copy I sent to the Gold Coast hasn't arrived yet.

'*Ja* …' he whispers in a drawn-out way.

'Bye, Pup,' I say. 'I love you.'

Very faintly, almost like I'm imagining it, he echoes: 'I love you.'

It's not right that my father, a champion boxer, is going out of the ring with two black eyes.

If the dog wants to be a fuckwit, we need to fix it

To take my mind off what's happening on the Gold Coast, I go with Rob to a party at Bernie and Jayne's. It's Jayne's birthday and Rob's band is playing. It's good to listen to their uplifting music, but after half an hour, I drift back from the crowd and stand on my own. Rob thought the party would be a welcome distraction, but the last thing I feel like is idle chatter. I'll drive back to the Gold Coast in the morning – that's where I need to be.

Above me, the sky is a cloudless, starry-lit tarpaulin. I tighten my coat and watch as Freddie comes out of the house, looking for me. He wants to run around the garden with a friend from preschool, but when I fetch his coat from the car, he refuses to put it on. 'You'll have to go back inside,' I tell him. He whines. I cajole.

Bernie, who is standing nearby, comes over and takes the coat. He kneels on the ground in front of Freddie. In the same way he'd talk to any of the boys at the shed, he says, 'Coat ... or no coat? You make the choice.'

Freddie shakes his head and laughs.

'Okay,' says Bernie. He takes Freddie by the hand and leads him into the house. Freddie struggles, but not much. A moment later, Freddie comes out, wearing the coat.

When Bernie wanders back over, I say, 'That worked well.'

He nods – 'Yep.' Then he looks right at me. 'How's your father doing?'

'Not so good.' My words catch in my throat. 'I shouldn't be here. I thought it would be helpful to have a break.'

'I haven't had a parent die,' says Bernie, his voice gentle, 'so I can't know what you're feeling, but I've had a lot of experience with death and dying. When I was young I lost a lot of mates through motorbike and car accidents, and probably should've been killed myself on at least half a dozen occasions.' He chuckles softly. 'But that was a tough time ... and working with those blackfellas in Central Australia – all the death around them, with kids who've suicided. But for some reason I've never really feared death.'

'I fear it,' I admit. 'I'm going back to the Gold Coast tomorrow and I'm scared of what I'm going to see.'

'Death isn't something to fear, Helena,' he says. 'Sure, it might be a bit unknown, but I look forward to it. I'm happy to be here in the physical world doing what I'm doing, but for me it's a cycle and death is just the next chapter.' Bernie grins. 'And it's probably going to be even better than this lot … and I love this lot!'

The sound of barking comes from the other side of the yard.

'Wait here a minute,' says Bernie, striding towards the kennels. A short time later he returns with a glass of wine, cradling something under his jumper with his free hand. I laugh as the head of a new pup pokes up from the neck of his jumper.

'What's a good little dog doing down here?' croons Bernie, caressing the puppy like it's a baby. 'Don't worry. I'll get you warmed up.'

Earlier, one of the bigger dogs had been barking at some kids who were playing nearby, getting in the way of their game and not listening when Bernie called it over. I'd watched as he caught it and gave the dog a tune-up before locking it in the kennel.

'You seemed pretty hard on that other dog earlier.'

After an awkward silence, Bernie says, 'I'd be one of the softer fellas around … but I also understand the dog is an animal and what needs to go on. We take on dogs in the program that are pretty damaged, and you have to be tough to bring them back into the dog world because the dog world's a violent place. When dogs bite and fight, things get hurt. I've seen kids bitten – ferocious big ugly stitching-up stuff – and I've seen dogs tearing down sheep. I might be going, shit, I love this dog, but if he bites one of those kids and I have to put the dog down … what's harder? If you talk about *hard*,' Bernie pauses, giving the word full emphasis, 'wait till you're squeezing the trigger of a gun to kill that animal and you have no choice. Kids have to be safe.'

I nod, unsure how to reply.

He nestles the puppy more securely under his arm. 'Dogs need to understand their role in the pack, and that business of dogs pulling their owners down the street leads to a whole chain of events. If I try and take a bone off a dog and he starts growling, that dog doesn't understand his place. So, I'll tell him – "I'm the top dog around here, and if I want that bone, well you just fuck right off."'

I laugh, picturing him speaking to his dogs like that. But Bernie is serious, very serious. He looks across to the fire, where people are no doubt chatting about much lighter topics than violence and killing. 'There are times when I know I'm too hard. I'm not perfect.' He stops for a moment and pats the puppy's head. 'People would say there are times when I'm too hard on the boys, too. Pretty similar thing, but you can be harder on kids with verbal exchanges than you can physically. Not so with a dog. With a dog you need to jerk him into line. They know what's okay and what isn't ... and if the dog wants to be a fuckwit, we need to fix it.'

*

The phone rings early the next morning.

'Pup died at six,' says Mum, her voice empty of emotion. She and my brother didn't make it to the hospital in time.

The guitar CD had arrived the previous day. My mother and brother played it for my father that afternoon, and he'd listened appreciatively, with closed eyes.

'We played the music when we sat with his body this morning,' adds Mum.

For the rest of the morning, I sit on the lounge and listen to the guitar CD. The kids come and go. I take my father's old guitar out of its rock-star case and hold it in my arms.

Joey comes by in the afternoon. I'd tried ringing him throughout the day, but he wasn't home.

'I'm locked out of my house,' he says, opening the fridge and checking what's inside. 'I forgot to take my key when I went out last night.'

'Joey ... Opa died this morning.'

'Oh!' He comes over to me. 'That's really sad ... but I'm glad I got to say goodbye.'

'Yes, you were lucky.' We hug and I smell alcohol on his breath.

Only ten people attend my father's funeral – my mother, my brother, my sister, three of my parents' closest friends and me – plus three of the staff from the funeral home. My oldest brother is in hospital, recovering from an urgently needed knee replacement.

My father didn't want the details of the funeral in the paper. I know it was his wish, but it doesn't seem right. Pup was an Olympic boxer, a successful migrant, a long-standing member of the Gold Coast Bridge Club ... people would want to be here.

So, for my family's sake, I stand tall and deliver the eulogy as if the room is full of people.

The four of us have dinner that night at a seafood restaurant near the beachfront. As we relax over wine, we discuss Pup's unfailing belief in medicine and doctors. 'He wanted to have both my legs broken,' my brother says with a wry smile, 'so I wouldn't walk like Charlie Chaplin.'

'He put me on a hormone program,' I remind them. By the time I was twelve, already the height I am now – five foot ten – my father was convinced I needed to go on a hormone program to stop me growing any taller. The program was barely trialled in Australia, but the doctors said I needed it and Pup believed them. I think I would have liked to be six foot.

He didn't do anything like that to my sister, apart from shouting at her about the dishes and the fruit picking. She was too hard to fix, to mould into what he wanted. Maybe he should have appreciated her unique qualities rather than trying to change and control her – just like I should have done with Joey.

We drink more wine and reminisce. Pup wanted us to be perfect. It wasn't easy to be his children – to live up to his expectations. Later, at the unit, when Mum gives my brother Pup's wedding ring, he says, 'I'll never be the man he was.'

The next morning, I drop my brother at the airport, and then drive home to Armidale. My sister is staying on the Gold Coast for another week. I leave her meditating on a pier overlooking the canal outside the unit complex. When I ring to let them know I arrived home safely, my mother tells me one of the residents came out and offered my sister a cup of tea because he thought she was suicidal.

She was in the lotus position, chanting.

Your husband loves you very much

In the weeks after Pup's death, the weather turns grey and bitter, like my mood. Because Rob missed a lot of work while I was away, he stays back late most afternoons. I don't have any teaching for the term, which makes it easier. On the days Freddie is at preschool, I try to re-engage with my thesis, but I have little enthusiasm or energy for academic pursuits. Also, on top of the normal household chores and the busyness of caring for an active three-year-old, the fire needs fixing all the time because the wood isn't burning well. Out the back near Rob's shed, I chop kindling, my fingers cracked and bleeding from the cold. Whenever I handle logs of stringy-bark, I end up with pieces of timber in my hands – huge dark lines lodged under the skin – that I lift out with a needle and tweezers. The other reddish-coloured wood is so heavy it's like hauling slabs of concrete inside. I become sad and weary. Anger sparks inside me like kindling catching alight in the coals of the fire. I find myself snapping at Rob and the kids at every opportunity.

'When was the last time you cooked dinner?' I ask Rob tersely.

He can't remember.

One afternoon, while Freddie is sleeping, I search through a box containing odds and ends from my father's study. I find his bakery certificates from Holland, notebooks of recipes for meat pies and sausage rolls, plectrums for his guitar, half-written letters of complaint, an old pair of spectacles, and some black-and-white publicity photos from his boxing days. I put one of the photos on the wall above the phone – a youthful, bare-chested Pup who faces the camera with a serious expression, boxing gloves raised into position. He's wearing shorts and a fancy silver belt. On his feet are handmade boxing shoes, the only luxury he ever allowed himself. He looks ready for any punch life is going to throw at him.

*

Two months after Pup's death, Rob develops a worrying rash on his inner thigh. He comes home from an appointment with the doctor looking concerned – 'I've got shingles.' Rob says he will need several weeks, perhaps months, off work. I boil the kettle for tea and we sit down and talk about the medication he's been prescribed, and what effect it might have on him in the months ahead. 'It'll be good to rest,' he tells me, before heading off to lie down. Rob's relief is understandable – he'll be able to graciously withdraw from some stressful business at work that's given him sleepless nights lately, but I'm worried about what this latest news will mean to our life. Shingles is a debilitating viral illness that can go on for years.

Over the next month, Rob loses much of his vitality and becomes slow and heavy in his movements. He spends long days outside, lying in a swag under the tree, or playing his ukulele in his shed. On weekends, I have to ask the children to be quiet because Dad is having an afternoon nap in a darkened room.

Within weeks of Rob getting shingles, Henry develops chicken pox. None of the children had chicken pox when they were younger, so, over the next two months, first Henry, then Theo, then Joey, then Freddie develop spots – with varying degrees of severity. After Joey's spots are healed, I don't see much of him. Maybe he senses that I don't have a lot to give. For a while, I carry the full load at home – I hardly go anywhere or do anything outside the house. I have one brief trip to the Gold Coast to pick up my father's car.

One day, after I've been shopping, I pull up at the shed. Bernie's yellow ute is there, so I go looking for him. I find him inside, working with some new boys. 'Don't give up on me,' I tell him. 'I'll come back and help again one day.' He's not worried. Rocket, the welding teacher from TAFE, is working at the shed three days a week now. When Bernie walks out with me to say goodbye, he notices my new car. 'You got mag wheels now?' he asks with a grin.

Another day, I run into Joey's TAFE teacher downtown. I discover that Joey's having ongoing issues with his enrolment because of his sporadic attendance. His teacher also mentions that Joey told her all about his birthday trip to Evans Head, and she was struck by an eighteen-year-old talking about how his mum had taught him to body surf – 'Joey's so lovable,' she says, smiling fondly. True, but sometimes I wonder if he'll ever finish the Year 10 course.

And then, in the early hours one morning, I'm woken by a strange noise. I find Theo kneeling on the wooden floor in the dining room, next to a pile of vomit. 'I don't know why I'm vomiting,' he says, his words a slur. I smell the rum straight away. 'You've been drinking,' I tell him. '*Bloody* drinking!' He had gone out without me knowing – jumped out of the bedroom window, an old trick I used to do when I was fifteen. But it's not until later the next day, when I'm still fuming about having to clean up vomit at four in the morning, that I remember my own teenage escapades.

During this time, an old friend of Rob's from Melbourne comes to visit. Terry is big and manly, sure of himself. He's like a breath of fresh air in our musty house. He cooks dinner every night and drinks mint juleps with me over games of Scrabble. When I marvel at his skills in the kitchen, he says, 'If you eat, you should cook.' At home in Melbourne, Terry is a house-spouse. His wife has a full-time job, they have one child, and Terry fills his days reading books and doing the shopping and cooking. Rob is envious. After Terry leaves, all he can talk about is giving up work and becoming a house-spouse as well. I worry when Rob speaks this way – he's only had a permanent job for four years, and I don't want to be hounded by financial insecurity again.

'Let's see what happens when you start feeling better,' I tell him.

*

Once life returns to normal – with Rob regaining some of his strength and the children back at school – I start escaping again. At the end of November, six months after my father's death, my mother and I go to Bali for ten days. We stay in a low-key beach-side resort in Sanur, the area where my sister lives. For several days I feel anxious – I've never been so far away from Rob and the kids. What if something happens? But I soon start to relax and enjoy the freedom. In Denpasar, my sister takes us to Jalan Sulawesi, a street crammed with fabric shops. We smoke *kreteks* and drink *kopi Bali* on the street, and I enjoy going to the tailor with the fabrics I buy. In the mornings, my mother and I walk along the promenade before the heat becomes too much for her, and then we eat tropical fruit and banana porridge for breakfast in the resort cafe.

One day, I stand on a black sandy beach at Sanur and watch my sister wade into the murky water. Her loose pants billow around her as soft waves splash against her hips. She carries a white Styrofoam box above her head – it holds the remainder of our father's ashes. The rest of his ashes were scattered in the sea at a family gathering on the south coast of New South Wales, held a month after he died, but my sister had returned to Bali by then. As part of her life in Sanur, she's involved with a Balinese yoga community, and emptying my father's ashes into the sea is the final part of a Hindu fire ceremony ritual that will liberate his soul. This is also my sister's time to say goodbye. My mother stands on a path overlooking the beach. She couldn't make it down the side of the stormwater drain that led to the sea. I should be out there with my sister, but the sewage in the drain stopped me in my tracks. I'm too used to Australian standards of cleanliness. Besides, it's right for her to be out there on her own – I had my last swim with my father five months ago.

Every night in Bali, we dine at beachside restaurants, where I see couples holding hands and leaning in towards each other over candlelit meals. When I look at them, I feel sad that Rob and I never have holidays away from the kids. We should try and come to Bali together sometime. Before I leave, one of my sister's Balinese friends, a fortune-telling priest, reads my palm and says: 'Your husband loves you very much.' His words leave me wondering why I'm overseas while Rob is at home, once again, with the kids.

Not long after the Bali holiday, I go to a Leonard Cohen concert in the Hunter Valley with some friends. Leonard is all that I expect him to be – gracious, generous, charming, digni- fied, humble and *sexy*, even as an old man. At one point during the concert, I find myself thinking: Rob should be here. In some ways, he's the most Leonard-like man I know – a romantic, with a deep sensual side. But, like all of us, he has a dark side that he struggles with as well – a shadow self that he boxes with in front of the mirror of life. I asked Rob if he wanted to come to the concert, but it was too hard for us to find someone to mind the kids, and the tickets were very expensive.

Bernie and Jayne also go to the concert. Their $450 VIP tickets include a shaded area to sit and a free bar, and when I see Bernie back at the campsite afterwards, he jokes that he drank back the price of the ticket. Over the following weeks, Rob and I share an obsession with Leonard Cohen's music – we listen to his CDs, read books about his life, watch documentaries. Rob's favourite Leonard Cohen song, which he sings with his band, is 'Tonight Will Be Fine'; mine is 'Hallelujah'.

And, for all this time, I grieve the death of my father.

V

Summer 2008/09

Taking care of important business

One morning, I find Bernie at my front door, wearing dark sunglasses and carrying a cup of takeaway coffee. We go outside so he can smoke. As I clear some junk off a couple of chairs, I notice Bernie doesn't seem his normal upbeat self. 'What's wrong?'

'Bad news about Skippa,' says Bernie, rolling a smoke. 'He's in the lock-up and not looking good for coming out any time soon.'

He mentions the name of a jail in a nearby town.

I shake my head, bewildered. 'Skippa's the one I thought that would never happen to.'

'Except they all have that potential,' replies Bernie with a shrug.

I think of Skippa's mother, the pain she must be going through. 'What did he do?'

'Skippa and another fella bashed the fuck out of someone,' says Bernie. 'So much alcohol involved we'll never know who did what.' He looks over at me. 'But what we do know is that the other bloke – Skippa's brother's wife's brother – had just got out of jail. He's a fella in his thirties and just did ten years for beating someone to a pulp. Skippa was with him and some shit went down in a flat where Skippa was staying for a few nights.' Bernie pulls the lid off the top of his coffee and takes a sip. 'I've seen guys busted up worse in a pub, but I suspect it's because of who Skippa was with that the cops went on a rampage.'

'Ten years is a long time in jail.'

'Yep,' agrees Bernie, yawning. 'And that fella will do another ten for this. Anyway, Skippa was with him – it was out of character, not something we'd seen before – but again, it's those quiet ones you've gotta watch ...'

A shiver goes through me as his voice trails off.

'Is that jail okay?'

'It's not too bad,' says Bernie, looking grim. 'But he'll be moved to another one soon and that's a fuckin' bear pit. He'll be mixing with some pretty hardcore fellas there.' He shakes his head and sighs. 'Skippa's not the jail type of kid, really. I just hope he doesn't do too much time.'

I remember how Skippa couldn't cope with his boss screaming at him. 'I can't imagine him in jail.'

'He'll do it in his own quiet way,' says Bernie. 'But if he doesn't get out soon he'll get quieter and quieter, get more and more depressed ... he'd be a great candidate for suicide.'

He stops and stretches, yawning again. 'It's a tough gig working with this crew. The reason we're successful is that we get involved in kids' lives, but when you're hearing shit like this all the time, it drains you. People say to me: "Just turn off your phone and have a break." But if I can stop a kid from being locked up by writing a court report, do I write the court report or do I let him get locked up because I need to feel better about myself?'

Bernie chuckles and shakes his head. 'Nah, I'm going to write that court report or whatever else is needed. Does that make me some sort of fuckin' hero? Nah ... probably makes me an idiot workaholic.'

Unsure of how to respond, I wait for him to continue.

'We had a mishap during the week.' Bernie lights the cigarette he's been holding in his hand for some time, and tosses the dead match into the bushes. 'I had to put one of the dogs down this morning.'

When I ask which one, he says, 'Not a dog you know.' He looks out over the back garden, and we sit in silence for a minute or two. 'Part of the stuff with the dogs is that they come and go. There's a lot for young fellas to learn from that, like when Banjo died. That shattered some of those boys.'

'Will you do a ceremony again?'

'Done it this morning,' he says, blowing smoke into the breeze. 'Put him down there with the other dogs – starting to get a fair dog cemetery out there.'

'Who was with you?'

'Just me today. It was a bit too serious for the boys.' His voice drops. 'It was a cock-up on my behalf, so it was something I had to go through. It'd be easier to run off to a vet and get the ground-room needle, but it's important for me to go through that process and check things are alright, meditate on it, look at it from another angle.'

I watch two rosellas hover over the sunflowers in the garden.

'It reminded me of a time when I had to shoot a few hybrid dogs for National Parks,' says Bernie, his voice still soft and low. 'Something happened one day with this dog. I had it there, ready to shoot, but I couldn't get a clear shot. And I thought, if only that dog would move forward three feet, I'd have a clear heart and lung shot. As I was thinking this, the dog moved forward and stood there.' Bernie looks across at me, but I can't see his eyes behind his dark glasses.

'I couldn't shoot the dog,' he tells me. 'I nearly quit my job over it. Shit … if you've got a touch with animals, should you be using it to kill them? I would've been laughed at for talking about that sort of stuff in a white fella environment, so I went back up to Tennant Creek and sat down with that old man who first started showing me dog tracks and went through it with him.' Bernie shakes his head. 'He was gobsmacked that I was there, asking him stupid questions, and said: "If you think you're bigger than the universe, then you've missed something very important. If that's meant to happen with that dog, then it'll happen, and it's not for you to question why."'

Bernie finishes his smoke, and takes another sip of coffee. He straightens his legs out in front of him, his boots covered with dried mud.

From inside comes the sound of Leonard Cohen singing 'Anthem'.

'I hadn't had much to do with his music prior to that concert,' says Bernie, nodding in the direction of the house. 'Slim Dusty is more my man. But I was really taken by Leonard Cohen and what he stood for. You got the feeling – same as those old men in Tennant Creek – there's more than one lifetime's learning in that fella. A few songs in particular touched me, and this is one of them – that line about how there's a crack in everything, that's how the light gets in.'

I ask Bernie what the lyrics mean to him.

'You think you're doing really well,' he says, 'but for some reason, it all falls apart, like with that dog I couldn't shoot in the Territory. For Christ's sake, here I was doing the most unbelievable job in the world, and all of a sudden the whole show came to a stop because I couldn't shoot one bloody dog! So, there's the crack – and it was time for me to go and learn another lesson that has multiplied a billion times on top of that through life, through dogs, through the boys. When things are going bad, it's back to that same stuff – the universe is bigger than what you are. If you learn to trust it, it knows better than you, and the right things happen for some reason or other. Why do things happen? Why do you get sacked from a job? Why do you stub your toe on a rock and then can't walk? Why does a kid like Skippa end up in jail? We spend so much time thinking, I've got something going really well here, this is the answer to everything, you know ... but wait! There's a big bloody crack, and you can either look at it as the whole show is fucked, or you can look at it as, that's where the light gets in. And when the light gets in, *whoa*! All of a sudden, it's just been one little stepping stone to something bigger and better.'

'Yep ... I reckon that's true.'

Bernie finishes his coffee and makes to leave. I follow him inside, watching his long legs stride up the hallway. I imagine him shooting the dog that morning, going through the smoking ceremony on his own – taking care of important business. At the door, I think about giving Bernie a hug or reaching out a comforting hand, but my arms hang loosely by my sides, not sure.

'See you next time,' he says.

I watch him walk to his ute. 'Hey, Bernie,' I call from the doorway.

He looks around, his eyes impenetrable behind his dark sunglasses.

'I ... um ...' There's so much I want to say, but I can't. Not today. 'Good luck with Skippa, and say hello to the boys at the shed for me.'

He nods. 'Yep, will do.'

Ice cream for breakfast

A week later, Joey comes over and tells me his housemate, Tim, is going overseas for two months. He wants Joey to live elsewhere while he's away.

'Maybe I'll move back home?' suggests Joey.

I shake my head. 'No, I don't think so. I'm still grieving for Pup, Rob's not well and I've got enough on my plate. Maybe we can look around for another share-house?'

Joey isn't impressed, but I can't have him move back home, not now. Not with everything else that's going on.

That same afternoon, Bernie rings. 'Want to come down to the shed this Sunday?' he asks. 'Some of the old crew are coming along and we're doing circle work with the new boys from TAFE.'

I almost say no. But maybe it'll be good to reconnect with Bernie and the boys, to escape from the house for a while.

'Okay.'

Bernie tells me he's been visiting Skippa in jail.

'How's he going?'

'It's fuckin' horrible,' says Bernie with passion. 'To see what's happened to that kid after a month – listening to his language, the whole head down shit, smoking White Ox crap and talking fuckin' jail-talk. I keep telling him: "Fuckin' wake up to yourself!" I understand why he has to do it, but it's like watching a living thing become something different. It's not right ... and I'm working on a plan to get him out of there.'

*

On Sunday, I put on my boots and King Gees and head over to the shed. Bernie is sitting outside with Blister, Jimmy and

210

some other blokes. I pull up a milk-crate and join the circle, feeling like the new girl at school. I nod hello to the others, recognising a few of the Aboriginal boys who've been working with the dogs.

Everyone is teasing a boy who's just had his tongue pierced – it's still swollen and he's having trouble speaking. Bernie teases him the most. Later, when Bernie asks why one of the boys hasn't arrived yet, someone tells him, 'He probably had too many cones this morning!'

'What's he doing eating ice cream for breakfast?' asks Bernie, with his wide-eyed innocent look. The boys laugh, and I start to relax. It's good to be back.

'Okay, let's make a start,' says Bernie. With a nod in my direction, he adds, 'This is Helena and she's going to be sitting in with us.'

The original group of Iron Man Welders help Bernie keep the younger boys in line. I notice Blister in particular has stepped up to the plate since I last saw him. 'This time is for going around, checking how everyone is, and to work on any problems,' he explains. 'One is shit, five is great.' He turns to the boy next to him, who is wearing baggy trousers, a crew cut and a 'fuck you' expression.

'Where you at, Danny?'

'One,' says Danny, rocking back on his milk-crate.

'Why's that?' asks Blister.

'My dad's always going out without me and I'm feeling shit.'

Bernie stops Blister before he goes on to the next boy. He looks around the circle. 'What do the rest of you blokes think might help Danny in this situation?'

The answers spill out: tell your dad you love him, you miss him, handcuff yourself to him, jump in the car with him.

When it's time to move on, Bernie looks at Danny with admiration. 'Congratulations for having the guts to speak out in front of everyone.'

Danny nods, his lips pressed hard together.

The new boys are happy to join in, and it works well having the older boys lead the way. I listen in, curious, as Bernie talks about taking responsibility for actions, helping the boys understand how if they *choose* to do things – like playing up in class, or talking rudely to a teacher – then they need to take responsibility for those choices instead of blaming the teacher, other kids or their parents.

'It's about changing the script,' says Bernie. 'We can't change what happened yesterday, we can only change from this moment on ... and I'm giving you the seeds of change today.'

I'm the last person in the circle. Blister looks over at me and gives me a kind smile. 'Where you at, Helena?'

His question takes me by surprise. 'Three and a half,' I reply, wanting to wrap things up. But really, I'm a one. Maybe not even that.

Before I leave, Bernie takes me aside and asks if I'm ready to attend a mediation session. In recent weeks, Rob and Joey have had two meetings with Bernie and another Family Support counsellor. Because of Pup's death and Rob's illness, I haven't had much time or energy to think about mediation, but I know it's important for me to face up to what's going on in my own family, to stop running away. Rob came home the other afternoon, wanting to talk to me about what happened in the session. I can only remember snatches of what he said – 'Joey and I were crying, Helena' ... 'It was very emotional'. Scared of facing up to the past, I pushed Rob's words aside and didn't ask any questions.

I stare back at Bernie, wondering if I'm ready. 'Not really … but I'll give it a go.'

When I get home from the shed, Joey rings and says he has no food. I drive around to his place and take him shopping. Over the last month, I've slipped back to helping him with his groceries again. None of this is easy … but I can't let him go hungry. Later, we go and see *The Dark Knight* at the local cinema – I've been trying to establish a regular movie night with Joey. Because we both enjoy films, it's something we can successfully do together, but I wish we didn't have to see action movies all the time. Heath Ledger's performance as The Joker is disturbing. When I leave the cinema, his leering clown-face is behind my eyes every time I blink.

On the drive home, Joey says: 'That was a really sad movie. Batman was all alone – the women he loved died, and he was taking the blame for someone else's wrongs. He'd become a castaway.'

I look across at him in surprise. Joey would see the depths of Batman's emotional life underneath all the violence and action.

You picking up what I'm putting down?

The day before Joey is due to move out of Tim's, with nowhere but our house as an option, we go up to the university together and look through the noticeboards for share-house accommodation. At home later, Joey rings one of the numbers about a room. A woman answers and says yes, the room is still vacant.

'Let's go and see her now,' I say, reaching for my keys. 'You're running out of time.'

'What do I say?' asks Joey in a panic when I pull up outside a weatherboard cottage. Wind chimes hang on the front veranda, tinkling in the breeze.

'Just say hello and see where it goes from there.'

I watch as he knocks on the front door. It swings open and he goes inside. Five minutes later, he comes back out and slides into his seat. 'Yeah,' he nods at my questioning glance. 'They were really nice and relaxed – a guy and a girl. They said I could move in tomorrow.' He keeps nodding to himself, like he's surprised by what happened inside the house. 'Yeah, I think I could live there.'

I look at him proudly. 'Well done, Joey. I'll drop you home so you can start packing.'

*

The mediation session is held in the front room of the Family Support building. Sparsely furnished with a couple of old lounges and an armchair, the room has a box of toys in one corner and a large mirror over the mantelpiece. Joey sits opposite me, looking like a character from an alien movie – his newly shaven head covered with wax. I had to laugh when he told me how that had happened. He'd wanted his head completely bald – the barber always left a soft covering of fuzz on the scalp. Tobias's mother and sister thought it would be a good idea to put wax on his head and pull the hairs out. Neither the hair nor the wax came off. The day before, I'd tried to remove the wax with a hot washer, but it was stuck fast. Even the barber couldn't help. Joey would have to wait until his hair grew, so he could cut the wax off.

During the mediation session, we mainly talk about our fraught years in Brisbane. For some reason, as I sit there, all I can think about is a picture Joey drew in one of the cartooning workshops he'd attended when he was in primary school. The drawing showed a muscly Tarzan-like character with a six-pack chest, hanging onto two vines in the jungle. He was wearing a loincloth and grimacing because half of one leg was caught in a crocodile's mouth while a second crocodile was zooming in on the other leg, the tails and mouths of more crocodiles below. At the time, I wondered what was going on for Joey – why he would draw such a picture. Now, as Bernie and the other counsellor recap on previous sessions, I begin to understand why. They describe how Rob initiated the mediation because he knew how much pain I went through over his problematic relationship with Joey, and how one of the first things they'd worked out was that both he and Joey loved me. They both wanted to make my life better – and also improve things for our whole family. Rob had admitted he was wrong in the way he had treated Joey as a child, and Joey had accepted his apology.

'Like a man,' says Bernie, glancing over at Joey, who nods in agreement.

With four people in the room talking about the past, it isn't easy for me to push aside the truth. A whole range of emotions that I've held down for years suddenly hit me in the chest. I start crying. I look across at Joey through my tears. My beautiful boy. Those years in Brisbane were *so* hard for him, and things continued to be very difficult for him when we came back to Armidale. I'm amazed that he doesn't hate us for being such hopeless parents; that he's forgiven us and has agreed to be part of these sessions.

Bernie takes charge of the rest of the mediation. And he makes me laugh, just like he does with the boys at the shed, by teasing Joey about the wax on his head. I've never laughed so much in a counselling session, yet here we are, talking about our history of pain. 'We can't change the past,' says Bernie. 'We can only work on what's happening now ... and probably the most important area right now is how to manage Joey's visits.' He suggests that we establish a 'no-go' zone from five-thirty in the afternoon to seven in the evening. That's the busiest time of the day for me, and also the time Joey usually appears wanting food, money, a lift and attention.

'And no more driving,' says Bernie, looking hard at me. 'You picking up what I'm putting down, Helena?'

I nod. 'Yep.'

At the end of the session, Bernie asks Joey: 'On a scale of one to five, how much a part of the family do you feel?'

'Two.'

Bernie asks me where Freddie would be on that scale.

I don't even need to think about it. 'Five.'

When Joey says he feels like a 'four' with my brothers and their families – his uncles who until recently he'd hardly ever seen – Bernie zooms in on how Joey behaved when he was with them, and how maybe his behaviour actually *changed* when he was with them. I tell Bernie about my oldest brother's phone call after Joey's visit, when he praised us for raising such a well-mannered boy. Bernie raises his eyebrows and looks at Joey.

Joey just grins and shrugs.

After the mediation session, I think back to a time when Joey had been living with Tim for a year or so. It was Henry's 11th birthday, and I said I'd buy milkshakes for the kids at the local lolly shop. We set off downtown – me pushing Freddie in his stroller, Theo walking beside me, Henry on his bike. Just past the first corner, I noticed Joey behind us, wearing his black shirt and jeans. I waved, but he didn't respond. I wasn't allowed to acknowledge him in public – he always said it was too embarrassing. So, for a heart-breaking five minutes, we walked downtown together – Joey on the other side of the road, some distance back. It had made me very aware of the chasm running through our family.

That's how it's been for far too long. I want Joey to walk with the rest of us now.

How do I clean a toilet?

'How do I clean a toilet?' asks Joey as I park the car behind Hungry Jack's.

A month has passed since the mediation session in which we agreed to implement the 'no-go' zone. Nothing much has changed. The 'no-go' zone isn't working – Joey's been coming around every day, sometimes more than once, and not always at the times we agreed on. I shouldn't be driving him at all, especially after what Bernie said at the mediation session: 'No more driving.'

So why am I still doing it?

I manage to convince Joey to attend a Defence Forces information session in Tamworth. We drive down early in the morning, with him eating takeaway fried chicken for breakfast. I'm trying to be more tolerant – just because I don't like takeaway food, it doesn't mean Joey shouldn't enjoy it. At the conference centre in Tamworth, he goes inside to complete an initial aptitude test. He'll enjoy that, I think to myself, as I wait outside in the car. He's always loved tests. I hope Joey chooses a job that uses his brain. I've spent hours studying the job descriptions in the brochures, and have underlined the ones I think he's most suited for – like cryptologic linguist or systems analyst. Sometimes, when I read through the brochures, I feel like running away to join the army myself.

We had another mediation session yesterday, during which I reminded Joey that I was, and still am, his strongest supporter. We're going to give the 'no-go' zone another try ... and this time stick to it.

*

I pop into the shed one afternoon to see how things are going. As I wander through the doors, I see Skippa working in one of the welding bays.

Bernie leads me back outside to talk with me, wiping his hands on his overalls, his eyes bright. 'We sprung Skippa from jail!'

'How did you manage that?' I ask, laughing with relief.

'I was just relentless,' he explains. 'After seeing him down there, I just went, nah – this is not fuckin' right. It's not right what he's done, but this is not a solution. This is only going to put him away for the next twenty years. So I didn't sleep until I had him out of there. I harassed solicitors and wrote court reports, brought in people like Peter Slattery to do assessments, called on all my contacts and wheeled in everything I had. I knew the credit union had a top solicitor, so I bashed on his door. I just kept at it and at it and at it – until a magistrate went, righto, with the strictest of bail conditions, we'll release this kid.'

'How long will Skippa be on bail?'

'For the next two years,' answers Bernie, running a hand through his hair. 'He's got to be at his mother's house from 7 p.m. to 7 a.m., and any other time he has to be in my direct company.' A crafty look crosses Bernie's face. 'But, by the time his bail term is over, not only will Skippa have done nothing wrong, he'll have done more fuckin' community service hours than a saint. We've got him training to become a youth worker, and the magistrate is already coming to the shed and watching Skippa doing circle work with the boys. He might still go back to jail after two years – that's up to a jury – but at the end of the day, is the community better off having Skippa locked up or out here doing what he's doing?'

'How's Skippa's mother?'

'She's tough, resilient,' says Bernie, stifling a yawn. 'When I look at her I think, hmmm, there's a heap of that resilience in Skippa as well. Everyone tells you that changing things with these kids isn't really possible ... but don't listen to what isn't possible. Let's just look at what we *can* do and what *is* possible. And when we stand in front of that jury, we're not going to talk about what happened. We'll talk about what he's done since, and there won't be anyone sitting in that jury who would have done as much for the community as what Skippa has done.' Bernie nods, more to himself than me. 'There won't be a button we can't push.'

Putting some of those tricks to use

While making dinner one night, I listen to a feature about Bernie and the boys on the local community radio station. The program host is reporting from the shed, and in the background I hear the familiar sounds of bashing, clanging, crackling and the shriek of the drop-saw. The reporter begins by asking Blister about his involvement in the program.

'I joined Iron Man Welders at the start,' answers Blister with pride. 'A few of us old fellas recently came back to help Bernie keep some of the young fellas in line.'

I smile when I hear him say that, remembering how Geraldine once told me: 'Those boys will be around Bernie forever.'

Blister is a dad now to a baby girl. When he's questioned on how fatherhood is going, Blister says: 'Being a dad – it's pretty good, but it's pretty hard at the same time.'

The interviewer moves on to Bernie. 'What is it you're doing that's working?'

'We sit and talk with young people,' says Bernie. 'Self-development is the most important thing. It doesn't matter whether a kid can weld or whether he can read and write if he doesn't know who he is and where he fits in life. So one of the things we work on is life and relationships – because those are the things that really matter to kids.'

I look up from chopping the onions, tears in my eyes. I always get a lump in my throat when I hear Bernie on the radio.

'The key to the stuff we're doing isn't coming up with new ways,' adds Bernie. 'It's going back and having a look at the old ways and at the things that really worked. I've spent a lot of my life working with Aboriginal people in the Northern Territory and learnt four or five golden rules. One is the auntie and uncle system. These days we use fancy names like "role models" or "mentors" – but it's just about having sensible older people around to show younger people how to grow up. Those Aboriginal people showed me some really clever tricks that have been around for thousands of years – I'm just putting some of those tricks to use.'

Before the program ends, the interviewer asks Bernie if he has a favourite song.

'A singer-songwriter called Tonchi McIntosh has a song that particularly touches me,' says Bernie. 'It's called "Kidman".'

I knew he was going to say 'Kidman' – it's the only song I've ever heard him sing at parties.

Bernie clears his throat. 'It's about Sidney Kidman, the biggest cattleman in Australia, who came and bought up all this country and got all the cattle. But he forgot about Mother Nature – everything was dying, they needed rain desperately, and Kidman had the insight to go back and talk to the people who had lived in that country for a long time. They got old man Tinder to come and sing his rain song and look out ... down it came!'

*

A few months later, Joey's share-house is sold and he needs to find somewhere else to live. He's not keen to go back to Tim's, so once again, we go up to the university noticeboards, searching for available rooms. We don't have any luck. With all the university students back in town, it's not easy to find a room to rent in Armidale. The day before he has to move out, I leave Joey with thirty dollars and the last of the phone numbers. 'I've got to go to work. Buy some credit for your phone and keep ringing until you get a place to live. You need to take whatever you can get, and tell them you'll move in the next day.'

The next morning, Joeys rings and says: 'I had a look at a room in someone's house, but they won't be deciding till the following week. That means I've got nowhere to go ... except your place.'

For the next six hours I help Joey clear the stuff out of his room at his share-house and clean it. Then we pile his boxes and bags into the car and drive back home.

'Just for a few nights,' I tell him. 'I love you and I want the best for you, but living together doesn't work for us. You know that.'

Put a spoonful of cement in your Weet-Bix

A few nights turn into eight. Joey falls into old patterns of staying awake late into the night and not emerging from the bedroom till noon. At breakfast, the five of us tiptoe around so we don't wake him. I start to feel tense again – like I'm waiting for something to happen, even when nothing does.

I ring Tim, who recently returned from overseas, and ask if Joey can move back in with him. 'Just for a little while,' I add, expecting Tim to answer, 'Yes, of course.'

But he doesn't.

'I'm painting the house,' he says apologetically. 'All the furniture is piled up in Joey's old room. He can come back when I'm finished, though, and that should be by Sunday.'

Sunday is three nights away. I know I'm being intolerant again. I think of Blister's mother telling him: 'If you're in trouble, you can come back.' Why can't I say this to Joey? I take a deep breath, loosen my fingers around the handset of the phone and steady my voice.

'Things aren't going so well here,' I tell Tim. 'I could really use one less person in the house – Rob and I are arguing, Freddie is waking up all through the night, Theo is being horrible and I'm stressed out of my brain. Please.'

'Okay.' Tim says he'll definitely have the furniture out of the room by Sunday, for sure. Joey can move back as a short-term option, but he'll need to be out for ten days over Easter because Tim's relatives are coming to stay.

Easter is weeks away. For now, Tim's words mean only one thing: three nights to go till I can breathe properly again. As I hang up the phone, I spot a photo of Joey on the noticeboard – blowing out candles on his 18th birthday cake, in high spirits after visiting his uncles in Sydney. If only he could be Mr Happy all the time.

*

On Sunday, I reach breaking point. It's still unclear whether Joey is going back to Tim's. 'For sure' has become 'maybe'. Joey hangs around the whole morning – lying in bed, playing with his portable PlayStation, not making any effort to pack up his stuff. Just normal teenage behaviour, but for some reason, it drives me wild.

When he comes into the kitchen to eat breakfast, I take the sheets off his bed, pick up the clothes off the floor, pack everything into bags and put them in the car. Joey doesn't comment. At six, I finally manage to convince him to leave his room. I drive him and his gear around to Tim's. Back home, I'm almost ready to collapse from emotional exhaustion. I sit on the lounge, eyes closed.

Five minutes later Joey reappears, asking for a lift to a friend's place.

Rob looks over in confusion as I snatch the keys from the top of the fridge. I know I'm not thinking rationally, but if I take Joey out now, then I'll be able to drop him back at Tim's and it'll soon be over. I drive him to his friend's house, hands tight on the steering wheel. Joey gets out of the car and knocks on his friend's door. Sick with impotent anger, I sit in the dark car, sobbing at the injustice of Joey's behaviour, while he happily chats with his friend for over fifteen minutes.

I push my grandmother's pendant along its gold chain. Why can't I say 'no' to Joey?

Guilt. That's it. I was too hard on him when he was young. I forced my own son to leave home at fifteen, and for years I've been trying to make up for it because I haven't been able to create a space for him to come back to. This driving business seems so much worse now that I have Pup's car – he would have hated to see me driving Joey around like this. I pull down the visor to look at a boxing photo I'd stuck on with Blu Tack. I don't like being so angry in his car. I can almost hear his voice: Is this what we came to Australia for? So *het kind* could be treated like a servant by her own son?

When Joey gets back in, I don't trust myself to speak. A torrent of rage will be released if I open my mouth.

Stay calm, breathe, I tell myself. We drive back to Tim's in silence.

At the house, I turn to Joey. 'I think we need a break from each other for a week or so. I need a rest.'

Joey doesn't reply. He gets out, half-slams the door and walks up the steps to Tim's veranda.

At home, I fall onto my bed and cry so hard my stomach hurts. The phone rings. I hear Rob's voice answer, the sound of his footsteps up the hall. He opens the door of the bedroom. 'Bernie's on the phone for you.'

I wipe my eyes and take the phone.

'Hey, Helena, how are you going?' Bernie's voice reaches out to me like a lifebuoy in a stormy sea.

'Not so good.' I burst into tears.

'Tell me what happened,' he says, like it's completely normal for me to be sobbing on the phone.

After I tell him, Bernie says, 'Joey has developed a pattern of behaviour where he threatens and intimidates you. Your behaviour perpetuates it. You both need to stop.'

'I don't know how.'

'I'll come over tomorrow and give you the words you need to use. Words that'll help you to be strong with him.'

I reach for the tissues. 'I just want Joey to join the army ... to move thousands of miles away.'

'We need to get him to move thousands of miles away from his behaviour,' says Bernie. 'And we need to work on your behaviour as well, Helena. It's time to toughen up. Put a spoonful of cement in your Weet-Bix tomorrow morning ... and for fuck's sake, stop driving Joey around.'

Bernie's right. Joey and I are caught in an unhealthy relationship. I'm not going to allow this pattern to continue any longer. I love him, but enough is enough.

VI

Autumn–Summer 2009

Staying here isn't an option

The shops are full of mandarins. Gleaming dimpled orange fruit. I have them in the fruit bowl at home, but I can't eat them. I tried. I peeled the skin off one but the sharp scent of citrus instantly brought back the image of Mum feeding Pup mandarins, segment by segment.

One afternoon, I walk past a nursing home and through the window I see an old woman lying on a bed with blankets tucked under her chin. She looks lost and lonely. The old woman stays in my mind for days. Is that all there is to look forward to? I don't want to be left to rot in a nursing home, my needs attended to by strangers.

In the meantime, I have more immediate concerns. Easter is less than a week away and Tim's relatives are coming. One morning, Joey rings and says: 'Hey, Mum. I need to be out of my room in three days. I'll probably stay with you for ten days while Tim's family is here.'

I don't comment but I know I can't let that happen. For many mothers, of course, this would be a normal request from one of their adult children – a request that most would happily accommodate. But that's not the situation here. As much as I love Joey and as much as I want to help him out, the time has come to put that spoonful of cement in my Weet-Bix. Although Bernie had said he would come around and tell me my 'lines', he'd never showed. He's busy with the boys at the shed, so I let it go. But now I need his help. I ring Bernie on his mobile and tell him about Joey's plan to move back for ten days over Easter.

'It's time for me to learn some new ways of behaving, Bernie.' I get my notepaper and pen. 'What do I say?'

First of all, Bernie apologises for not coming around earlier: 'Just got caught up,' he says. Then he gets straight to business. 'Okay, the next time you ring him, ask Joey: "What are your options?" He'll say your house. Then you say, "That's one option but let's think of some others." Tick them off with him – "You get the dole so Centrelink may be able to help, or you could pitch a tent at the caravan park, couch it, or stay at the youth refuge." Tell him, "Staying here isn't an option, Joey, but this is what I can do. I can give you a hand to get in touch with any of those places on the list, but choosing to shout at me is not one of the options." Don't engage with his arguments about the past. Just keep saying, "This is what I can do. I can help you come to a decision, but staying here is not an option."'

'Yep,' I say, writing furiously. 'Thanks, Bernie.'

The next morning, when the house is quiet, I ring Joey. 'Let's talk about your options for where you're going to stay over Easter.'

'Your place,' says Joey, in a tone that implies it's the only option.

'Where else?'

He can't think of anywhere else, so I start reading through the list of choices I'd prepared.

'There's no way I could stay at the youth refuge,' says Joey. When I mention the caravan park, he asks: 'You'd prefer me to stay in a caravan park with murderers where I might get my throat slashed?' There had been an incident a couple of weeks before where one of Joey's friends had witnessed a man getting his throat slashed in an altercation at one of the local caravan parks.

'Staying here isn't an option, Joey,' I tell him, calm and steady. 'But I'll support you with whatever you decide.'

He hangs up on me.

That afternoon I write a letter outlining all the options Bernie and I had discussed. I put the letter inside an envelope, walk around to Joey's house and slide it under his door.

Joey comes around later in the evening, when I've just put Freddie to bed. 'I want to talk about things,' he says with a hint of belligerence. 'What are the reasons why I can't stay here?'

I have told Joey the reasons a hundred times already – how his behaviour creates enormous tension and affects everyone in the house, how he refuses to do any jobs and help with the house-work, how he plays loud rap music while Freddie is sleeping, how he sometimes shouts at me so loud that the neighbours are worried. I have two other boys in their teens, and I don't want Joey's behaviour to be their benchmark.

I take a deep breath. *Come on, Helena. You can do this.*

'I'm not going to discuss that now, Joey,' I tell him. 'Staying here isn't an option, but I'm prepared to help you with whatever you decide.'

A stubborn look crosses his face. He sits on the couch. 'I'd like you to tell me the reasons before I leave.'

Bernie's voice sounds in my ear: *Don't engage.*

I'm not sure what to do. Bernie said to ring if I need help, so I walk over to the phone and dial his number.

'Hey, Bernie,' I say when he answers, keeping my voice level. 'Joey's come over to discuss things, but he doesn't want to accept he can't stay here.'

'Okay,' says Bernie. 'Tell him – "Now is not a good time for me, Joey. I'd like you to leave. We'll talk about it tomorrow at a time that suits me, but staying here is not an option." I'll stay on the phone while you talk to him.'

I repeat these words to Joey, working hard to maintain an unruffled appearance. My legs are shaking. I'm not good at confrontation. Knowing Bernie is listening makes me feel a little self-conscious. When I lift the receiver to my ear to check if he's still there, I hear him say, 'You're winning, Helena. You've seventy per cent won this. Keep going.'

Joey pulls the phone cord out of the wall, hanging the line up on Bernie. Now it's just Joey and me.

I stand my ground. 'Now is not a good time for me, Joey. I'd like you to leave.'

I'm sounding like a broken record, but the words come easier every time. 'I'll talk to you tomorrow.'

In the end, I have to force him out the door. Clearly unnerved by this change in my behaviour, he doesn't know how to deal with the new me. The side gate clicks shut. I wait for him to come back, to start arguing with me again like he'd normally do. But he doesn't.

I plug the phone back in and call Bernie. He answers on the first ring. 'How'd you go?'

'I did it.'

'He's probably gone home to lick his wounds,' says Bernie. 'No doubt he still thinks he'll be staying at your place. But we've introduced him to choice theory, which doesn't leave him any room to debate and argue and win. Write out a list of reasons why he can't stay. When you ring him tomorrow, have the list near the phone. Don't engage, just keep telling him – "I'm prepared to help you with whatever you decide to do, Joey, but staying here isn't an option." You're going to have to be strong, Helena, but this'll lead to a more honest relationship with Joey. It'll release his life to him.'

Later, lying in bed, I feel a twinge of guilt about how I behaved with Joey. But then I remember what Bernie said about the dogs the night before Pup died – there are times when you need to be hard, especially when the dog needs jerking into line.

This is one of those times.

Don't engage

Meanwhile, Rob seems to be retreating more and more into a world of his own. No doubt it's the lingering effects of the shingles, but I'm concerned about the change in his behaviour. Although he's back at work, and is slowly regaining his energy, he isn't his normal self. He becomes very critical – commenting on the way I dress, the way I stack the cookbooks, the way I like the lights to be soft, and the way I salt the potatoes. I know I'm not an easy person to live with – I wipe benches too much, I don't stack the cookbooks neatly, I'm too abrupt, too *Dutch* – too culturally different for a dairy farmer's son. And probably too complicated for most people. But I know Rob is struggling with his health, so I try to ignore his complaints.

Besides, I have other things to think about. The day after

making it through the first round with Joey, I type out a list of reasons why he can't stay – such as his unwillingness to help with the housework, his sleeping habits, the fights and the tension – and put them by the phone.

At midday, after reading the list out loud several times, I ring Joey. When he answers, his voice thick with sleep, I start to explain why he can't stay. By the time I reach the second reason, he hangs up.

Okay, fine.

The next day, at three in the afternoon, Joey calls and says he's coming around to talk to me.

'It's not a good time for me,' I tell him. My pulse begins to race. 'I'm about to pick up Freddie from preschool.'

'I'm coming around.'

Joey has caught me off-guard. I rush around the house, closing doors and windows, finding my keys, hoping to leave before he arrives.

Too late. I hear knocking on the front door. I stand back against the wall, like a rabbit caught in a spotlight, and pretend I'm not home. Ridiculous. Hiding in my own house. Anyone else would stop knocking and try again later. Not Joey. He walks around the side, banging on the windows, shouting: 'Mum! Mum!'

Worried he'll break the glass, I race over to the back door.

'I didn't hear you,' I say. 'I was in the bathroom.'

Joey explains to me that he needs to bring his gear around the next day.

I breathe deeply and slowly, trying to regain my composure. I remember Bernie's words: *Don't engage.*

'Sorry, Joey,' I tell him. 'Staying here over Easter is not an option.'

'Fuck you!' he yells, inches away from my face. He races outside, grabs the trunk of the nearest rose bush and rips it out of the garden. His face wild with fury, he spots one of my favourite pottery dishes on the back table. Crash! The plate lies smashed on the concrete path. Satisfied, Joey marches up the side of the house, his body an exclamation of injustice. The gate slams. Bang!

My hands shake so much I can barely hold the dustpan and broom as I sweep up the broken crockery. I throw the rose bush in the compost heap. Then, a mess of nerves, I find my helmet, lock up the house, and ride my pushbike across town to Freddie's preschool.

Later, when I'm home again, I call Bernie. 'I had an awful scene with Joey this afternoon.'

'Tell me what happened,' he says.

Shamefully, like I'm releasing a long-held secret, I recount the events of the afternoon. Bernie doesn't seem surprised or shocked by anything I tell him. When I say that mine might be a hard case to fix, he says he's seen much worse.

'I think I'll write Joey a letter,' I say, when I've finished explaining. 'I'm better at writing than speaking.'

'Good idea,' agrees Bernie. He helps me work out the words I need to use.

Dear Joey, I write the next morning.

*You come asking for help and wonder why you can't stay here? The answer is the way you behaved yesterday afternoon. From now on, if you want to come over you need to **ring first** and check if it's a good time. If I say no, it's not a good time, then don't come over. Simple as that. And when you do come over, the behaviour has to be normal. Same as at anyone else's house. Bashing on windows, swearing, smashing* *plates and ripping rose bushes out of the garden is not normal or appropriate, and I'm not accepting it anymore. When you visit other people's houses you don't behave like that. This is my house, my life, and I don't want people abusing me and damaging my property. As I said yesterday, and also today, staying here is not an option over Easter.*

Love Mum

I walk around to Joey's house and push the letter under his door.

As I prepare dinner that night, I listen to a radio program I recorded when Triple J featured Bernie and the boys at the Armidale Wool Expo a while back.

I recognise the voice of Wayne, one of the Aboriginal boys, as the program starts: 'Yeah, some people just go around and break into houses and everything, iPods, laptops ...'

The reporter's voice follows: 'A bunch of teenage boys from Armidale on the New England Tablelands of New South Wales, who've been well known to the cops for ages, are now on a first-name basis with farmers on the dog-trialling circuit. Now, in case you're not familiar with dog jumping, basically it's like the canine equivalent of high jump and these boys have won every dog jumping competition they've entered. It's day one of the dog jumping competition here at the Wool Expo in Armidale ...'

I boil water for pasta, smiling at the sound of barking. Someone says, 'Come on, boy! Come on ... *good dog!*' and I'm suddenly filled with an intense desire to return to the world of the shed, to Bernie and the boys. I didn't know they'd been doing so well with the dogs.

Skippa comes on next. 'I'm nineteen,' he tells the reporter. 'Been working with the dogs for about a year and meeting new people all the time. It's real good fun – the dogs give us something to look forward to.'

Then the reporter introduces Bernie. 'I can only call it dog magic,' he says earnestly. 'The boys love these dogs and the number of comments we've had about the way they handle the dogs is something special. I've never seen anything like it. There are farmers here with third generation–bred dogs and fancy LandCruisers talking to this mob of boys who wear their caps on back to front – telling the boys what a fantastic job they're doing with the dogs. It was one of the most amazing moments I've had in youth work.'

The reporter swings back to the boys. 'Wayne, you and your dog won today. How does it feel?'

'Good. I was confident.'

'Have you come first place in any other competitions?'

'At the Armidale Show,' answers Wayne in a cocky manner. 'And every comp we go to!'

'So now you're just used to winning.'

'Starting to get sick of it!' Then he laughs. 'Nah!'

Doing the right thing

Rob and I had planned to take the kids to the coast for Easter, but it pours with rain. Rob admits he doesn't have the energy to go anyway. Joey comes around on Good Friday, waltzing around the house like he owns it.

'I'm staying at Lenny's,' he says, and asks me to drop a mattress around. 'I slept in Tim's tent in Lenny's backyard last night, but it rained and now everything's soaked.'

Joey jumps into the shower, without asking. By turning up unexpectedly like this – not ringing like I asked – he has the upper hand again. I decide to let it go, for now, but when Joey leaves, I call Bernie.

'He's introduced the third trick,' says Bernie. 'Carry on like nothing has happened. He has to understand it's not like that anymore – "You need to ring before you come over, Joey. Don't come in and make yourself at home. Is it okay if I do that at your place? If you need a hand finding a place to have a shower, I can help you with that. We can talk about your options, but you're not coming in if you haven't rung." Give him clear guidelines.'

I scribble down some notes. 'He's asked for a mattress. I was going to lend him a comfortable one, but I think I'll just give him a thin camping mat and a sleeping bag.'

'Yep,' agrees Bernie. 'Take a mattress around, but don't give him the comfy one. He's only thinking about what's best for Joey. He needs to know you'll help him, but the help isn't unconditional. That's not the way it works – it's a two-way street. If he comes around like that again, tell him: "You can either choose to leave, or wait here for the police."'

'The police?'

'Ripping rose bushes out people's gardens and bashing on windows and doors isn't acceptable, Helena. He needs to learn that ... maybe the hard way.'

Straight after talking with Bernie, I write the next letter.

Dear Joey,

The way you behaved when you came over here this afternoon is not the way it works anymore. This is not a place where you can make yourself at home, open the fridge, have a shower and go into other people's rooms. Would it be okay if I did that at your house? I don't think so. From now on, you're not coming into this house if you haven't rung. If it suits me, you can come over, or I can help you with something. I said I would support you, but my help is not unconditional. You play by the game and I can give you help. At the moment you seem to only want to do things your way, but this is my house and I make the rules about what goes on here. If Lenny's place is too uncomfortable, ring one of those other options on the list. I've dropped off the camping mattress, your sleeping bag, the pillow you left here and some milk. We can have another crack at things some other time – remember to ring first.

Love Mum

I drive around to Lenny's with the bedding and the letter. No one answers the front door when I knock. I walk around the back to the shed where Lenny sleeps. It looks like a home-less shelter – bottles and mess cover the concrete floor, bare mattresses and filthy-looking pillows. It's hard to think of Joey sleeping here in this cold rainy weather. But I have to be tough otherwise Joey will never take any responsibility for his life. I put the letter, the mattress and the old sleeping bag near the door, so Joey will see them when he returns.

Later that night, at a party where Rob's band is playing, I spot Bernie across the room. It's disconcerting to see the 'real' Bernie after the intensity of our phone conversations over the past week. He knows so much about me. I wave to him from where I'm standing and he nods in my direction, but at the end of the night, I can't leave without saying goodbye. He's sitting with a crowd of people, so I don't want to say too much. I bend down to speak in his ear. 'Thanks for everything you've done this week … you really make it a lot easier.'

He stands up and gives me a hug. 'No problem, Helena. I'm always happy to help.'

*

Joey comes back at seven the next night. Although he's remembered to come after the 'no-go' zone, he didn't ring first. Rob and I are exhausted from being up during the night with Freddie, who had his worst bout of croup ever. I'm resting in bed when I hear voices in the kitchen – Joey asking Rob if he can use the computer, if he can make a call to a mobile, if he can pick up his shoes that were left in Theo's room.

He's completely ignored my letter.

Is this what our life is going to be like forever?

I think of Bernie's advice to Skippa, when he was having that trouble with his boss – 'Time to do something different'. If we just do the same as what we've always done, nothing will change. I want to help Joey find the right path in life.

I go to the kitchen where Joey and Rob are standing.

'I'd like you to leave my house now,' I tell Joey. 'You can choose to do that or I'm going to ring the police.'

'Why would you ring the police?' he asks. 'I'm just going to put on my shoes and then I'm leaving.' He heads into Theo's room.

I watch him walk away. He always has a reason for not listening to what I say. It's time to change the script.

I ring the police. An officer comes on the line.

My voice feels like it belongs to someone else. 'My eighteen-year-old son, who doesn't live here, is refusing to leave my house.'

When I give my name, the officer asks, 'Is this in relation to Joey Pastor?'

They know him well. This is why I am ringing the police – because I don't want my son to go to jail.

Joey bursts out of Theo's room.

'How could you ring the police?' he shouts. 'I'm leaving, aren't I? Just getting my fucking shoes! Do you know what they'll do? They're just waiting to find an excuse to send me to jail! Is that what a mother does?'

From a distance, like I'm watching a scene from a play, I think, what drives a mother who loves her son to this point?

Bernie's voice rings in my ears: *Don't engage.*

'That's not my problem, Joey,' I tell him, fighting back the tremor in my voice. 'I asked you to leave. You didn't. Now you can deal with the police.'

I hear Freddie crying in his bedroom, woken by the shouting. I notice Theo and Henry have come out of their rooms. They look frightened. My heart aches, but I feel like I have to finish this. 'Go sit with Freddie,' I say to Rob. 'He needs someone with him. I can deal with Joey.'

I'm doing this for all of us, but mostly for Joey.

The police are at the front door within a minute or so. They had told me on the phone that they were just at the corner and would be there in no time. Rob asks them to go down the side, so they won't alarm Freddie. Joey runs through the back door as the side gate opens. He leaps over the back fence like an Olympic hurdler. We've had the police here before, but this time I don't care about the neighbours hearing the noise, or whether they see a police car parked out the front. I'm not collapsing like I usually do when the police arrive. I'm strong enough to deal with this.

Two police officers search through the backyard with their flashlights. Then they come to the back door and ask what I want to do next.

'I told Joey to ring and check if it's a suitable time to visit,' I explain to them. 'I don't want him charged, but if he doesn't ring before he comes over, I will keep calling you until he gets the message.'

After the police go, I phone Bernie. 'Is this a good time to talk?'

'Any time is good.'

'I just had another scene with Joey.'

'Tell me what happened.'

I don't need to hide anything from Bernie, or pretend that we're some happy family who have got it all together. I tell him about the police, half-expecting him to say I went too far.

'"Fuck off, Joey,"' says Bernie, like he's the one talking to Joey. '"You didn't ring. We're not having this conversation." Next time he comes over, tell him, "You didn't ring. Here's fifty cents so you can make a phone call." You're doing the right thing, Helena. Even if he doesn't talk to you for ten years, you're doing the right thing. You're a good mother.'

I need to hear this.

While I'm on the phone, Theo comes over and asks if the police are chasing after Joey. He looks worried.

'Let me talk to him,' says Bernie. He talks to Theo for a long time. I stand in the kitchen, listening as Theo says, 'Uh huh ... yeah ... uh huh.' I drink three glasses of water while they're talking. My mouth is as dry as a desert.

When Theo gives me back the phone, Bernie says, 'Tell the kids I'm helping you to do this, Helena ... and that we're doing it for Joey.'

Drawing a line in the sand

Weeks go by with no sign of Joey. During this time, Rob's knee begins to ache and he starts using a walking stick around the house. As it turns out, he needs an arthroscopy – just like my father had – which makes me remember Pup's kneecap being removed while he was supposed to be having a simple arthroscopy. Although Rob's knee improves after the operation, he won't be able to walk without a stick for some time. On the weekend, when we take Freddie out to Dumaresq Dam, Rob stays behind with him in the playground, while I walk around the dam by myself.

Meanwhile, Henry is suspended from school and misses out on a three-week camp to Fraser Island. The suspension letter is the first news I've had of any troubling behaviour, but it seems that Henry and five other thirteen-year-old students have been repeatedly warned about playing up at school and consuming small amounts of alcohol on the school grounds. I know Henry's done the wrong thing, but the severity of the punishment is very hard for me to accept. I write letters to the school council, but nothing changes. So, while the rest of their class enjoy three weeks on a tropical island, Henry and the other children under suspension are given the opportunity to join in with activities at the welding shed. Bernie's first question to the group is: 'Who else was doing what you were doing and got to go on the camp?' There were several others, of course, and the injustice burns hot inside me. But, when I tell Bernie how I'm feeling, he says, 'There's a reason why Henry didn't get to go on the camp, Helena … it might not be apparent yet, but the universe works in mysterious ways.'

On the day before Joey's 19th birthday, I give him a call. 'Maybe you want to go out for dinner or see a movie …' I offer, but before I get any further, he says: 'I don't want to talk to you.'

Afterwards, I ring Bernie. 'It's hard not seeing Joey for his birthday.'

'There'll be other birthdays,' he says.

'I know, but it still hurts.'

The next day, late in the afternoon, Joey rings. He explains how he's angry about the way I'm treating him, and that he feels my behaviour is unfair. Joey admits that he's starting to see things from my perspective, but doesn't feel that I'm seeing things from his. He says that I treat him differently from the other members of the family, and that he couldn't enjoy his birthday while feeling so secluded from his family.

In many ways he's right. I have treated him differently, but what he doesn't understand is that I've always loved him and that I've always done my best.

'I'm sorry you feel that way, Joey,' I say cautiously. 'But I did ask if you wanted to go to the movies or out for dinner. Maybe we'll try again next week.'

After the call, I take my cup of tea into the backyard, where I sit in the sun and remember how the birds twittered outside the window when Joey was born in Darwin.

A baby is born! A baby is born!

I'm weakening, I know it.

I call Bernie.

'Don't go there,' he says. 'This is the next strategy – the guilt trip. He's been walking all over you. Now you're drawing a line in the sand and he can't cope. These are some of the things you can tell him – "Joey, you choose to be secluded by your actions. Would you accept it if I started pulling plants out of your garden and punching on windows? If you spoke to your mates like you speak to us, or treated your mates the way you treat your family, you wouldn't have any mates." It might be time to do some mirroring with him.'

'What's that?'

'When he says, "I'm your eldest son, how can you act like this?" you say, "But I'm your mother, how can you act like this? As a son, you choose to treat me the way you do. You've chosen to go too far, so I'm treating you accordingly. If Rob, Theo, Henry or Freddie start bashing on doors and knocking tables over, they'll have similar restrictions set in place. Because of the way you behave, I've instigated the phoning up business. Treat me with the same respect you expect – if you want to be treated differently, act differently." Joey stepped up to the plate with that mediation between him and Rob. You asked him to try mediation again and he didn't want to. So, now we're doing it this way, and you'll meet in public places until his behaviour changes.'

'Okay,' I say, taking lots of notes. 'Thanks, Bernie.'

That night I write Joey another letter.

Dear Joey,

I've been thinking about some of the things you said on the phone – about how I wasn't being fair and how I have treated you differently. For years you've been walking all over us – turning up at the house anytime you like, searching through people's bedrooms for things you need, yelling and shouting, expecting to be driven around town and have me wait in the car while you catch up with friends. Then, when you don't get your own way, you threaten me and damage my property. I'm not having this anymore. Because of the way you behave I have chosen to make things different from now on. If the other people in the family behaved the way you have,

I would treat them exactly the same way. This is why I have put the phone option in place – you've chosen to go too far and I now have to treat you accordingly. That is why you need to ring and arrange a convenient time to see me or anyone else. You didn't want to attend the mediation session that I suggested so I am now doing it this way.

If you want to be treated differently, act differently.

From now on, I want to see you in public places – parks, coffee shops, restaurants – somewhere neutral where we are both relaxed. We'll do this until you can show me your behaviour has changed. You need to fit into this set of boundaries now.

I love you, Joey. You're my son and I want us to have a better relationship ... but a lot of things have to change. No more compromising.

Love Mum

I'm drawing a line in the sand.

*

The first anniversary of Pup's death is only thirty days away. The date has become my self-imposed deadline to have things sorted with Joey. The other week he asked Theo to grab some leftovers from our fridge. Another night, he came over without ringing. I gave him fifty cents so he could go to the pay phone four blocks away to call me first and forced him out the door. Joey shouted and became angry. After he left, even though I was upset, I didn't ring Bernie. I need to stand on my own two feet.

I explain to Theo that I have to be like this because otherwise Joey will still be coming around when he's forty-five, asking for food and money. His life will be a mess because he never learnt to take responsibility for anything.

I have become the Mistress of Tough Love.

Dear Joey, I write the next morning, hoping this will be my last letter.

> *What happened last night is not the way it works anymore. Ringing Theo is not the option if you want to come around here. You need to speak to me first. Also, you are still shouting at me when things don't go your way, so until this behaviour changes, no house visits. I love you and I want to improve our relationship, and I'm keen to meet up with you in public places (which is why I invited you to the movies), but coming around here like you did last night is not an option.*
>
> *Also, it is not my responsibility if you don't have food or didn't get to Coles on time. How would you feel if I came around to your house and took food out of your fridge, or if Tobias or Lenny came around and did that to you? If you need more money to buy food and pay for other expenses, put more effort into finding a job or finishing Year 10.*
>
> *This is the second time you have come to the house without ringing. If you try it a third time, I will phone the police immediately. I'm happy to meet up with you in a public place – ring first.*
>
> *Love Mum*

Shortly after I push the letter under his door, Joey rings. 'Stop writing those damn letters,' he says, more in exasperation than anger. 'If you feel the need to write a letter, you can read it over the phone.'

'Okay, fine ... but no interrupting.'

'We can discuss each point,' says Joey. He sounds like he's prepared to make a big effort to be reasonable. But I only get as far as the second paragraph before he hangs up.

*

The next day, I come home from dropping Freddie at preschool and listen to a message from Bernie on the phone: 'Joey rang and we had a very interesting conversation. Talk later.'

I call Bernie straight away. 'What happened?'

'Joey said I had to stop telling you to write letters,' answers Bernie. 'He didn't like this "ringing-up" business with the fifty cents. I said I was free to help you out as a friend, and that he'd been given the opportunity to have mediation and knocked it back, so this was how you were doing things now. Joey said he'd changed his mind about mediation, so I asked him to choose where we could have the sessions. He suggested MacDonald Park. Is Thursday at two okay with you?'

'That's one of my teaching days ... can we change it to another time?'

'Joey will have to work that out,' says Bernie, unconcerned. 'But he's definitely feeling the pressure, Helena. He's bending in the right direction.'

In my head is an image of a sapling, bending towards the light.

Like a parrot on a pirate's shoulder

On the first anniversary of Pup's death, I buy a new bra, make my first ever pot roast in the slow-cooker, and bake a Greek New Year's cake. I also ring Joey and ask him to come to the movies. He agrees, with just a moment's hesitation. That evening, we walk down to the cinema together to see *Defiance* – a movie about two brothers who hide Jews in the forest during the war. Later, as we walk home through the cold dark streets, I tell Joey how years ago I read through a list of Jewish families who died in the Holocaust, and I saw the surnames of both my parents listed among the dead. Recently, my sister discovered our mother's great-grandmother was a German Jew, and that our father's ancestors were Spanish Jews who fled to Holland in the fifteenth century.

'It's a part of our history that I don't really know anything about,' I say to Joey. 'But I'd like to find out more one day, just as you will probably want to know more about your Syrian connection. It's important to know where you come from.'

Before we go our different ways, I ask Joey if he wants to sort out another time for the mediation session with Bernie. He doesn't. On the way home, I think of how his offer to meet with me in MacDonald Park was probably a 'once only' opportunity. I should have taken it.

*

Bernie is in the paper again for the second time in two weeks. He's taking a team of six Aboriginal boys and their dogs to an elite dog jumping championship in Victoria. In the photo, Bernie and the boys are rigged out in jeans and black cowboy shirts with *Paws Up* – the name of the dog program – embroidered on the pockets. Good for them, I think to myself.

I haven't heard from Bernie since the last episode with Joey. After I suggested again to Joey that we meet for mediation, with no response, I let it go.

The next day, I pop in to the shed, hoping to catch Bernie before he leaves for Victoria. Only Blister is there, working with Rocket, the old welding teacher from TAFE.

'Bernie's at the rural skills shed,' says Blister.

By the time I reach the rural skills shed on the other side of town, Bernie and the boys are just about to start circle work. This new lot of boys are wild, but Bernie keeps them in line, mostly with humour. One of the boys hasn't been going to school, hasn't been going to Youth Link at TAFE, and hasn't handed in his work experience form. He asks Bernie if he can do work experience with him.

'I was hoping you'd ask me that,' says Bernie. 'How about —'

He's interrupted as a figure in a white pantsuit and high heels sashays through the door. I watch in amusement as Geraldine puts her hands on her hips and tosses her hair back from her face.

'Alright,' she says, looking around at the group of boys, some of whom are already cowering in mock-fear. 'Who's been eating sugar this morning?'

The boys start dobbing on each other – pointing their fingers and calling out names. One boy has the misfortune to be caught with a can of Coke, and before he can run out the door, Geraldine grabs him and wrestles him to the floor. He calls out to the others for help, but they just stand back and laugh.

'You know the rules,' Geraldine tells him sternly, holding him down and putting her knee in the small of his back. 'No lollies, no soft drink and no junk food before twelve!' When she pulls his ear – *hard* – the boy cries out in pain. He's half-laughing, but obviously feeling the pressure. 'What's good enough for my daughter is good enough for you!' she pants, still holding his ear. 'If I catch you drinking Coke again next week, I'll beat you!'

The others whoop and holler, while Bernie sits back and lets it all happen in front of him. Before Geraldine can deal with any more rule-breakers, two drug and alcohol lecturers from Tamworth arrive. They've come along to see the boys work with the dogs.

Geraldine releases her grip and the boy goes back to his seat, grinning madly, even though he's followed by calls of 'Shame!' Soon after, Bernie and the boys take the visitors down to the grassy area at the back of the rural skills centre. As Geraldine straightens herself and tidies her hair, I wait behind with her for a moment: 'I think he enjoyed having his ear pulled!' I say, with a nod towards the boy.

'They love it,' she says with a giggle. 'Someone is actually giving a shit about their health and how they are – but not coming down on them like a teacher would. I give them permission with boundaries ... and they can apply that to lots of things in life.'

Geraldine shouts out her goodbyes to Bernie and the boys, warning them that she'll be back next week, and then totters off to her car. I smile to myself as I walk down the hill to join the others – although Geraldine has a weird way of showing it, I feel like I've just witnessed an act of love.

While the dogs have a run, a rural skills staff member wanders over and tells Bernie not to let the boys and dogs jump around on the hay bales – 'They might put holes in the plastic,' he says.

'We don't go many places where we don't do something we shouldn't be doing,' Bernie tells the visitors from Tamworth. 'The boys will give you a demo on how much control they've got over these dogs. Take Badger off the lead, Skippa. We train the dogs with hand commands, whistles ...'

One of the other boys calls out to Badger to see if the dog will be distracted.

Bernie whips around to face the group sitting on the bales. 'Don't call him if you're mucking around ... it fucks up the dog!'

The boys are quiet.

'It seems funny at the time,' says Bernie, 'but it just fucks up the dog.'

Bernie turns back to the two men. 'They're all pretty young dogs,' he explains, 'and socialisation is really important with them.' He walks over to join Skippa, who is kneeling down next to Badger. 'This dog is one the boys have been starting – Skippa's been doing some work with it. When we got Badger, he had never walked on a lead and you couldn't catch him.' He knelt down and called to the dog: 'Here, Badger! Sit, good dog!'

The others are silent while Bernie works the dog.

'Good dog!' Bernie looks up at the boys gathered around him. 'He wants to roll over, so we just ignore that. Here, Badger, come on, good dog! What a *good* little dog!'

I love Bernie's dog voice.

Afterwards, Bernie lifts Badger up onto his shoulder, like a parrot on a pirate's shoulder, laughing at the expression on the dog's face. 'I'll just let it look around,' he says. 'It thinks it's a bird ... *good* dog!'

*

I ring Joey the following week. 'Want to go to the movies again?'

'Yeah, okay,' he says grudgingly. 'Is *Alien vs Predator* still on?'

'That's not the sort of movie I want to see,' I tell him, 'especially if I'm paying for the tickets. *Into the Wild* is on at six. I'll meet you at the cinema if you're interested.'

I hang up before he can ask me to give him a lift.

Later, walking to the cinema, I think of how Joey is often reluctant to see the movies I suggest. How many action movies have I sat through to keep him happy? I wait for him in the foyer, watching the clock, not really expecting him to show. At one minute to six, he wanders through the door with a slight nod in my direction. He still doesn't like to talk to me in public. I buy our tickets and we go inside.

Based on a true story, *Into the Wild* is about Chris McCandless, a headstrong young American man with high ideals. After finishing college, he gives away all his money, changes his name to Alexander Supertramp, and drives, then hitchhikes to Alaska without telling his parents where he's going. His mother almost goes mad with worry and wonders if her son is still alive. McCandless sets up camp in a deserted bus in the Alaskan wilderness at the beginning of spring. A few months later, when he runs out of food and is ready to return to civilisation and perhaps even reunite with his family, he can't make his way back across a flooded river. Stranded, he spends his last days huddled in his sleeping bag, getting thinner and thinner, his face sunken and gaunt, watching the blue sky outside the bus window. He didn't believe in maps, but if he'd had one he would have known that only half a mile away was a cable spanning the river that he could have used to transport himself across.

As Joey and I walk home together through the dark streets of Armidale, I can't stop crying, thinking of the suffering parents go through with their children.

Beside me, Joey sighs heavily. 'This always happens when you choose the movies, Mum. We should have seen *Alien vs Predator.*'

Are you really Superman?

Over the next few months I don't see much of Joey, even though he's back living around the corner with Tim. We have the occasional flare-up where Joey steps over the line, but most of the time we're softer and kinder with each other. By August, things are going so well I invite Joey to Freddie's fifth birthday ceremony at his preschool. Rob is at work and can't make it.

'That's if you can be ready by ten,' I tell him.

When I knock on Joey's door the next morning, he opens it immediately, dressed and ready to go.

'Good on you,' I say, impressed. 'Freddie is really excited about you coming.'

We drive to the Steiner preschool – Joey's first trip in the car for months – and wait outside till the class is ready. I sit on a bench in the garden. Joey, in his black cap, baggy black jeans, and black and silver Superman T-shirt, stretches out on the slippery dip, his rap-style appearance out of place in the preschool's serene bush setting. Then Clara, the young preschool teacher, opens the door and beckons us in. Her rosy cheeks and Germanic looks remind me of Julie Andrews in *The Sound of Music*.

Inside, orange walls glow like sunlight. Freddie and his class-mates are gathered in a circle, sitting cross-legged on the floor, almost bursting with excitement and anticipation. In the middle of the circle are a cake and a treasure basket full of stones and shells, with pieces of coloured cloth strewn about. Clara gestures for Joey and me to join the circle – we sit either side of a golden cushion – and Freddie sits opposite us with a big smile on his face.

Once Clara takes her place on the floor, the children begin to sing: *'Freddie's birthday, he's turning five, shining with his heart of gold.'*

Clara drapes a golden cape around Freddie's shoulders. He closes his eyes as she places a silver cardboard crown on his head. A lump forms in my throat as the treasure basket is passed around, each child solemnly selecting a stone or shell to put on the cloth near the birthday cake.

'Once upon a time,' begins Clara in a soft storytelling voice, 'a little angel and a big angel lived happily in a heavenly garden. One day the little angel said, "I would like to go and live on earth."

"Yes," said the big angel, "I will look after your wings until you return." So, the little angel and the big angel looked for a home on earth. At this time, there lived a woman and a man who loved each other very much, and their names were Helena and Rob. One day they made a wish for a child. The big angel caught the wish and brought it to the little angel and said, "Now your time has come to live on earth." The little angel went over the rainbow bridge to live on earth.'

As she says these words, Clara spreads a rainbow-coloured cloth across the centre of the circle. Freddie stands and walks across the cloth, taking his place on the golden cushion between Joey and me. I sneak a glance at Joey – his face is rapt.

Clara and the children begin singing again, their voices earnest and high: '*Welcome, welcome brand new day, flowers bright and sunshine gay, with painted birds that sing their song, make me kind and good and strong.*' Tears fill my eyes. Birthdays always turn me into an emotional wreck.

'The parents were overjoyed to receive the child,' continues Clara, 'and they called him Freddie.'

Freddie beams at me, his eyes shining with happiness.

Afterwards, we sit together around a low wooden table to eat cake and drink water from pottery mugs. The kids, fascinated by Joey, ask heaps of questions. 'Where do you go to school?' ... 'Are you really Superman?'

Joey smiles at them, eyes twinkling, and cocks an eyebrow. 'What do you reckon?'

Later, when it's time for us to leave, the kids wave madly through the open windows. 'Bye, Joey! Bye!' He turns and waves back.

'That was pretty cool,' says Joey thoughtfully, as he puts on his seatbelt. 'Clara's definitely doing the right job.'

I look over at him – Mr Mellow. I decide to take the long way home, through the back streets of east Armidale. As we pass the welding shed, I ask Joey, 'Why didn't you stick with the shed?'

'There was nothing there that really interested me,' he answers, stifling a yawn. 'I liked the people there, and I liked the dogs, but ...'

'It wasn't your scene?'

'Nah.' Joey looks out the window, and we drive in silence for several minutes. 'It wasn't for Lenny or Tobias either. In fact, all my close friends, none of them stuck with the shed.'

Leave him be

It isn't long before Joey moves on again, into a garage at Tobias's new house in Girraween. Tobias has just been released from the juvenile detention centre again for getting into another minor scrape with the law. Joey asks me, very politely, if I can help him move. Loading his gear into the car, I notice he's still carting the box of soft toys around with him – Sleepy Bear, Dino, Sharky, Dolphin, Little Dino and Rabbit.

Once Joey is living with Tobias, I see less and less of him.

I miss him in my life. I worry about him, too.

One day, when Bernie rings, I begin to express some of my concerns about Joey. He cuts me short.

'You need to chill, Helena ... he'll be right. Stop worrying.'

'Okay.' I'm reassured by his words. 'That's going to be my new motto – chill.'

A few months later, Joey rings and tells me he has to move again because Tobias and his family are moving to a smaller house. I fully expect Joey to ask if he can move back home, but instead he says: 'If you can help point me in the right direction that'd be really great.' He wouldn't mind finding a flat, he tells me, but he doesn't want to go into one of those cheap places where 'every other unit is full of drug dealers'.

'I'll check the university noticeboards,' I say, hardly able to believe that, firstly, Joey is taking on the job of finding a place by himself and, secondly, he isn't leaving it till the day before he needs to move out. Little under a year ago – the time of the big 'showdown' over Easter – this sort of conversation would have been unthinkable.

But the following week, I send this email to Bernie:

Just got to get this off my chest … feeling worried about Joey. I helped him move from Tobias's yesterday to another house in Girraween. He's renting a room from an older woman – weathered face, looks like she's lived an extremely rough life, and she has another boarder as well. I KNOW it's great that Joey organised somewhere for himself … but I just feel like he's living a down-and-outer's life. What's he doing sharing with that sort of person? She's probably salt of the earth in that rough-as-guts way, but I don't know … I thought of him sleeping there last night and felt very sad. It's brought up these terrible feelings within me, that I've abandoned my own son.

Bernie's reply set me straight:

Everyone's trip is different and the universe throws stuff at us that makes no sense at the time. Who knows why Joey has ended up living where he is, or for how long it will last. I think he needs to run his own race and it sounds like he is by finding somewhere to live himself. Might not be what you or I would choose – but his choice will involve what he can handle and what is comfortable for him. I don't think many parents would agree with the choices their kids make. You can't change what he does – so you need to either accept it or don't look. I don't think you really believe that shit about abandoning your own son – it certainly isn't what I see from the outside! But it seems as though you have a vision for how Joey should be living his life – and when he lives his life in his way, then it won't pass muster in your head. This will keep going round in circles – a constant state of sadness, disappointment and worry. My advice would be to leave him be – let him make his choices and live his outcomes – love him and be there to help if he needs it. Try not to decide in your head what is best for him – he is a young man and needs to sort this for himself. Hope I haven't been too hard on you. Talk soon. B.

And, so, I leave him be. Joey often rings me from the shopping centre, asking if I can drop him home with his groceries.

'It's a long way to walk,' he says.

I sometimes think of Bernie's words – *If it becomes a use, back off* – but it doesn't feel like a use, not yet. I'm just happy to see Joey and help him out. When I drop him off at Girraween, I try not to notice the rusted-out car in his neighbour's front yard, or the overflowing garbage bin spilling onto the street.

This is Joey's choice, I tell myself. Or the choice I imposed upon him.

Leave him be.

VII

Autumn–Summer 2010

A swollen heartbeat

My mother comes to Armidale for a four-day visit. Within an hour of picking her up from the airport, we are in the travel agency, buying tickets for another holiday to Bali. On the phone in recent weeks, we had begun planning a second visit to see my sister, so we could be with her for the second anniversary of Pup's death. I am high on coffee and cake, and as I hand over the money to pay for tickets for Theo and me, I suddenly remember that I haven't fully discussed the proposed Bali trip with Rob. During my mother's visit to Armidale, she also puts a deposit on a house in a newly built retirement village two blocks away from us. There seemed no reason for my mother to remain on the Gold Coast, and we both thought Armidale would be a good place for her to settle now that she was on her own.

In May, Theo, my mother and I go to Bali for a two-week holiday. At the airport in Denpasar, we meet up with my sister's oldest son and his four-year-old boy, who will be in Sanur at the same time. Theo and his cousin get along fine, but my mother, my sister and I start arguing about various factors related to my mother's move to Armidale, which is set to happen shortly after we get back from our holiday. None of us had put enough thought into the timing or organisation of the trip to Bali, and my mother is struggling with the heat and a sore leg. The tension increases as each day passes. From Armidale, Rob sends curt emails. 'How much is this costing?' he asks, when I cry on the phone. For some reason, I grow fearful that I'll never see Rob and the children again. He wasn't happy when he heard about Theo and me going on the trip, and now the distance – both emotional and physical – seems huge. My heart starts to feel like it's racing all the time, and I can hardly sleep because of severe headaches. I notice a visible lump in my chest, thumping away like a swollen heartbeat. A Balinese doctor checks me over and then informs me I have heart palpitations. When I ask what causes this to happen, he says: 'A lot of stress.' All I want to do is go home.

At the airport in Armidale, it's a relief to see Rob and Freddie – both alive and well – but Rob still seems distant, even when he's standing right next to me. Henry and Joey are waiting for me at home. 'I've missed you *so* much!' I tell them. Joey has grown a beard and is effusively happy, while Henry's hair has been transformed into spiky dreadlocks during my time away. It's good to be back in my own house, even though I sense something brewing with Rob.

Less than a week after we return from Bali, my mother moves to Armidale. By the end of her second day in the retirement village, we both know it's a mistake. Armidale doesn't have the distractions of the Gold Coast – no department stores, no Megaplex cinemas, no Swarovski crystal shops. Suddenly there is nowhere for her to escape from the reality of my father's death. When she starts crying on the second day, she can't stop. I've never seen her so broken. I do what I can to help – I fill her freezer with meals, I take her for drives, I invite her around to our place for dinner – but her grief is overwhelming. I ask Rob and the kids to pitch in as well – Theo helps his oma with the shopping, Henry spends a few hours at her house after his guitar lesson each week. She likes it when he plays classical guitar for her. Once a week, my mother shouts me dinner at an Italian restaurant in town where Theo is doing a school-based apprenticeship. We drink martinis, talk about the events of the week, and eat gnocchi with creamy blue cheese sauce. Comfort food.

One night, I invite Joey to come along to the restaurant with us. I'm in the shower when he arrives. Within minutes, I hear him and Rob arguing out in the kitchen. 'Bloody hell,' I mutter as I quickly rub a towel over my body. 'Why can't you two leave each other alone?' I throw on some clothes and bustle Joey out the door, but on the three-minute drive to my mother's house, we have an argument about money. 'I don't want you to come out for dinner with us anymore,' I tell him. I turn the car around and drop him downtown, but not before stopping off at the bank so I can get him twenty dollars. It's the first time I've slipped back into the old way of behaving with Joey – I need to be careful it doesn't happen again. By the time I arrive at my mother's house, I'm in tears and need a large whisky before I can go out in public. At the restaurant later, I look at the couples having romantic candlelit dinners and think: why aren't I here with my husband?

The punch I didn't see coming

Over the next few months, Rob starts retreating into a quiet space of his own. Most nights he's in bed by nine, which is too early for me. At times, I worry about how withdrawn he's becoming. He never wants to go anywhere.

When I'm out and about – on my own – people start asking: 'Where's Rob?'

My older brother comes to Armidale to stay with Mum for a week. After they've been around at our place for dinner, he takes me aside. 'There's something wrong with Rob,' he tells me. 'He's not his normal self. I think he might be depressed.'

I encourage Rob to go away for a weekend, to get out of Armidale and visit an old friend in Brisbane. When I pick him up from the airport, he turns his face aside as I go to kiss him. Later that night, when Freddie is asleep, and Henry and Theo are watching a movie in Theo's room, Rob says, 'We need to talk, Helena.'

Once we're settled in the lounge room, Rob says, 'I'm leaving you.'

He tells me that, one – he raises a finger – he's had enough of our marriage. And, two – he raises a second finger – he's met another woman who is the same sort of person as him.

Bile rises in my throat. I put my hand over my mouth, worried I'm going to be sick.

Another woman?

I'd always trusted Rob completely. How could he have another woman?

'Nothing's happened,' he adds, 'but she's also married, and she's going to leave her husband for me.'

I can't get my head around what Rob is saying.

The other woman is married, too? Nothing has happened, but she's going to leave her husband as well? Surely, something must have happened if two people decide to leave their partners and families for each other.

When I ask Rob who the woman is, he won't tell me. Coward, I think to myself, lurching to my feet – to deliver a punch like that, and then back away and hide in the corner.

In a daze, I go around to Tim's house, hoping to bum a rollie from one of his housemates. No one is home. As I walk up the street, though, I suddenly realise who the other woman must be – someone from his department at the university. A few days previously, Freddie and I had dropped in unexpectedly at Rob's work and found the two of them having morning tea together. She seemed nervous when she took me down to the kitchen to show me where the tea bags were kept. She'd been at the restaurant the previous week – having dinner with her husband. I'd introduced her to my mother.

Back home after my walk, I brace myself and confront Rob. He's still sitting in the lounge room. I ask him if it is the person I suspect.

'Yes,' he admits. I notice a gleam of happiness in his eyes. 'We're similar sorts of people.'

In his self-published life story, my father wrote: 'It is always the punch one doesn't see which does the most damage – if one sees the punch, the defence mechanism in one's brain and body prepares for the impact and withstands the force.'

I knew my marriage was in trouble, but the other woman is the punch I didn't see coming.

Rob leaves me crying in the lounge room. He goes in to talk to Theo and Henry. They come out, distraught. I've never seen them so upset.

Henry hugs me, hard.

'We'll be okay,' I tell him, through my tears. 'We'll be okay.'

Later, when I've calmed down, I ring Joey and explain that Rob and I are separating. I want to make sure he knows before anyone else.

'Are you alright?' I ask.

'I'm okay,' he replies. 'But are you okay?'

'Yes,' I tell him. 'I'm just very sad.'

That night, Rob goes to sleep in Freddie's room. We never sleep beside each other again. Our nineteen years together – with all our bumps, hurdles and unforeseen obstacles – are over.

The next morning I'm a shaking wreck, my mouth dry with shock. I spent most of the night awake, working through the past. No wonder our marriage had fallen apart – we have a history of pain and struggle – and those years in Brisbane had created a divide in our relationship that was hard to repair. For a long time now, I've known that Rob has wanted more from me than I can give. It's not surprising that he's looked elsewhere, but even though there's little hope, I'm still desperate for a solution. I write Rob a letter, from my heart, while Freddie is watching *Play School*. I don't want our marriage to end. I don't want our family to break apart.

It's school holidays. Theo stays home and minds Freddie so I can meet Rob at the university. We drive to a dirt road on the edge of the campus and I give him the letter I'd written that morning – my last attempt to save this marriage, this family. But after he reads it, he doesn't react. My letter makes no difference to him at all. When I suggest counselling, he reluctantly agrees to attend a session. Deep down, though, I already know that counselling isn't going to work.

I drive home, sobbing all the way. Pulling over to the side of the road, I ring Bernie's mobile. He doesn't answer. I go to the shed. He isn't there.

'It's his day off,' says Blister.

I ring Bernie's mobile again. No answer. I ring Bernie's home number. I know he isn't answering because it's his day off, but

I really need his help. He's the only person in Armidale who understands my history. It will be too hard to try and explain it to anyone else.

Bernie finally answers the phone.

'Bernie ...' is all I manage before I begin crying again. 'I ...'

'Have you got wheels?' he asks. 'Can you come out here?'

And then I'm in the car again, driving out of town like I'm never going to stop, slugging from a water bottle the whole way. When I get to Bernie's place, I wait outside on the back veranda, near the sliding door to his lounge room, and take several deep breaths before I knock. Jayne and her sister Sally are inside with Bernie.

'Come inside, Helena,' Jayne says, her voice soft and welcoming.

I shake my head, not trusting myself to speak. Bernie comes out and we stand together on the veranda, some distance away from the lounge room. I tell Bernie how Rob wants to leave me, how he has another woman, how I want to have counselling and can he recommend a good counsellor.

I look at him and wait for his response.

Bernie kicks at some small stones near his feet. 'This is always difficult, Helena,' he begins, 'especially if ...'

But before Bernie can finish his sentence, I am leaning back against the wall and crying because I suddenly realise that Rob is just putting a full stop on a sentence that I began long ago. It is time for this marriage to end, and it is time for me to accept the truth.

It's not important to know what else Bernie and I speak about that morning as we stand against the back wall of his house, but Bernie is very funny, and even though I'm crying so hard I'm using one of Freddie's old cloth nappies to soak up the tears, I'm also laughing so much my cheeks are aching. One of the saddest days of my life – just like that mediation session – yet here I am, laughing all the way through it.

Before I leave for home, Bernie looks me in the eye, straight and steady. 'Kids get through these things, Helena. It'll be hard, but just keep focusing on getting them through it first and you'll come out the other side of this … bigger, better and happier.'

Breakdown material

When I tell my mother my marriage is over, she sits down, shocked. 'But I came here to be with a family,' she says, looking concerned.

'We're still a family,' I manage to say, before I fall apart again.

She stands up and fetches the whisky bottle from the top of the cupboard, finds two glasses and brings them over to the table. Then she lays her hand over mine and says: 'At least you've got your mother here, Helena.'

Rob stays in the house for a few more days while he searches for a flat. Because it takes longer than he'd expected, he moves out to a friend's place for a couple of weeks. I only see Rob show emotion once, on the last night, after he's read stories to Freddie. I go over and put my arms around him and Freddie, and the three of us stay on the lounge together for some time, hugging each other and crying.

But on the day Rob comes back to shift the rest of his gear to his new flat, he almost skips through the front door. I can't bear to watch, so I sit outside in the sun, pretending to do a crossword. Rob leaves the house with pretty much the same stuff he had when he arrived in my life. As I give him the cane blind – the same one he had in his bedroom when he lived with the philosopher – I remember the night Rob laid Joey's clothes out in preparation for bed. The night I fell in love with him.

Rob takes his bookshelves, and I let him have the encyclopaedias, but not the piano. Rob gave me the piano for Christmas, our first year back in Armidale – when our life was full of renewed possibilities

'It's mine,' I remind him, even though I don't play piano.

The house feels a lot lighter when his belongings are gone. I vacuum and shift things around so it won't look so empty when the kids come home from school. When I finish cleaning, I nod to myself with satisfaction. We'll be okay. In the bedroom, Rob's side of the cupboard is shockingly empty, like he's died, but I stack all my journals in there and fill up the space with words. Then I make chicken curry for dinner. When Henry and a friend of his come home, they move the old falling-apart lounge outside. Henry's friend says he will take it with him to his place, and that feels like a huge relief.

Later, as I sit at the table with Freddie, Theo, Henry and several of their friends, I begin to cry.

'Do you know many people at school whose parents are separated?' I ask Theo.

He's surprised by my question, and looks over at his friends and then back at me. 'Mum, nearly everyone's parents are separated.'

And that makes me cry even harder because I feel like I've failed my children. My parents managed to stay together – they loved each other till the end. But I hadn't been able to do that with Rob.

*

Over the next few weeks, I go under, down for the count of ten, and I can't pull myself back up. I cry everywhere, even in front of strangers. One day, shopping downtown, dressed in green clothes and feeling like crap, I see Joey walking up the street towards me, smiling broadly.

'You look like Kermit the frog,' he says, laughing. But when I burst into tears, he hugs me and is very kind.

I know I'm as much to blame as Rob for the problems in our marriage – I'd been escaping for years – but, even so, I feel hurt and angry. It's not easy to be the one left behind. I can't stop thinking of all the struggles we had in Brisbane, all those years I stood by him.

Another day, when I'm very low, Bernie rings. We chat for a while and I tell him how I'm feeling. 'I should have left Rob years ago.'

'Ah,' replies Bernie, 'that's like saying you wish you'd picked up that chop bone off the lawn that you just stood on.'

'What do you mean?'

He chuckles. 'You see an old chop bone on the lawn and you walk past it for several months and each day you think, shit, I should pick that up because one day someone will step on that. Before too much time passes, someone eventually does step on that old chop bone – and it turns out to be you! After the initial shock of stepping on a sharp chop bone has past, you get to thinking: "I wish I'd done something about that fuckin' bone months ago." But alas, nothing will move that bone *after* you have stepped on it.' He laughs again. 'Working that out is the easy bit … where it gets hard is what to do now. You can either continue wasting time and energy wishing you'd done something different, even though there's no chance of changing that now, or you can learn from it and be happy that even though it was a painful lesson, never again will you fall for the same trap. Then go forth and find a new lesson and always remain vigilant in your perusal of the lawn for old chop bones.'

I want more from Bernie than this chop bone story. I want sympathy.

'I feel like I'm having a breakdown.'

'You don't sound like breakdown material to me, Helena. You'll come out the other side of this ... no doubt about it.'

*

For the rest of the year, I support my children through the pain of their father leaving. For the first time in ages, I focus entirely on them and stop running away. Most of the finances are sorted for the time being, so I'm able to lessen my teaching workload; Rob says he will continue to pay the mortgage, the house and car insurance, and the rates so that I can concentrate on finishing my PhD over the next year or so. He also agrees to a property settlement, which leaves me with the house and the knowledge that the children won't have to undergo any further moves – at least while they're with me. Rob and I develop a complicated and ever-changing roster, where Freddie and Henry stay at Rob's flat a couple of nights a week, while Theo goes on one of the nights he's not working. Rob's flat isn't big enough for them all to be there together. When the kids are with me, I sleep in the spare bed in Freddie's room because he has terrible stomach pains and has become very fearful. I move the bed so it's right next to his, and we make up a song that we sing at bedtime: *'Archangel Michael / come and protect me / with your sword and your shield / Give me courage / give me strength / with your sword and your shield.'* Sometimes I sing it to myself as well. One day, as we're riding home from preschool, Freddie starts sobbing – deep, gasping sobs – and says: 'I don't know why I'm crying.' Family break-up is huge and confusing for children. My mother tells me that Henry asked her: 'What is going to happen to us, Oma?' She told him that his mother and father still love him very much – they just don't live together anymore.

At home, Henry grows quiet. I often think of what Bernie said: 'It's the quiet ones you've got to watch', so I work hard to get Henry out of his bedroom as much as possible. 'Come and play guitar for me,' I say to him after dinner. We develop a repertoire; I sing and he plays guitar – teenage songs like 'Hey There Delilah' and 'I'm Yours', old favourites like 'Nobody Knows You When You're Down and Out', and a heap of Jack Johnson songs. I speak to the deputy principal at Henry's school and ask her to keep an eye on him. Theo seems to be handling things okay – it's hard to know. He's still doing his school-based apprenticeship at the restaurant four nights a week, and is completing Year 12 – busy is good, I think. He loves his job. Joey pops around from time to time. He doesn't seem to be too upset about Rob leaving, but, once again, it's hard to know.

I miss having a partner in my life, but I focus on the kids and I put their needs first – I stay home, I cook, I invite their friends to dinner, and I develop an obsessional interest in Jamie Oliver. I talk about him so much that Freddie asks: 'Mum … are you going to marry Jamie Oliver?' That makes me laugh. At night, though, while everyone else is asleep, I have panic attacks, wondering how I'm going to hold it all together. I often wake in the middle of the night – frantic – thinking: *I forgot to take my pill!* It's always a long time before I realise that I don't take any pills.

Meanwhile, when Rob comes to pick up Freddie and Henry, he bounces up the steps, full of smiles and renewed energy. He looks years younger. He goes on a series of 'coast trips' with his new partner – constantly asking me to change the roster to accommodate his weekends away. He heads off to a conference in New Zealand, visits his old friend Terry in Melbourne, and goes to see his family on the south coast. Fair enough, I think. I left him behind for many years. I try not to be bitter and twisted. I try to behave with grace. But it's not always easy.

It's not a general store!

Not long after Rob leaves, Joey moves into a flat next door. The woman he'd been living with at Girraween was evicted from her house. Unsettled by this turn of events, I don't tell anyone, not even my mother.

'Chill,' I remind myself.

For the first week or so it seems okay, but then Joey starts dropping over whenever he needs toilet paper, milk, cereal – and it feels like we're slipping back to old ways. One night, when Bernie rings to see how I'm going, I mention that Joey is living next door and that he's started popping in a lot.

'That's interesting,' says Bernie. 'Rob's out and Joey's in.'

'I can't help feeling anxious whenever he comes over.' I start outlining all the reasons why it will never work with Joey next door.

'Drop the "anxious", Helena,' interrupts Bernie. 'See it as a good thing. I reckon he's looking to heal the relationship.'

'Maybe,' I say, not convinced.

'And it's a good thing that Joey's out of Girraween,' he tells me firmly. 'But it sounds like you need to apply the brakes a bit and keep this period a positive experience. Remember, it's the driver's responsibility to decide when and how far to push the brake pedal – and *you* are the driver. If he starts overstepping the boundaries, you can get back into some mirroring.'

A few days later, Joey comes over and asks if he can borrow my vacuum cleaner.

I hesitate. Joey has a habit of breaking things.

'My vacuum cleaner is very precious to me,' I explain. 'It's worth five hundred dollars. I don't really like lending it to people.'

'I'll be *careful*, Mum!' he assures me as he goes off with my Dyson.

I try to relax – 'Chill!' – but after he's had the vacuum cleaner for more than an hour, I ring to check when he's bringing it back.

'I *knew* you'd be over there worrying about it,' he laughs. 'It's fine … although I dropped it on the concrete on the way over and the plastic cracked a little.'

'What!'

He's joking, thank goodness. A short while later, when he brings the vacuum cleaner back, I ask Joey if he wants to go dancing with me that night.

'A good band is playing at the Armidale Club,' I tell him. 'I could shout you a drink … we could have a dance.'

'Maybe,' he says, and then he's off again, after taking two litres of milk out of the fridge.

After dinner, when I call his mobile to see if he's ready to come down to the club, Joey says, 'I'm at a mate's place … I'll be there later.'

I'm disappointed that we can't go in together. I haven't been to the Armidale Club as a single woman yet – and feel a bit nervous – but I suppose there has to be a first time for everything. Opening the door will be hard, walking inside on my own. I'm not sure if I can do it.

I ring Tim, to see if he can come with me, but he says, 'I might see you there later.'

So I walk down to the club on my own. *Sterkte*, Helena, I tell myself as I approach the building. I take a deep breath and open the door. Once inside, I see a friend at the bar and it's easy after that. An hour or so later, I'm on the crowded dance floor when I feel a tap on my shoulder – it's Joey and one of his friends, Red.

'Hey, Mum!' Joey's face is open and friendly. When he leans across to yell in my ear, I smell rum on his breath.

'Let's have that dance,' he shouts, his voice suddenly too loud as the song ends, 'and then you can buy me a drink.'

The band starts to play a slower song – a heartfelt soul number from the past – and half the people on the dance floor wander off. But Joey and I stay on, dancing side by side to the beat of the music. Out there on the dance floor, in front of the band, I can't stop smiling. I am *dancing* with my son at the Armidale Club.

I want to raise my fist in the air and tell everyone – 'This is my boy!'

*

On Christmas Eve, Joey, Theo, Henry, Freddie, Mum and I gather in the lounge room. My mother and I drink advocaat with cream; the kids drink soft drink and beer and eat chips. We don't make a big fuss at Christmas, but I'm touched by the way everyone has put a lot of thought into the presents they have chosen. Joey's gift to me is particularly special: 'The Leonardo DiCaprio Mixtape' is a compilation of songs by Nas, the rapper Joey and I talked about in the car when we were driving back from the Gold Coast.

'You have to listen to it on your own,' Joey says when I open the present. 'It's not the sort of music you have playing in the background.'

Along with the CD, Joey has typed out a list of the songs, with his personal response included under each title. 'I'm going to read this later,' I say, hugging him tight. 'When the house is quiet.'

When we finish giving out the presents, Joey and Theo head off to the pub to meet some friends. I take Freddie, Henry and my mother out to see the Christmas lights.

That night, before I go to sleep, I read the accompanying notes for 'The Leonardo DiCaprio Mixtape'. In the opening paragraph of the notes that Joey – my rare orchid – has written, he describes some of the song concepts, the artistic imagery, and the poetic nature of the compilation that he has made for me. I read through the notes, barely able to see the words through my tears. It's one of the most beautiful presents I have ever received.

But after Christmas, I have to push my foot down hard on the brakes because Joey is coming over at least once a day to borrow things that he needs and it's starting to feel like a 'use'. So, in early January I give Joey one last letter, which I write with just a little bit of help from Bernie:

Dear Joey,

I'm really happy that you've moved in next door and that it's working well. I think it's also a great opportunity for us to improve our relationship. However, there are a few things that aren't working for me right now. First of all, I'd like you to imagine a group of friends who meet in the park every week for a drink, the same four mates each week. They share a few bottles of beer or whatever and have a great old time. But one of these mates never buys any beer – he always relies on his friends to bring it along. You can imagine that sooner or later the other three friends are going to get pissed off with this bloke for not putting in any money or shouting them any beer. They'd probably get together and ask each other: 'How can we get this other bloke to pull his weight?' ... That's pretty much the place where I'm at right now.

My house is not a general store – it's not an option for you to come over here when you run out of milk or bread, or can't find a pair of scissors.

My house is not a drop-in phone / internet centre. I'm on my own now – a sole parent with three kids at home for most of the week – and am struggling to pay the bills. It's not an option for you to use my computer / internet anymore. You have the ability to organise credit in your phone, set up your internet at your place, or go to the library. If you need a hand to look at other alternative options for free user sites, ask the librarian. Your birthday is coming up in a few months – we could discuss assisting you to get a laptop, but in the meantime you'll have to manage elsewhere.

My house is not a shower centre, or a place to come after you've had a messy head-shaving session. Ditto if you need to look at your-self in the mirror. If you need a hand to find a way to purchase a cheap mirror, I have a friend who saw one at the second-hand shop that cost about the same price as a can of coke.

I'm trying to finish my PhD. I have an enormous amount of work to do and it is very important that I have uninterrupted study time. Dropping in whenever it suits you doesn't suit me. Here's what I can do:

I'd like us to have dinner on Monday nights – starting this Monday. Come around about 5.30 p.m. We can play Scrabble, chat and enjoy a meal together – this is the sort of thing that I can partici-pate in to improve our relationship.

I'm happy for us to meet <u>one</u> other time during the week – at a time that suits both of us. But it's no longer an option for you to *'drop in' when you choose. If you need to talk to me about anything else during the week, I'd like you to ring (just as I ring you). We now share a backyard fence; let's find a place where I can leave a 50 cent piece which you can use to ring me if you don't have credit.*

I love you, Joey. You're my son and I really want to improve my relationship with you. I also want to see you move ahead in 2011. You have a lot to offer the world. This year is about moving towards your hopes and dreams, knowing what you want and where you can take your life … or alternatively, it's hanging around your mother and waiting for me to sort out your life. I'm not sure if this is what you're asking me to do.

Love Mum

When Joey moves again a couple of months later, he won't tell me his new address.

'East-side' is the only information he gives me.

Fine. Leave him be.

VIII

Autumn–Winter 2011

Ducks on the pond

One Monday afternoon, driving back into Armidale after a weekend at the coast with an old friend, I notice the leaves on the poplars lining the highway have turned golden. Here we go again, I think, winter is coming – frosty mornings and wood fires, coats and boots, dry chapped hands. With half an hour to spare before I'm due to pick up Freddie from Rob's, I stop in at the shed on my way past. A chill wind hits me as I step out of the car. Grabbing a turquoise cardigan from the back seat, I walk over to a small brick building near the shed that has become the BackTrack 'office'.

Rocket, the welding teacher from TAFE, has recently begun working at the shed. He and some of the boys are sitting at the table inside. I nod hello.

'Where's Bernie?'

'Here,' says a voice from the other side of the room. Bernie is working on the computer. He stands, stretches, and then wanders over to me, chuckling to himself.

'What's so funny?' I ask.

'You wouldn't want to get lost in that cardigan,' he says, still laughing.

'It's a different world at the coast.' I'm suddenly aware that my cardigan, summery skirt and sandals look ridiculously out of place in this environment. 'Have you got a few minutes?'

We go outside where I tell him about a dream I had the previous night – about a talking cow that kept saying 'Warramunga', the name of the Aboriginal tribe who Bernie worked with in the Territory years ago.

'It was really weird,' I say, laughing it off.

Bernie is interested, and doesn't think it's weird at all. 'Maybe the Warramunga are sending you messages.'

'Maybe,' I agree. 'Also, I've been thinking about that conversation we once had about dogs and I'm wondering whether Joey is a leader, a follower or a lone wolf.'

'Hmmm,' Bernie says, giving the matter some thought. 'Dogs have different roles in the pack ... but I think he's a leader.'

I'm surprised by his answer. 'Why not a lone wolf?'

Bernie shakes his head. 'Think back to when he was hanging out with Tobias and Lenny – he was a leader with them. And think about that whole army idea you had for him. Is Joey the sort who's going to take orders or give orders? Like when he comes over to your house.'

'Not anymore,' I say, but when Bernie raises his eyebrows at me, I look away.

A boy pokes his head out of the office and Bernie asks him to find one of the new shirts the dog jumping team will be wearing at the Royal Easter Show in a few weeks. The boy pops back inside and comes out with a shirt, proudly holding it up for me. The bright red shirt is cowboy style, embossed with the Paws Up logo and the names of several sponsors.

'We've got black cowboy hats as well,' says Bernie. 'We're making a statement.'

A white car pulls up outside the gates, full of Aboriginal girls. 'Hey, Bernie,' someone calls. 'Sarah here?'

'Nah.' Bernie checks his phone for the time. 'About five minutes.'

The girls wait in the car. I hear squeals coming from the shed. BackTrack has started a girls' program, and Sarah, another youth worker, is the coordinator. Bernie glances over at the shed and grins: 'I don't think I want to know what's going on in there.'

Blister, a portly father of two now, wanders out from the side of the shed. Along with Skippa, he's become a trainee youth worker. He smiles as he comes over to stand with us.

'You know what they call women in the shed?' I ask them. 'Ducks on the pond – it's from that movie, *Sunday Too Far Away*. The shearers always said it whenever a woman approached the shearing shed.'

'Ducks on the pond, eh?' says Bernie, and I can tell he likes the expression. 'Never heard that one before.'

He turns to Blister. 'How are the ducks going?'

'Good,' says Blister. 'They're hooking in and doing the work.'

One of the girls comes out of the shed, carrying a metal butterfly. 'Hey, Bernie!' she calls, holding it up for him to see. 'I'm not going to sell this one!'

He takes the butterfly and twirls it in his hands. 'That's crackin',' he tells her. 'You could maybe add a few metal buttons on the end, to bring about an up-curve in the tail.'

The girl walks over to show the butterfly to the others waiting in the white car.

Then a four-wheel drive pulls in next to us and a strong-bodied woman jumps out. She looks full of energy.

'I'm Sarah,' she says, shaking my hand heartily.

As I introduce myself, I think about all these young women at the shed. I don't really have a place here anymore, but a lot of other women do. And that's a good thing. The shed is bursting with life and, as always, it fills me with happiness. But it's time for me to go, so I say my farewells and reach for my keys. Bernie walks me to my car.

'Hey, I heard you're selling wood,' I say to him. 'Is it good wood?'

He stops in his tracks and gives me a look of amused exasperation.

'We're about to get a *huge* funding grant from Tony Windsor, the Paws Up team is heading down to the Royal Easter Show, my whole game plan is coming together ...' Bernie shakes his head. 'Do you really think I would sell shit wood to anyone, let alone one of my friends?'

'Okay!' I laugh and open the door of the car. 'I'll order a load then.'

He nods, and then shakes his head at me like he thinks I'm crazy. 'See you next time, Helena.' As I watch him walk back to the others – to Skippa and Blister and Sarah – who are still standing outside the office, I feel that familiar pang. I miss coming along to the shed.

'Hey, Bernie,' I call, aware of tears pricking my eyes. He turns, shielding his eyes against the glare of the sun.

'Keep an eye out for Joey on your travels.'

He grins. 'I always do.'

The getting of wisdom

Joey pops in one night while I'm having dinner. He tells me he's been catching up with Tobias and Lenny, who've both just got out of a minimum security prison. When he recounts some of their experiences, I think how their tales don't quite match what Bernie once told me.

'Were they trading things?' I ask.

'A little,' admits Joey, before changing the subject. 'I still don't know where to have the party, Mum.'

Weeks ago, when we'd first discussed his 21st, I'd agreed to contribute money so Joey could have his party elsewhere. But because most of his friends lived in flats, finding a suitable venue wasn't easy. Joey never asked me directly if I could host the party, but whenever he came over, he'd sit at the table with his head in his hands and say: 'I'm still having trouble finding a place, Mum.' Then he'd look at me with those big brown eyes. Each time, I fought off feelings of guilt – 'You know what I'm like, Joey.' And he'd nod in a resigned way: 'Yeah.'

I eat a few mouthfuls of dinner. 'What about the park across the road?'

'You can't drink in Armidale parks,' he says. 'But maybe we could have the party down behind Hungry Jack's. We had a barbecue there one night and put all the beers in plastic bags in the creek.' He nods to himself. 'Yeah, we could go there, and it's only a twenty dollar fine if the police catch us …'

I start to think about having the party. 'How many people are coming?'

'Just my closest friends,' says Joey, sitting up straighter in his chair. 'About fifteen people.'

Fifteen isn't many. Surely I can cope with that?

Sensing my interest, Joey leans forward, his face earnest. 'They're all good people, Mum,' he says, writing out the list of names on a piece of paper. 'The only ones to worry about are Nat and Courtney – they get a bit loud after a few drinks, but we'd calm them down.'

'If it's only fifteen, I might have the party here,' I say, getting up from the table to put my dishes in the sink. 'I could make the birth cake.'

'No cake, no food,' says Joey firmly. 'We just want to drink.'

'But I was making that cake the day you were born,' I tell him, turning around. 'It's special.'

Joey laughs. 'You can't come out with cake at my 21st! What would my friends think about that?'

'They'd probably like to eat it.'

He shakes his head. 'You don't understand. No cake ... no food. There'll be drink, there'll be loud rap music – I don't want you coming out with friggin' cake and candles and spoiling everything.' Joey looks at me, one eyebrow cocked. 'Are you sure you're going to be able to cope with this?'

No, I'm not sure. To tell the truth, I'm suddenly freaking out.

Joey stretches his arms over his head and yawns. He gathers his gear, ready to leave. 'Hey, have you got any spare milk?'

'General store?' I ask, raising my eyebrows.

Joey chuckles. 'One of the people on that party list is Tara. You know in that letter you wrote ... she's the one who always says to Jeremy when he never chucks in, "Four friends go to the park, but one of them never buys any beer." That's Tara.'

That final letter I wrote Joey has become a part of Armidale folklore. He shared it with his friends and they all joke about it now – and if someone takes something out of another person's fridge, someone else is sure to say: 'Hey, it's not a general store!' I laughed when he told me that. His friends all think I'm a dragon-mother but, like most parents, I've always done my best. And really, this whole book is a love letter to my son.

I give him the milk and agree to drive him home because it's raining. I still don't know where he's been living since he moved out of the flat next door. 'Just swing by Tobias's,' he says, once we're in the car.

Out the front of Tobias's house, Joey leans over and kisses my cheek. 'Bye, Mum, I love you,' he says. 'I'll come around tomorrow sometime ... for my birthday!'

On the drive home, I wonder whether it's foolish of me to have the party. It's not that I don't like celebrating birthdays, but a 21st is different and I don't know how to go about managing one. My parents never made a fuss over birthdays. My mother, who had recently decided that Armidale wasn't right for her, had moved back to the Gold Coast. When I rang her to ask whether I should have a party for Joey, she said, 'Why would you make so much work for yourself, Helena?' She couldn't remember her family doing anything special for any of her birthdays, even her 21st, and added, 'My parents just said – "Happy birthday. You're twenty-one. Bye!"' But that had been in the 1950s, when the Dutch had still been recovering from the war. Things are different now.

I haven't done anything special for Joey's birthday this year. Normally I do so much. I guess I'm still finding my feet. On a whim, I turn the car around and go to the supermarket, where I buy balloons and streamers and ask the cashier for a crisp fifty dollar note. At home, I ask Henry to help blow up balloons, but he has a sore throat so I do them all myself. Theo is at work and Freddie is at Rob's for the night, so the house is nice and quiet. After tying the balloons in groups of three, I string them around the corners of the dining room. I drape streamers over the doors and windows and across the ceiling. By the time I'm finished, it looks like the birthday fairies have been.

Once the room is done, I set to work on Joey's collage card. As I flick through magazines for words and images, a picture of two men wearing Star Wars helmets and black clothes catches my eye. The men are holding BMX bikes in front of a corrugated iron shed. The picture makes me think of a photo that Joey once showed me of him and Tobias, dressed up as bandits for a fancy-dress party, handfuls of Monopoly money in their pockets. As I begin to sort through the words I've cut out of the magazines, I think long and hard about which ones are about me and what I want for Joey, and which ones are actually about Joey: *Risks and riches / ambition / perfect pitch / late bloomer stands on good stead / dark past / the getting of wisdom.* In the end, I only stick *the getting of wisdom* over the pictures of the Star Wars figures, and those words probably refer more to me than him anyway.

While I work on the card, I play 'The Leonardo DiCaprio Mixtape' that Joey gave me for Christmas. I thought of how Joey had said: 'You have to listen to it on your own,' when I opened the present. Over the last few months, I've tried several times to listen to the CD, but I never made it past the first track, with its heavy beat and even heavier language. Joey often asked me about it, and whenever I said, 'No,' annoyance sparked across his face.

Now I'm determined to play the whole CD before his birthday. I turn up the volume – it seems appropriate – and although I become stressed and agitated by some of the songs, I keep it playing while I finish the card.

At one stage, Henry comes out of his room and looks around like he expects someone else to be there. 'No,' I tell him. 'It's only me.'

Just as I'm sticking down the last letters of Joey's name, a song comes on that I recognise: 'I Know I Can'. Children sang the chorus, and I'd often asked Joey to play it on our drives around town because of its positive message. I pour myself a glass of wine, and sit on the floor next to the stereo, where I can listen to the words. The next track is 'One More Dance' – one of the songs Joey talked about in the car after we said goodbye to Pup for the last time. 'One more dance with you, Mama ...' and it has a different, softer beat and suddenly I'm crying and can't stop. All the sadness and fallen hopes from the last twenty years pour out of me as I listen to Nas sing about his mother's death. She hadn't had an easy life either. I think back to that car trip with Joey, and to all the things that have happened between me and my boy since then, and I cry and cry, like I'm grieving someone's death, not preparing to celebrate their birth.

I wanted it to be so different, Joey.

Are you cool?

On the morning of Joey's 21st party, I ring Rob and leave a message, asking him if he wants to organise a barbecue for the party.

He calls back soon after and says he'd like to be involved. I can tell from his voice that he wasn't expecting me to invite him around. 'I'll borrow one of the Iron Man barbecues from Bernie and Jayne,' he says, his tone friendly and sociable.

After Henry mows the lawn, I organise the outdoor furniture into a cosy circle, and put a table near the back ramp for Joey's music system. Then I make brownies and hummus, and buy dips and chips and crackers at the supermarket. I also buy sausages and bread. When I come back from shopping, I spot the barbecue – one of Jimmy's designs – in the yard. Theo and Henry have set it up, ready to be lit. At four in the afternoon, I still haven't heard from Joey, even though he said the party would start at noon.

Joey walks through the door at five, with Tobias and Lenny in tow. They've both filled out and become men since I last saw them. They greet me warmly with hugs and smiles, and then they help Joey set up the music system. Other people start to arrive at dusk.

A short while later, I'm standing by the kitchen sink when I hear the side gate – *click!* I watch Rob and Freddie wander down to where Joey and his friends are gathered, and pause for a moment before joining them outside. I look at Rob through the kitchen window, toying with my grandmother's pendant. He was my best friend for a long time, and there are some things I miss, but he'll probably be much happier with his new partner – someone who is the same sort of person as he is.

Then I take a deep breath and dry my hands on a tea towel. *Sterkte*, Helena. I haven't yet reached the stage where I can speak comfortably with Rob, but I know time will make it easier. We've been through too much together to remain embittered. There's no point in that. Besides, we have four beautiful children who need the two of us to remain supportive parenting partners.

Loud popping noises, like fireworks, suddenly sound from the backyard. Down by the fire, Freddie has opened a bag of party poppers he'd given Joey, and he and the other guests are setting them off – *Pop! Pop! Pop!* I laugh as Freddie finds the Super Soaker water gun and runs through the yard, squirting Joey's friends. He's having a ball.

The kids will make it through this family break-up, just as I will. On the phone the other day, my sister said to me, 'The best metal is forged in the hottest fire.'

We'll be okay.

I head down to the backyard and say hello to Rob, although my smile feels stiff and unnatural. Freddie leaps into my arms while Rob busies himself with the fire. It's an awkward moment. They stay at the party for about half an hour longer, and after they leave, I go back inside and make cherry *clafouti* – cherry pie – from Julia Child's French cookbook. Along with a sudden passion for Jamie Oliver, French cooking has become one of my food-based obsessions over the past six months. Joey walks into the kitchen while I'm blending the batter and hisses: 'Will you stop bringing out food!'

But his friends have eaten the food – the brownies gone in a flash, the chips, the dips, the sausages, even my mother's Dutch shortbread recipe that I made. All gone.

While the cherry pie is in the oven, I bum a rollie from someone with a packet of Port Royal and stand near the fire with the others, who warmly welcome me into their circle. One of Joey's friends, gracious and charming, offers me his seat. When he asks what I do, I say I'm a writer, and he tells me he wants to write a book, too, about a debilitating disease he has. And then I talk with Lenny and Tobias about how they're feeling now they're out of jail. I mention how Bernie said eighty per cent of people end up back inside, so they have to try really hard to stay out. They both agree, nodding their heads vehemently, and admit they've learnt a lot from the experience.

I look around and notice Joey and some others huddled by the music system, where the songs seem to be changing every minute and the volume has been pushed up loud. The voices are getting louder, too; everyone is shouting, and empty spirit bottles are strewn over the grass. But I'm okay. We're having a party.

A young woman comes into the kitchen as I'm taking the cherry pie out of the oven. When she sees the decorations I put up the night before, she smiles happily and says, 'You can't have a party without streamers and balloons!' She and another fellow eat some cherry pie with ice cream, and then we stand together around the piano and sing while Henry plays 'After the Gold Rush'. While I'm serving second helpings of cherry pie, Joey comes over and asks me to mind his wallet. His face is relaxed and happy, and he's unsteady on his feet. 'I think I'm a bit drunk, Mum,' he says. 'Are you cool?'

'I'm cool, Joey,' I tell him. 'You just don't realise.'

He squints across at me, swaying a little, and then nods in agreement. 'Yeah ... you *are* cool.'

After knocking his shoulder against the door jamb, he turns and heads back to the garden. By the time I make it out again, Joey is falling over the outdoor lounge and Tobias and Lenny are murmuring kind things to him, that sort of 'I love you, man' and 'You're a good mate' drunken talk – but they're so tender with Joey, so loving, it almost makes me weep. I make an excuse to go back inside for the rest of the cherry pie, which is very popular with all these people who, according to Joey, aren't interested in food. Then a song comes on by the Wu-Tang Clan and Tobias calls out to me, 'Hey, Helena, remember when we listened to this on the way to Evans Head?'

I smile at him. 'Yes, I do remember.' We'd listened to it so many times that I'd been singing along with the lyrics. I think back to that weekend, remembering how I taught Joey and Tobias my way of body surfing at Chinaman's Beach. So much has happened since then – Pup died, Joey and I had all those confrontations, Mum came and went from Armidale. My marriage ended.

But Joey and I are still here.

He reels over to me while I'm thinking all this. 'I might need to sleep here tonight, Mum,' he says, his words slurring together. 'Is that okay?'

'Yes,' I tell him. He's not going anywhere.

People begin to leave. When I check the time, it's not as late as I thought it would be. I'm getting off easy, even though my head is throbbing from loud rap music and shouting voices.

Nearly everyone has gone by the time I help Joey up the ramp at the back of the house. As he's talking to Lenny, Joey lurches backwards and nearly falls over the railing. It would be so easy for him to flip over and die, or to become a paraplegic for the rest of his life, but I pull him back. I pull him back from the danger and lead him to the spare bed in Freddie's room where he mumbles, 'I might need a bucket, Mum,' and then goes to sleep. I fetch a bucket from the laundry and put it next to his bed.

Later, after about ten minutes of cleaning up – yes, only ten minutes of putting bottles in the recycling bin is all I have to do because people have butted their cigarettes in the tins of sand I'd provided and burnt the rest of the rubbish in the fire – I go back to check on Joey, hoping he hasn't fallen off the bed or anything like that. He was the only one who didn't eat – *no cake, no food, we just want to drink* – and he was the only one who got really drunk. I was having normal conversations with all the other people, right up to the time they left. But Joey is fine – he's stretched out on the bed, fast asleep. Then, because he's using the sleeping bag as a pillow, I throw an extra blanket over him.

'Goodnight, Joey,' I whisper, leaning down to kiss his cheek. 'Happy birthday.'

I don't sleep well because I keep worrying about Joey getting up in the night and crashing into things. Alone in my bed, I think about his birth, about how he entered the world in a room of fading light, with sunset birds singing outside the window.

A baby is born! A baby is born!

Why do those words make me cry, I wonder? So much hope and love put into one baby.

My beautiful boy.

My firstborn.

When it's still dark outside, I notice a light shining in Freddie's room. I get up to check what's happening. Joey is lying across the bed, playing a game on his computer. He looks up at me and smiles.

'I was a bit drunk last night, Mum,' he says. 'I think it was the tequila. I've never been like that before.'

He sounds completely normal. I can't believe he's sobered up so fast. He asks me about the party and I tell him it was good. He doesn't remember when everyone left, but I comment on how his friends were all so polite and friendly.

'I told you they were good people, Mum.'

'Yes, Joey,' I say, hugging him. 'You did.'

And, for that moment at least, Joey and I understand each other.

EPILOGUE

Summer 2014

Years have passed since the events in this story took place. Looking back, I now realise how very hard it was for Joey to be living away from home so early. He was only fifteen when he first left, and apart from a few short visits in times of need, he never lived at home again. Like many of the boys at the shed, Joey really struggled to be independent at such a young age. When I read over this story, I can see how much he longed to be at home with his family – a family who loved him, but who, for complex reasons, found it hard to live with him. Joey showed enormous strength and resilience to make it through that time, to reach a good place in life, and he touched a lot of hearts along the way, especially mine. I'm very proud of what he has achieved, and I know my father would be, too.

Joey and I still have a way to go, but we'll get there. In the meantime, I'm just happy to know he's doing well. At twenty-four, he has a loving partner – a good, strong woman – and they're the parents of a beautiful five-month-old baby boy. Joey also has a secure job, and he and his family live in a flat in a quiet part of town. I sometimes think of that affirmation I wrote for Joey on the night before his 17th birthday:

Joey is caring, kind and happy. He is busy with work, friends, love and life. Joey is sensible and aware of other people's feelings. He loves and is loved. Joey is great to be around and knows his family loves him. Joey is calm and settled within himself. Joey has all the money he needs. Joey is my beautiful boy.

It all came true, even though I made so many mistakes along the way. I wish I could go back and do it all differently, but that's not possible. Like Bernie says: 'We can't change the past – we can only work on what's happening now.' I learnt a lot when Bernie began helping me heal my relationship with Joey. During that time, there was no need for anyone to be a winner or a loser – Joey and I just needed to come to a better place of understanding. I know he still thinks I was too hard on him with some things, but I did them because I thought they were the right things to do at the time. Perhaps others will learn from my story and avoid similar years of heartbreak with their children.

Over the years, Bernie has also gone from strength to strength. Although the original team of BackTrack volunteers has moved on from what was a rough and ready program back then, Bernie has continued to work tirelessly to improve the lives of over four hundred young men and women. He's been supported in his efforts by a wide range of people and organisations. BackTrack now has a team of paid staff and a number of programs that include Iron Man Welders, Paws Up, AgLads (a rural skills program) and Links 2 Learning (a mixed gender program that helps young people re-engage with education). Because of the organisation's phenomenal success, people all over Australia are now sitting up and taking notice of what goes on down at the shed. Researchers from several universities are now evaluating the program, and its progress, to help other youth organisations that are starting out.

Like Joey, the seven boys who feature in this story (who are now known as the 'Magnificent Seven') have all gone on to achieve good things in life – they have trades, they're buying their own cars and houses, they're bringing up their own families, and they're passing on the lessons they've learnt. Some of the boys still live in Armidale, some have moved away, but they all keep in touch with Bernie and they drop into the shed whenever they can.

The BackTrack boys, past and present, come from loving families. They're all good boys, but if they hadn't found their way to the shed, many would be unemployed, struggling, in jail or dead. Family conflict remains a recurring theme – even in loving families – and sometimes it's easier for people like Bernie and the BackTrack team to step in and become a surrogate family for a while, to help the boys make it through adolescence in one piece.

Back in 2007, when I first joined the Iron Man Welders, I was struck by the amount of *love* I saw in that dusty, dirty welding shed. That love is still there. Those early years were tough, with hardly any money or structure, but BackTrack achieved what it set out to do. Much of what happens today is the same as what I've described in this story – the only thing that's changed is that Bernie and the current BackTrack team are doing it better.

We've all grown from the experience.

Where the boys and dogs are at now:

The 'Magnificent Seven'
(in order of appearance)

'Thommo' moved to Victoria in 2011 and is about to complete his final year as an apprentice butcher. He's in a long-term stable relationship and is the proud father of two children. He and his partner are expecting another baby soon. Thommo still goes about his business with the same quiet dignity he had when he was at the shed, and the lesson he remembers is: 'Just keep showing up and don't worry about the mistakes ... if you keep trying, shit will just work out.'

'Gazza' has had a full-time job for over six years, and he is now a supervisor in a thriving foundry business near Armidale. Through his work at the foundry, Gazza has provided a successful pathway to employment for other BackTrack boys, and he is a caring mentor in this role. He and his long-term partner are expecting their first baby soon. About those early years with the Iron Man Welders, he says: 'Everyone needs to find a place ... and from there you can grow. The shed gave us that place.'

'Freckles' finished his trade in metals and engineering a year ago. He moved workplaces three times during his apprenticeship, but always maintained full-time employment and now owns his own house. Although he's still a bit mischievous, Freckles is a hard-working young man who is always well-liked by his work-mates and others in the community. During his time at the shed, Freckles says he learnt: 'Stick in, show up, give it a go, and put in effort.'

'Tye' moved to the Northern Territory in 2009 and has enjoyed a range of full-time jobs in welding and hospitality. With his cheeky, fun-loving nature, Tye attracts a lot of good people into his life, and he is always willing to help others. He says he learnt a number of important lessons at the shed, such as: 'How to overcome a problem without acting out and not giving up ... you can achieve anything if you put your arse down and keep your head up with a grin ... if you get your hands dirty, it pays off ... learn from mistakes – we are all human, and just as long as you learn from that, you become a better man.'

'Blister' continues to be a 'care-taker' at the shed. He has completed certificates in engineering and agriculture, and he has also completed his Certificate IV in youth work. In 2010, Blister began a traineeship in youth work at BackTrack, which led to him becoming a full-time staff member. He is now married to Emma, and they have two girls and another baby on the way. At the shed, he says he learnt: 'Always have a go ... and whatever it is, it's always easier in the end.'

'Jimmy' completed his trade in engineering and has had ongoing full-time employment with several welding workshops in New South Wales. He's also done some paid work at the shed – like making a tray for the back of Bernie's ute – and the current lot of BackTrack boys really appreciate the way Jimmy is still hanging around like a cobweb. He says his biggest lesson at the shed was learning: '"I dunno" isn't a fuckin' answer.'

'Skippa' began a traineeship in youth work at BackTrack, but then worked for some years doing solar installation throughout New South Wales. He now has a social work position near Armidale, and one of his strengths remains his quiet, gentle nature. For Skippa, the shed was about learning: 'Don't worry about what's in front of you, don't worry about what's behind you, just worry about what's happening now.'

The dogs

'Girl' is still the boss dog of the whole pack, and she keeps the others in their place with a nonsensical approach to dog behaviour. She learnt this approach from her grandmother, Jay, and also from Bernie's daughter, Maeve, who helped her raise many litters of pups. Girl remains one of the highest jumpers on the Paws Up team, and she always gives a hundred per cent to whatever she's doing.

'Lou' has retired from the jumping team. She's worn out from giving so much to the boys, but she's still a deep thinker. Lou helps out at the shed from time to time, and particularly enjoys the 'Reading Books to Dogs' literacy program.

'Banjo' is buried in Bernie's dog cemetery. He's a reminder that not all the dogs (and not all the boys) make it through in one piece. Banjo joined the jumping team in an era when the dogs had to work really hard. He was always 'Mr Consistent' and is fondly remembered by all, but most especially by Skippa.

'Geordie' (Banjo's brother) retired from jumping a couple of years ago. He's a pensioner now, and is known as the 'grandfather' of all the dogs.

'Zorro' was injured a year ago and has now retired from jumping. He's still known as the 'legend' that started the dog jumping craze.

'Badger' moved to the Northern Territory with Bernie's son, James, who rescued him from the pound when Badger was two years old. Badger is still doing crazy things, but getting more sensible with old age.

'Bindi' is a kelpie who came in from the outside and now belongs to Blister. She's a champion jumper and is known as the 'New Zorro'. Her success is an important part of Blister's development as a youth worker.

ACKNOWLEDGEMENTS

I have travelled a long way to reach the end of this book. I am weary, in need of rest, but first I must give thanks to those who helped on the road to publication. Early encouragement from Peter Bishop and the team at Varuna Writers' House was invaluable, as were several residencies and a 2010 HarperCollins Varuna Award with editorial Warrior Woman, Anne Reilly. The Australian Society of Authors awarded me a 2010 mentorship with the wise and wonderful Judith Lukin-Amundsen, and Bundanon Trust gave me a glorious two-week residency in the Writers Cottage at Bundanon.

Over the years, Edwina Shaw has offered me editing advice, warm friendship, fabulous food and much, much more. Antonia Banyard, Katherine Howell, Michelle Dicinoski, Victor Marsh, Anna Zagala and Isabel D'Avila Winter also gave me vital support, inspiration and guidance. In Armidale, more friends than I can name here have helped along the way, and I am grateful to them all. At the University of New England, Donna Lee Brien, Russell McDougall and Dugald Williamson provided insightful feedback on my writing about the Iron Man Welders. *Griffith REVIEW* and the Australasian Association of Writing Programs both published early chapters.

My agent, Brian Cook, brought my work to the attention of my publisher, Alexandra Payne at UQP. The warmth and professionalism of the team at UQP has been heartening, and the astute editorial talents of Jo Jarrah, Kristy Bushnell and Pamela Dunne helped me to see what was missing in the story and bring about its completion. Christa Moffitt's cover design is spot on, and thanks also to Rob for permission to use his poems.

Most importantly, I am indebted to the people who feature in this book. I especially hope that my family, the original BackTrack crew – Bernie Shakeshaft, Jayne Schofield, Geraldine Cutmore, Andrew Simpson, Sally Schofield and Justin Flint – and the boys at the shed feel that I have treated their stories with sensitivity and respect. I am also thankful to Bernie Shakeshaft for so generously sharing his wisdom, and for his unwavering belief in me.

Finally, I thank my own boys for their love and tolerance – they've helped me through some hard times over the years – and I am especially grateful to Joey for his brave, true heart.

298

A word from Bernie

'If you are not willing to learn, no one can help you. If you are determined to learn, no one can stop you.' (author unknown)

The 'Magnificent Seven' were determined to learn, but it didn't always look like that. The boys taught us – by their actions, not their words – what might be possible when we hang in there and never give up. They chose an alternative direction to where they were heading. Our job was to make sure they always had an alternative.

Together, we developed a new way of being that was supported by a community, a mob of wild dogs and some extraordinary people who were determined to learn and who never gave up. This winning combination – where we used a 'village to raise a child' – has led to over four hundred children being raised.

The methods used are simple: live in the 'now' and don't focus on the past or the future; provide opportunities for learning; reward positive behaviour; and be responsible for one's own actions. Slowly, inch by inch, a new reality is formed.

My unrelenting desire is to make a difference to the lives of young people who are toughing it out, trying to find their way. To be part of something you care about is the first and most important step, then dream big.

Whether you think you can, or whether you think you can't, you're probably right.